This book on women's health is a m
hood. Although it is impossible to
a young girl to know, Dr. Farhart and Dr. King ...
covering the most important issues. I would recommend this book for women of all
ages. They will find this book enlightening and full of good practical information.

—Don Colbert, MD
*New York Times* best-selling author, speaker, and practicing physician

*The Christian Woman's Complete Guide to Health* is many years overdue. What a
blessing to the young generation, a woman's handbook that will carry you through
every phase of being a woman. I have floundered my way through most of these and
still have a lot of questions. Now I have a source for the healthy answers, knowing
they are with the knowledge from the Word of God.

—Elizabeth Travis
Wife of country music star Randy Travis

In a world of ever-changing values, godly principles have remained true. Societal pressures on our daughters to compromise those values have never been stronger. As a board
certified OB/GYN and proud father of two daughters, I am pleased to see a resource
covering the time from puberty to menopause that extols those godly standards. Godly
decisions made in adolescence will benefit future relationships and fertility, as well
as both physical and spiritual well-being. "For you were bought at a price; therefore
glorify God in your body and your spirit, which are God's" (1 Cor. 6:20, NKJV).

—William R. Lile Jr., MD, FACOG
Founder, ProLifeDoc.org

Thank you, Dr. Farhart and Dr. King, for equipping and empowering women to
manage their health! This book is like a private consultation, filled with wisdom and
understanding for the issues, decisions, and struggles women face throughout their lives.
What a marvelous resource for the women we are and for the women we mentor.

—Dondi Scumaci
International speaker and author of *Designed for Success: Ten Commandments*
*for Women in the Workplace*

As a specialist in teen issues and sex education, I believe that young ladies need facts
to build a strong foundation in health and wellness. Dr. Scott Farhart and Dr. Elizabeth King's book offers just that. It empowers young ladies to take responsibility for
their own health with solid biblical instruction.

—Gabe Salazar
Youth motivational speaker and teen sex educator

# THE
# Christian Woman's
# Complete
# Guide to
# HEALTH

THE
# Christian Woman's
# Complete
# Guide to
# HEALTH

## SCOTT FARHART, MD
## ELIZABETH KING, MD

SILOAM
A STRANG COMPANY

Most STRANG COMMUNICATIONS/CHARISMA HOUSE/CHRISTIAN LIFE/EXCEL BOOKS/FRONTLINE/REALMS/SILOAM products are available at special quantity discounts for bulk purchase for sales promotions, premiums, fund-raising, and educational needs. For details, write Strang Communications/Charisma House/ Christian Life/Excel Books/FrontLine/Realms/Siloam, 600 Rinehart Road, Lake Mary, Florida 32746, or telephone (407) 333-0600

THE CHRISTIAN WOMAN'S COMPLETE GUIDE TO HEALTH
    by Scott Farhart, MD, and Elizabeth King, MD
Published by Siloam
A Strang Company
600 Rinehart Road
Lake Mary, Florida 32746
www.strangdirect.com

Design Director: Bill Johnson
Cover Designer: Judith McKittrick
Author Photograph: © Paul Wharton

Library of Congress Cataloging-in-Publication Data:

Farhart, Scott, 1959-
   The Christian woman's complete guide to health / Scott Farhart, Elizabeth King.
      p. cm.
   ISBN 978-1-59979-207-1
   1.  Women--Health and hygiene. 2.  Women--Health and hygiene--Religious aspects--Christianity.  I. King, Elizabeth. II. Title.
   RA778.F36 2008
   613'.04244--dc22

                                    2008018858

First Edition

08 09 10 11 12 — 9 8 7 6 5 4 3 2 1
Printed in the United States of America

We would like to dedicate this book to our patients at Northeast OB/GYN Associates, whose lives have instructed and inspired us.

# Acknowledgments

WE WOULD LIKE TO THANK ALL THOSE WHO MADE THIS PROJECT POSSIBLE. First and foremost, we want to thank our spouses, Sandy Farhart and Dr. Aaron King, for their sacrifices while we toiled away at our computers. This book is as much theirs as it is ours. To our children, Jordan and Jared Farhart and Daniel King, for giving up time with us while we completed this book: thank you, and we love you.

We are grateful to Pastor John and Diana Hagee for their unwavering support of us, and to the production staff at John Hagee Ministries for their tremendous help with our promotional spots. Our appreciation goes to the Siloam and Strang groups for helping make this book a reality for the body of Christ, specifically to Debbie Marrie and Lillian McAnally, who faithfully guided this book with their considerable managerial and editorial skills.

Our thanks to those who have endorsed this book: Dr. Don Colbert, Elizabeth Travis, Gabe Salazar, Dondi Scumaci, and Dr. William R. Lile Jr. Your encouragement is greatly appreciated. Thanks also to Niky Scragg and Nucleus Medical Art for their fine illustrations, and to Dr. Francisco Arredondo and Dr. John Pilcher for lending us their charts on fertility and body mass index, respectively. Thanks also to Ethicon for the use of their Gynecare TVT-OT illustration. A special thanks to a woman known only as "Jilly" who let us share her Web site on post-abortion stress syndrome.

Finally, we would like to thank the physicians and staff at Northeast OB/GYN Associates for creating such a rewarding and fulfilling place to work. It is a joy to come to the office each day where a group of dedicated people allow us to do what we love best.

# Contents

List of Abbreviations . . . . . . . . . . . . . . . . . . . . . . . . . . . . . . . . . . .xiv

Foreword by Diana Hagee . . . . . . . . . . . . . . . . . . . . . . . . . . . xv

Introduction . . . . . . . . . . . . . . . . . . . . . . . . . . . . . . . . . . . . xvii

## Section 1
## Puberty: Your Changing Body

1   Woman as Designed by God . . . . . . . . . . . . . . . . . . . . . . . .1

2   Body Image . . . . . . . . . . . . . . . . . . . . . . . . . . . . . . . . . . . 14

3   Sex and Teens . . . . . . . . . . . . . . . . . . . . . . . . . . . . . . . . . 20

## Section 2
## The Healthy Woman

4   Your Gynecologist and You . . . . . . . . . . . . . . . . . . . . . . . . 27

5   Emotional Health . . . . . . . . . . . . . . . . . . . . . . . . . . . . . . 35

6   Diet and Exercise . . . . . . . . . . . . . . . . . . . . . . . . . . . . . . 42

## Section 3
## Sex and the Single Woman

7   Dating and Sex . . . . . . . . . . . . . . . . . . . . . . . . . . . . . . . . 53

8   Sexually Transmitted Diseases . . . . . . . . . . . . . . . . . . . . . 59

9   STD Prevention . . . . . . . . . . . . . . . . . . . . . . . . . . . . . . . 74

10  Abortion . . . . . . . . . . . . . . . . . . . . . . . . . . . . . . . . . . . . 84

11  Post-Abortion Recovery . . . . . . . . . . . . . . . . . . . . . . . . . .90

## Section 4
## The Married Woman

12  The Wedding Night . . . . . . . . . . . . . . . . . . . . . . . . . . . . 99

13  Methods of Birth Control . . . . . . . . . . . . . . . . . . . . . . . . 105

14  Sacred Sex . . . . . . . . . . . . . . . . . . . . . . . . . . . . . . . . . . 122

15  Female Sexual Drive . . . . . . . . . . . . . . . . . . . . . . . . . . . 132

## Section 5
## Congratulations! You're Going to Be a Mother

16  When You're Ready for a Baby . . . . . . . . . . . . . . . . . . . . 143

17  Infertility: Causes and Treatments . . . . . . . . . . . . . . . . . 151

18  The First Trimester . . . . . . . . . . . . . . . . . . . . . . . . . . . . 163

19  The Second Trimester . . . . . . . . . . . . . . . . . . . . . . . . . . 172

20  The Third Trimester . . . . . . . . . . . . . . . . . . . . . . . . . . . 178

21  Childbirth . . . . . . . . . . . . . . . . . . . . . . . . . . . . . . . . . . 187

22  The Postpartum Mother . . . . . . . . . . . . . . . . . . . . . . . . 198

23  The Life of a Perimenopausal Soccer Mom . . . . . . . . . . . . . . . .208

## Section 6
### Living Life at Midlife and Beyond

24  Everything Menopause . . . . . . . . . . . . . . . . . . . . . . . . . . . . . . . . . . 217
25  Surgery 101 . . . . . . . . . . . . . . . . . . . . . . . . . . . . . . . . . . . . . . . . . . . 228
26  Life Beyond Forty: Maintaining Your Health . . . . . . . . . . . . . . . . . 239
27  Women and Cancer . . . . . . . . . . . . . . . . . . . . . . . . . . . . . . . . . . . . . 247
28  Aging and Intimacy . . . . . . . . . . . . . . . . . . . . . . . . . . . . . . . . . . . . . 257

Notes . . . . . . . . . . . . . . . . . . . . . . . . . . . . . . . . . . . . . . . . . . . . . . . . . 267
Glossary . . . . . . . . . . . . . . . . . . . . . . . . . . . . . . . . . . . . . . . . . . . . . . . 282
Index . . . . . . . . . . . . . . . . . . . . . . . . . . . . . . . . . . . . . . . . . . . . . . . . . 288

## List of Abbreviations

Below is a list of abbreviations commonly used in this book.

ACOG: American College of Obstetricians and Gynecologists
AIDS: acquired immunodeficiency syndrome
AMA: American Medical Association
CDC: The Centers for Disease Control and Prevention
FDA: Food and Drug Administration
HIV: human immunodeficiency virus
HPV: human papillomavirus
HRT: hormone replacement therapy
JAMA: *Journal of the American Medical Association*
NIH: The National Institutes of Health
NIAID: The National Institute of Allergy and Infectious Diseases
NSAID: nonsteroidal anti-inflammatory drug
OB/GYN: obstetrician/gynecologist
PAS: Post-Abortion Syndrome
PASS: Post-Abortion Stress Syndrome
PID: pelvic inflammatory disease
PMDD: premenstrual dysphoric disorder
PMS: premenstrual syndrome
STD: sexually transmitted disease

# Foreword

WITH THE ENDLESS NUMBER OF TITLES ON THE SHELVES OF BOOKSTORES everywhere, what makes this book on health different from all other books? Why should you read this book? Allow me to explain.

It is not the truth that will set you free, but the *knowledge of the truth* that will set you free. The truth about women's health issues has been available since the beginning of time; however, this truth has been clouded by the fallacies of a humanistic world. When searching for fundamental knowledge, women need not be driven by fear, old wives' tales, or political correctness. The time has come for the Christian woman to liberate herself from the secular world and obtain knowledge concerning her body from balanced, reliable, and godly sources.

Christian women must not be intimidated to search out the truth. We must become proactive when caring for our bodies. I have exciting news! *The Christian Woman's Complete Guide to Health* is the tool that will help you accomplish your search. We ought to seek out knowledge from a multitude of godly counsel. The authors of this vital health guide book, Doctors Scott Farhart and Elizabeth King, are wise vessels who have dedicated their life's work to bring healing to the thousands of women they serve within their practice.

Dr. Farhart continually strives to attain a deeper knowledge of his profession, bringing healing to those he serves through his expertise and through prayer. I know him to be one of the most compassionate advocates of women's health care. Pastor Hagee and I also have confidence in him to teach thousands in our congregation and the tens of thousands that comprise our television ministry outreach throughout the world.

I have the privilege of knowing Scott Farhart first as a man of God who has devoted himself to serving in church leadership for the past thirteen years. Second, I know him as my brother-in-law, a man lovingly committed to my beloved sister and their children for nearly twenty-five years. Third, Scott is my doctor. He is an outstanding physician who has served as the chief of staff for one of San Antonio's foremost hospitals, and I trust him to direct my path in making wise choices regarding my health. He is also the doctor for three of our children and has delivered five of our grandchildren!

Dr. Elizabeth King is the wife of a physician and a mother of a toddler. She knows what concerns women from firsthand experience. She also delivered our youngest grandson, Will, this past year. She gave our son and daughter-in-law guidance during a complicated pregnancy, and for that she has our eternal gratitude.

Our children have placed their utmost faith in these fine physicians to bring our grandchildren into this world, and that, dear friend, is the highest endorsement I can give the authors of this book.

Our lives are but a vapor in the span of eternity; it is time for us to live life to the fullest, with wisdom, joy, and good health. *A Christian Woman's Complete Guide to Health* is different from all other health books in that it will be a torch of truth that will light your path on your journey to becoming a better you.

—DIANA HAGEE
Wife of Pastor John Hagee and
chief of staff of John Hagee Ministries

# Introduction

WHEN WE FIRST THOUGHT OF WRITING A WOMEN'S HEALTH BOOK, WE looked at the available resources for Christian women on the market today. Most came from an academic perspective that emphasize secular humanism with a liberal bias toward women's health. Chapters were often included on such topics like "lesbian health" and "abortion as birth control." While the scientific information was generally sound, many Christian women would not want to navigate through the liberal opinions and secular advice that permeated most of the text.

What we hope to bring to you is a medically accurate and spiritually sound resource your whole family can use. The sections are purposely arranged so each generation can find the information they need. Each phase of a woman's life is represented: from puberty to singlehood, from womanhood to motherhood to senior adulthood. Undoubtedly some of you will find that certain phases in your life may overlap. For example, you may be raising children at the same time you are going through menopause.

While there are specific sections for reference, information important to all women is found in every chapter. This book is meant to be a resource you can use to find the answers you need in every situation you will face. We hope that mothers and daughters, grandmothers and granddaughters can find within these pages medical information from a trusted source.

Between the two of us, we have practiced obstetrics and gynecology for over thirty years and have treated several thousand women of all ages. Within the day-to-day practice of our medical profession, we regularly address the subjects we have placed in this book. The latest research and medical opinion are tempered with a solid knowledge of the Word of God. Where there are differences of opinion within the medical community, we have acknowledged it and given our own opinion as well. Where there are areas of controversy, we have addressed the various factions and given enough information for you to form your own opinion. In areas where Christians may disagree, we present the facts to you so that you can take ownership of your health-care decisions.

As you read this book, we want you to feel as if you are having a personal consultation with us. If you are having a difficult time finding sound, biblically based medical advice from a pro-life OB/GYN in your community, we hope to serve as a medical resource to many of your questions. However, we are not a substitute for your own physician who has the benefit of direct contact with you and the ability to run specific tests to determine what is best for you. This book could serve as a starting point to gather the information you need to ask your physician important questions and make informed decisions about your health care.

You will find anecdotes interspersed throughout the book. While we have taken great care to obscure patients' identities, most of you will encounter each of these situations at some point in your lives. You may even identify with the struggles these women have faced. If not you, then someone you know will need this advice. As you mentor the next generation of godly women, stay informed of the latest medical information.

We have included additional features such as:

- "Mom Never Told Me!"

- It's in the Word (biblical examples)

- Did You Know?

When you see the following symbols, you will find:

 For More Information

 Digging Deeper

 Remember!

 Risks and/or Side Effects

Finally, understand that we cannot possibly place all of the information regarding women's health into one book. The resources we have used are listed with each chapter to allow you to further explore the information for yourself. The Internet has been of great benefit in helping everyone access information at home. But be careful to stay with respected medical Web sites and away from sites that are written by "laymen." Otherwise, you may become victims of their own hidden agendas.

It is our hope that this resource book is one you will recommend to your friends and neighbors, your women's groups, and your churches. We are here to serve you as you seek the truth about God's most precious creation: women!

—SCOTT FARHART, MD, and ELIZABETH KING, MD

# SECTION 1

## PUBERTY: YOUR CHANGING BODY

# Chapter 1

# WOMAN AS DESIGNED BY GOD

WHEN GOD DESIGNED WOMAN, HE CREATED SOMEONE VERY SPECIAL. Developing from a girl to a woman, however, is complex and filled with ups and downs. Most young women deal with painful periods each month, as in the case of one of our patients, Sarah.

*The summer before heading off to college, seventeen-year-old Sarah came to the office for her first gynecological exam. Her periods were regular, but she was suffering from severe pain the first two days of her menstrual cycle. The pain was so bad that not even over-the-counter pain medications provided much relief. The only way she could get some relief was to climb into bed, apply a heating pad to her lower abdominal area, and assume the fetal position. She missed many days and events during her senior year in high school because the pain was so excruciating. Now she would be attending college, and she was afraid her painful periods would affect her class attendance and social events with friends.*

*We placed her on a low-dose birth control pill to decrease the severity of menstrual cramping. Over the Thanksgiving break, she came back to the office and was happy to report she did not have to miss any classes or sorority events. Her period was significantly lighter and her cramping was minimal. She was able to enjoy her life away from home during her freshman year in college.*

## Overview of Female Anatomy

From the very beginning, we read that women are unique creations:

The Lord God made a woman from the rib he had taken out of the man, and he brought her to the man. The man said, "This is now bone of my bones, and flesh of my flesh; she shall be called 'woman,' for she was taken out of man."

—Genesis 2:22–23

Though the Bible states that females are formed from males, a developing fetus will automatically take a female form if not influenced early on by the male hormone testosterone. It is testosterone that closes the vagina, makes the labia turn into a scrotum, and elongates the clitoris to form a penis. Without it, a normal-appearing female will be formed, complete with breast development and a vagina, even if that person has the chromosomes of a male. So being female is no "accident" or "mistake.""

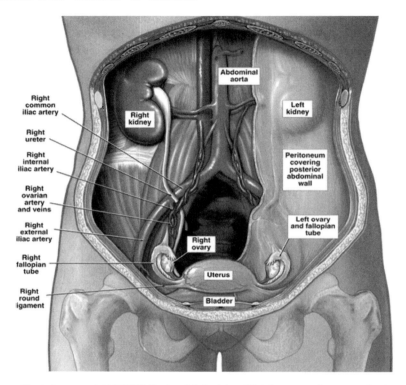

Illustration copyright © 2008 Nucleus Medical Art. All rights reserved. www.nucleusinc.com.

## Your ovaries

The ovaries are the dominant organs in women. Nearly all of the sex hormones come from the ovaries, and they hold the key to much of what it means to be female. These almond-sized oval structures are located on each side of the uterus. They produce the female sex hormones estrogen and progesterone, and they store all of the eggs needed for later reproduction. Each month, dozens of eggs compete with each other to select the one egg that will be released for fertilization in a process called *ovulation*. In a complex interaction between the brain and the ovaries, one dominant egg reaches maturity and is released into the pelvic cavity where the fallopian tube takes it into itself. There, one of the waiting sperm fertilizes it. The resulting new embryo journeys into the uterus to begin its new life.

The ovaries make a hormone called *estrogen*. From the onset of puberty to menopause, the ovaries produce this hormone daily. It's what keeps the female voice high, develops breasts, changes the shape of the pelvic bones to accommodate pregnancy, and grows a uterine lining for later use in reproduction. This hormone has been found to interact with almost every organ of the body in a powerful way. It causes calcium to bind to bone (the loss of estrogen is the primary cause of osteoporosis in women). It increases the good cholesterol and lowers the bad cholesterol, delaying the onset of heart attack and stroke in women compared to men. And this doesn't mention the effects on the brain!

When the egg is released in the middle of the menstrual cycle, a second hormone, called *progesterone*, is made. Its principle job is to prepare the uterine lining to receive an embryo. Without this preparation, the embryo would float by and fall out of the cervix, never implanting and never causing pregnancy. If an embryo does not implant and signal its existence to the ovary, the progesterone levels will fall and the uterine lining will tear away, beginning the familiar process of *menstruation*.

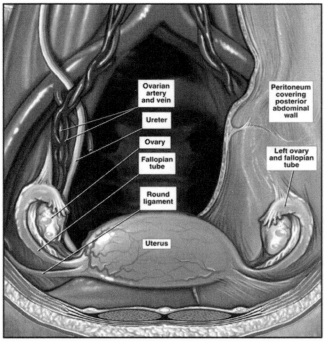

Enlarged View Of Uterine Region

## Your uterus

The uterus, commonly referred to as "the womb," is the place where the embryo develops into the fetus and then is delivered by a series of contractions as a live baby. The end of the uterus that protrudes into the vagina is the *cervix*. While the uterus and cervix have different functions and different cellular makeup, they essentially blend together into one organ. Think of them as the uterus being the "house" and the cervix being the "door" to that house. The uterus is primarily muscular in nature, responsible for menstrual cramps that shed the old lining, making a place for the placenta to attach during pregnancy, and causing labor contractions during delivery. Damage to the cervix from surgical procedures to correct abnormal Pap smears, or from past abortions, can weaken its ability to hold a pregnancy to term and cause loss of the fetus. When a woman is not pregnant, the cervix is a source of lubrication for intercourse. It also releases its own unique secretions during the fertile phase of each cycle that nourish the sperm and aid their passage into the uterus.

## Your fallopian tubes

Attached to the upper sides of the uterus are the fallopian tubes that bring egg and sperm together and transport the created embryo to the uterus. The fallopian tubes are among the most delicate of the female organs and vitally important. Scarring of the tubes from previous infection is a common cause of infertility, which is a topic for another chapter.

## Your vagina

The vagina is a three- to four-inch muscular tube leading from the cervix to the outer labial opening. It is lined by cells that secrete lubrication to aid in intercourse and is capable of expanding during sexual excitement to hold the erect penis. The vagina is able to accommodate any size penis, and a fully developed baby can journey through it during birth. It is surrounded by the bladder above and the rectum below. Childbirth injuries to the vaginal walls, as well as aging of the muscles, can cause the uterus, bladder, and/or rectum to "fall" into it, as we will discuss in a later chapter. While the vagina is the main location of intercourse and is capable of feeling its own unique sensations, it is not the primary place where a woman experiences the pleasure of intercourse—that is left to the clitoris.

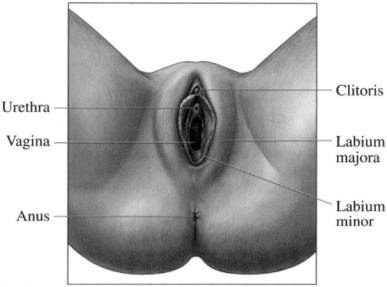

Urethra

Vagina

Anus

Clitoris

Labium majora

Labium minor

## Your clitoris

The clitoris is the most sensitive receiver of sexual pleasure in a woman's body. Its counterpart in men is the head of the penis. The clitoris is filled with sensitive nerves that transmit pleasurable sensations. It is also capable of an erection, and when erect, it protrudes from under a hood of skin formed by the joining of the tops of the labia (or lips). During intercourse, the inward thrusting of the penis pulls on the labia, and the hood of the clitoris rubs against it, causing sensation to be transmitted to the clitoris. With enough sensation, a woman will achieve orgasm.

# What Is Puberty?

Puberty is the physical, emotional, and sexual transition from childhood to adulthood. This transition occurs gradually and contains a series of well-defined events and milestones. The brain contains two structures—the hypothalamus and pituitary gland—that are responsible for turning on and regulating the secretion of hormones from the ovaries in women (the gonads). This is referred to as the *hypothalamic-pituitary-gonadal axis* and is initially active in the fetus and during the first few years following birth. It then becomes inactive until the onset of pubertal development. At approximately age eight, the adrenal glands send a signal that turns on the gonadal sex hormone production approximately two years later. The process of pubertal development requires approximately four years to achieve full sexual maturation. This process takes place in an orderly fashion of breast development, pubic hair growth, menstruation, and growth spurts.

Three critical elements that play a role in the timing of a girl's sexual maturation are adequate body fat, adequate sleep, and vision. Without adequate body fat, the body cannot turn on the developmental process. This is a protective mechanism because a woman's body cannot support a pregnancy without a certain amount of reserve. This is why you will notice that as you approach puberty you gain weight, often in new places. Girls begin to develop hips, and their proportion of overall body fat increases. Likewise, puberty is delayed in girls who participate in strenuous exercise before puberty. Adequate sleep is also important in hormone signaling and production. During the sleep cycles in puberty, there is an increased secretion of both follicle-stimulating hormone and luteinizing hormone (two hormones produced in the brain to stimulate the ovaries). Visual exposure to sunlight is necessary for sexual development. Blind children have delayed puberty, and pituitary hormone secretion is suppressed in hibernating animals.

Mood changes are very common during pubertal development and may lead to periods of depression or violent outbursts. Although this can be difficult for both adolescents and their parents, be reassured that these mood changes disappear with time.

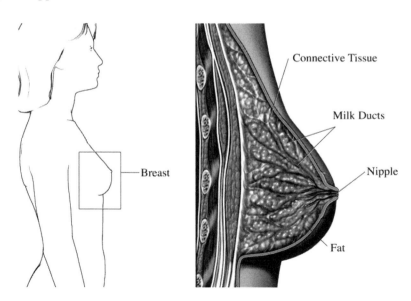

Connective Tissue

Milk Ducts

Breast

Nipple

Fat

## Development of breasts and body hair

The initial sign of breast development is a darkening of the areola (pigmented skin around the nipple). The breast tissue underneath it will begin to grow into a mound, which is commonly referred to as a breast bud. Shortly thereafter, pubic hair will start to develop. It will initially be a few long, downy, slightly darkened hairs. Breast development continues past the edge of the areola. Girls will also develop darker hair in the axillary region (armpit). The pubic hair then begins to darken, increase in amount, and become coarser. At this stage it is confined to the *labia majora* (the outer lips of the vagina) and *mons pubis* (the raised fatty area above the labia). It will then begin to spread to the inner thighs. Around this time, most girls will get their first period (*menarche*). Breast development continues past the areola mound and the breast takes on a rounder shape. The breasts may have initially grown at different rates, with one larger than the other, but they should eventually even out.

## Menstruation

About a year following initial breast development, most girls will get their first period. This occurs on average at age twelve, but it can begin as early as age nine or ten, or late into the teen years. As stated earlier, the hormones estrogen and progesterone regulate the menstrual cycle. When a pregnancy does not occur, the uterine lining is shed. This monthly process is commonly known as your *period*.

On average, the menstrual cycle is twenty-eight days, with some girls bleeding for only three to four days, while others will experience bleeding for five to seven days. When you first start having menstrual cycles they may be erratic, sometimes occurring twice in one month and skipping a month at other times. Your body usually just needs time to get used to the new signals it is receiving. If erratic cycles persist beyond the first year, you should consult a doctor for evaluation.

The menstrual cycle is divided into three phases. The first stage is marked by the first day of bleeding (referred to as Day 1 of your menstrual cycle) when your body sheds blood and the endometrium (or lining of the uterus). Many women will develop problems with this stage, such as dysmenorrhea (painful periods) and/or menorrhagia (heavy periods), which we will discuss in detail later on.

The second stage of the menstrual cycle is the follicular/proliferative phase. The pituitary gland releases a hormone, FSH (follicle-stimulating hormone), which in turn stimulates the ovary to develop a follicle (egg sac). This follicle contains an ovum (egg), which matures during this phase. FSH also stimulates the ovary to produce estrogen. The increasing amounts of estrogen cause the endometrium to grow and reach its maximal thickness at the time of ovulation.

## "MY GIRL" CARE KIT

A girl's first period is a rite of passage as she moves from puberty to womanhood. It can be an exciting time, but it can also be an awkward stage in a girl's life—not quite a little girl, not quite a woman. Aside from talking to a trusted Christian woman, a simple emergency care kit can make most girls feel at ease.

Find a nice toiletry or cosmetic bag (something discreet that will easily fit in a backpack or purse), and fill it with things needed for the first period. Here is a sample list, but you can create your own.

- A small calendar (to keep track of menstrual cycles)
- 1 sanitary pad and 1 panty liner
- Feminine disposable wipes
- Antibacterial hand wipes
- A small note of encouragement with a favorite Bible verse
- Two to three chocolate kisses (what girl doesn't love— and need!—chocolate at this time)
- The phone number or e-mail address of a trusted Christian woman to answer questions and offer support

The third stage of the menstrual cycle is the luteal/secretory stage. This is marked by the production of LH (luteinizing hormone) in the brain, which triggers the release of the egg (ovulation). Some women can actually feel when they ovulate, sensing a twinge of pain on one side or the other. The empty follicle becomes a sac known as the *corpus luteum*. This sac grows in response to LH and begins to secrete progesterone, causing the endometrium to convert from a proliferative state to a secretory state. The endometrial glands contain fluid that will support a developing embryo should pregnancy occur. If pregnancy does not occur, the corpus luteum begins to deteriorate, progesterone levels fall, and the lining of the uterus is shed. Estrogen levels fall along with progesterone, and this drop in hormones signals the body to start the process over again.

When a girl first starts having her period, she may wonder about using a pad versus a tampon. It is really a matter of preference and comfort. There are certain instances when wearing a pad is not feasible, such as going swimming.

Anyone can use a tampon, even virgins. You can use a tampon during your very first cycle if you wish. It is important to remember to change your tampon regularly, however, because you can develop a condition called toxic shock syndrome if a tampon is left in too long. If you have difficulty inserting a tampon, let your doctor know. It could be a symptom of a condition called

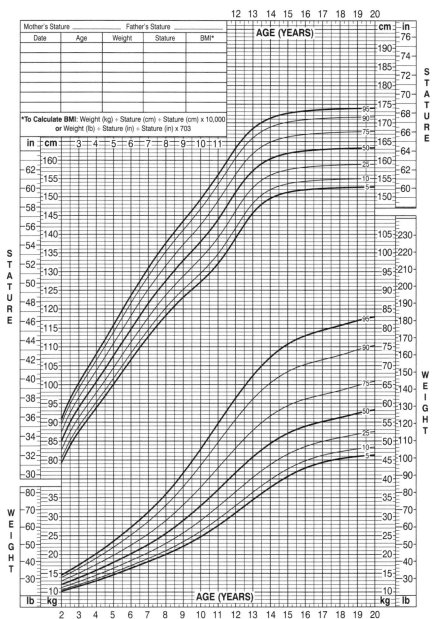

## 2 to 20 years: Girls
## Stature-for-age and Weight-for-age percentiles

NAME _____

RECORD # _____

*To Calculate BMI: Weight (kg) ÷ Stature (cm) ÷ Stature (cm) x 10,000
or Weight (lb) ÷ Stature (in) ÷ Stature (in) x 703

| Date | Age | Weight | Stature | BMI* |
|------|-----|--------|---------|------|
|      |     |        |         |      |
|      |     |        |         |      |
|      |     |        |         |      |
|      |     |        |         |      |
|      |     |        |         |      |

Published May 30, 2000 (modified 11/21/00).
SOURCE: Developed by the National Center for Health Statistics in collaboration with
the National Center for Chronic Disease Prevention and Health Promotion (2000).
http://www.cdc.gov/growthcharts

SAFER · HEALTHIER · PEOPLE™

"imperforate hymen," which can be fixed surgically.

Tampons and pads come in various sizes, and some are even scented. You should be able to find something you are comfortable with.

### Growth spurts

When puberty arrives, adolescents experience an intense amount of growth in large spurts. Girls begin their growth spurt at age ten or eleven, then peak at age twelve; by fifteen or sixteen, their growth stops. During growth spurts, limbs may grow at different rates, causing a girl to be clumsy or uncoordinated. Growing pains can occur from the tightening of tendons and ligaments. Many teen athletes will experience these pains, especially if they do not stretch adequately before and after sports. Girls can grow as many as three and one-half inches in one year. (Refer to the standard growth chart on page 9 for growth percentiles per age.)

The first sign of a growth spurt is when new shoes are needed, as the hands and feet grow first. The lower legs, forearms, upper arms, and thighs grow next, and then the spine. The hips and pelvis are the last areas to grow.

## Things to Watch Out For

As stated earlier, becoming a woman is a challenging physiological process. Here are some of the most common physical issues that a pubescent girl may encounter.

### Abnormal menstrual cycles

Like our patient, Sarah, sometimes menstrual cycles can be abnormal, interrupting a girl's ability to do even the simplest things during that time. The cycle can be stabilized with an oral contraceptive (birth control pill), which provides a stable dose of both hormones that control the menstrual cycle.

*Dysfunctional uterine bleeding* (DUB) is defined as excessively heavy, prolonged, or frequent bleeding that is not caused by a uterine abnormality. It is caused by hormonal alterations, which often lead to anovulation (the inability to ovulate on a regular basis). Some women experience painful periods known as *dysmenorrhea*. Others have mood and behavioral changes that occur in a regular, cyclical pattern known as *PMS* (premenstrual syndrome) or *PMDD* (premenstrual dysphoric disorder).

Heavy menstrual periods are defined by either the amount of blood lost, known as *menorrhagia*, or an excessive number of days (more than seven) bleeding (polymenorrhea). A woman has menorrhagia if the blood loss exceeds 80 ml. One way for you to quantify this is by how frequently you have to change a tampon or sanitary pad. If it is more than every hour while awake, then you are bleeding too much. Passing large clots can also be a sign of heavy bleeding. It is normal to pass clots, as long as they are no larger than a dime.

DUB is a common problem at the "bookends" of your reproductive life—at the beginning and the end. In anovulatory cycles, the estrogen levels rise as usual, but since an egg is not released, a corpus luteum is never formed. Therefore, progesterone is not produced. The endometrium continues to proliferate and eventually outgrows its blood supply. This leads to irregular bleeding as part of the lining is sloughed. Nearly one-half of all adolescents in the United States will experience irregular bleeding in the first year following menarche, and 20 percent will experience irregularities for up to five years.

## Painful periods

Menstrual cramps are common, especially during the first few days of the cycle. Chemicals called *prostaglandins* are released that stimulate the muscles in the uterus to contract. Over-the-counter pain medications such as ibuprofen block prostaglandins and can be helpful in relieving this pain. It is uncommon to experience pain with the first three to six menstrual cycles, before ovulation is established. Dysmenorrhea is more common during the early reproductive years and causes significant disruption in life in 15 percent of women.[1]

Primary dysmenorrhea is pain without an anatomic cause, while secondary dysmenorrhea results from an abnormality within the uterus. In primary dysmenorrhea, there is an excess production of prostaglandins. Symptoms include:

- "Labor-like" pains in the lower abdomen that come and go
- Fatigue
- Low backache
- Headache
- Nausea
- Vomiting
- Diarrhea

Girls may assume the fetal position or use a heating pad on the lower abdomen in an attempt to gain relief from the pain. Nonsteroidal anti-inflammatory drugs (NSAIDs) are often prescribed for symptom relief. If the pain is persistent, oral contraceptives can be used to prevent ovulation.

## PMS and PMDD

Premenstrual syndrome (PMS) is a group of physical, mood, and behavior changes that occur in a regular, cyclic fashion during the later stages of the menstrual cycle. Most women will experience symptoms one to two weeks before the onset of their period, and their symptoms will resolve near the end of their period. Hormonal fluctuations are responsible for symptoms such as:

- Weight gain
- Breast tenderness
- Bloating
- Mood swings
- Irritability
- Acne
- Fatigue
- Body aches
- Nausea
- Diarrhea
- Difficulty sleeping and concentrating
- Craving sweet or salty foods

Every woman is different in the type of symptoms they experience, but all share the common timing of their symptoms. It is difficult to estimate the number of people who suffer from PMS, but it is believed that up to 85 percent of women will experience PMS at some point during their lifetime.[2] It is not clear what causes PMS, so the treatment is directed toward the symptoms. There is some evidence that a multivitamin with folic acid and calcium supplementation can help. Aerobic exercise, relaxation techniques such as yoga, and dietary changes such as avoiding caffeine, salt, refined sugars, and alcohol are beneficial.

Premenstrual dysphoric disorder (PMDD) is a type of depression where a woman experiences depressed mood, anxiety, mood swings, and decreased interest in activities beginning the week prior to menses, or the menstrual flow. It is a severe form of PMS and requires specific criteria to make the diagnosis, including at least five of the following symptoms beginning in the two weeks prior to menses and ending within four days of the start of your period:[3]

- Feeling hopeless or sad
- Feeling tense, anxious, or "on edge"
- Moodiness or frequent crying
- Constant irritability or anger
- Lack of interest in things you normally enjoy
- Difficulty concentrating

- Appetite changes, overeating or cravings
- Trouble sleeping
- Feeling overwhelmed
- Physical symptoms such as swollen breasts, headaches, bloating, and weight gain

PMDD is usually treated with antidepressant medications called selective serotonin reuptake inhibitors (SSRIs).

# Chapter 2

# BODY IMAGE

ONE OF THE DIFFICULTIES FACING TODAY'S YOUNG WOMAN IS BODY IMAGE. Hollywood and the fashion industry offer a false identity of "true" beauty by parading lanky, waif-thin models on magazine covers, runways, and television shows as the standard to which all women should aspire. Although nearly every marketing venue targeting young women portrays beauty as a size-zero woman with sunken cheek bones, few young girls and women are naturally "waif-thin."

What most women do not realize is that the very faces and bodies presented to them in the media are products of clever manipulation and surgical enhancements. As physicians, we can spot breast augmentation, Botox, lip enhancement, rhinoplasty, and face-lifts a mile away! But most women, especially younger ones, believe that what they see in the media is real.

*Like most fourteen-year-old girls, Laura was concerned about her appearance. Despite her attempts to control her weight, Laura was gaining weight, and her five-foot-two-inch frame was now supporting 180 pounds. Her mother brought her to our office because, aside from weight gain, Laura had developed facial hair on the sides and her acne had worsened. The previous year Laura had only one period, and her cycles were irregular.*

*Upon examination, we noticed stretch marks over much of her abdominal area and the beginnings of darker hair rising from her pubic region upward. A series of blood tests showed that Laura had a condition called polycystic ovarian syndrome, or PCOS, which causes an imbalance in the ovarian production of male-like hormones combined with an insensitivity to insulin. This could cause her to gain weight and stop menstruating. PCOS is a common condition, and we later discovered that Laura's mother suffered the same symptoms in her teen years but was never diagnosed.*

*We discussed possible treatment options and selected oral contraceptives, which would suppress the production of abnormal hormone levels by her ovaries and regulate her flow. Laura's acne cleared and her periods became predictable, a benefit of birth control pills. Through diet and exercise, she eventually lost some weight. In the future, she might need medical help conceiving a child, but for now, this was not an issue.*

# The Dangers of Obsessing Over Body Image

An American Psychological Association task force found that virtually every media form studied showed evidence of the sexualization of women. These included television, music videos and lyrics, movies, magazines, sports media, video games, the Internet, and the various advertising outlets associated with these media. The American Psychological Association went on to conclude, "In study after study, findings have indicated that women more often than men are portrayed in a sexual manner (e.g., dressed in revealing clothing, with bodily postures or facial expressions that imply sexual readiness) and are objectified (e.g., used as a decorative object, or as body parts rather than a whole person). In addition, a narrow (and unrealistic) standard of physical beauty is heavily emphasized. These are the models of femininity presented for young girls to study and emulate."[1]

Studies show that sexualization is linked with three of the most common mental health problems of girls and women: eating disorders, low self-esteem, and depression.[2] Research in teenage and adult women has shown associations between exposure to thin women as the ideal of female beauty and the development of eating disorders.[3]

## Eating disorders

According to body-image researcher Sarah Murnen, professor of psychology at Kenyon College, "The promotion of the thin, sexy ideal in our culture has created a situation where the majority of girls and women don't like their bodies....And body dissatisfaction can lead girls to participate in very unhealthy behaviors to try to control weight."[4]

This has led to an explosive increase in what experts call "disordered eating," a term used to describe a range of eating problems, including frequent dieting, anorexia nervosa, and bulimia.

"We know seeing super-thin models can play a role in causing anorexia," says Nada Stotland, professor of psychiatry at Rush Medical College in Chicago and vice president of the American Psychiatric Association. "Because many models and actresses are so thin, it makes anorexics think their emaciated bodies are normal."[5]

Research is confirming that younger and younger girls are being affected by the media message that thin is beautiful. According to Sarah Murnen, an expert on eating disorders for over fifteen years, "We have done studies of grade-school girls, and even in grade 1, girls think the culture is telling them that they should model themselves after celebrities who are svelte, beautiful and sexy."[6] Murnen and her colleagues reviewed twenty-one studies that looked at the media's effect on more than six thousand girls, ages ten and older, and found those who were exposed to the most fashion magazines were more likely to suffer from poor body images.[7]

According to psychologist Sharon Lamb, coauthor of *Packaging Girlhood: Rescuing Our Daughters From Marketers' Schemes*, even very young girls are being bombarded with the message that they need to be super-skinny to be sexy. The gaunt images of celebrities such as Nicole Richie, Paris Hilton, and Kate Bosworth are frequently on magazine covers that young girls buy. Lamb, a psychology professor at Saint Michael's College in Vermont, says that, "Girls are being taught very young that thin and sexy is the way they want to be when they grow up, so they'd better start working on that now."[8]

**Anorexia nervosa.** According to the National Alliance on Mental Illness, anorexia nervosa is defined as "a refusal to maintain minimal body weight within 15 percent of an individual's normal weight." Estimates suggest up to 1 percent of the U.S. population suffers from anorexia, with 90 percent of the cases occurring in adolescent or young women.[9] It is a serious, often chronic, and life-threatening eating disorder. Even when they become extremely thin, anorexics continue to think they look fat. Other characteristics include an intense fear of gaining weight and a distorted body image.

Women who are anorexic drop body fat so severely that most of them will stop menstruating due to the lack of ovulation. This, of course, hinders a woman's ability to get pregnant. If she does get pregnant, the anorexic will have a difficult time dealing with the expected weight gain of pregnancy, and the developing fetus will often suffer malnutrition, which leads to low birth weight, preterm birth, and other pregnancy complications. Anorexia leads to bone loss, or osteoporosis, plus heart and brain damage from malnutrition. According to the National Institutes of Health, anorexia leads to death in 10 percent of cases.[10]

Here are certain signs of anorexia that mothers, coaches, teachers, and friends should be aware of in the lives of all girls:

- Anorexics often cut their food into tiny pieces.
- They refuse to eat in front of others.
- They prepare food for others but do not eat it themselves.
- They may exercise obsessively.
- They are often involved in activities that place pressure on them to be thin, such as ballet, gymnastics, or modeling.

The majority of women suffering from anorexia are Caucasian and begin shortly after puberty; however, some severe life events can turn women in their sixties and seventies into anorexics.

Treatment of anorexia can be difficult because the patient is often in denial of her problem. Since she sees herself as too heavy, it is difficult for her to accept that she must gain weight. Also, eating under the prescription of others represents loss of control over her body.

Those who are diagnosed and treated early in the disease process have the highest rate of success. Patients who accept their disease and are willing to undergo treatment may be able to reverse most of the medical complications of anorexia when their weight is restored. But because most anorexics remain in denial for some time, they are usually fairly advanced in the disease before entering treatment.

Some patients can be treated as outpatients, but others who have a delayed diagnosis will need hospitalization to stabilize their dangerously low weight. These include those whose weight has fallen below 30 percent of their normal weight. Severe and life-threatening malnutrition may require intravenous feeding. Experienced treatment programs have a two-thirds success rate in restoring normal weight, but relapse is common.[11]

Antidepressant drug therapy is often used for treatment. Some form of psychotherapy is needed to deal with underlying emotional issues. Behavioral therapy, group therapy, and family therapy are all important aspects of care. A nutritionist is helpful in guiding those with anorexia toward proper eating habits. Support groups are also helpful and break the social isolation so many with anorexia experience.

Even with treatment, most anorexics will prefer a thinner weight and continue some preoccupation with food and calories. We see this in our pregnant patients who have a history of eating disorders. They will commonly request that they be told no information about their current weight or the weight gain they experience during their pregnancy for fear that the normal twenty-five- to thirty-pound increase will cause a relapse in their disorder.

**Bulimia.** Bulimia is an eating disorder characterized by cycles of excessive eating (bingeing) followed shortly thereafter with purging. This can be in the form of forced vomiting, laxative use, or excessive exercise.

Bulimia is usually a disease of adolescent girls and young women. They often are of normal or nearly normal weight. Since they commonly exercise, these women appear to others to be healthy role models. In contrast with anorexics, however, bulimics feel a loss of control over their eating habits and tremendous guilt in the purging.[12]

Causes of bulimia are felt to include societal pressure to be thin and undiagnosed depression. Because bulimia is done in secret, it may be difficult to diagnose unless the person is "caught."

Medical complications from bulimia include dental cavities and loss of tooth enamel from exposure to stomach acids. These signs are often detected by the woman's dentist or dental hygienist. Some women have cuts and scars on their knuckles from forcing themselves to vomit. Physicians often detect cardiac arrhythmias and muscle weakness from loss of potassium due to vomiting or laxative abuse.

Because patients suffering from bulimia feel shame from this activity, it is easier to treat than anorexia. Underlying depression treated with medication and counseling about proper body image usually cure them.

## Polycystic Ovarian Syndrome

While not a psychiatric disorder, polycystic ovarian syndrome (PCOS) is a medical condition that causes weight gain after puberty and impacts body image. PCOS can be a trigger for eating disorders as women try to gain control over their changing bodies. The cause of PCOS is unknown but is primarily an endocrine (hormone) disorder. In PCOS, the ovaries do not ovulate properly, creating cysts that secrete too much testosterone, which leads to increased acne and thickening of facial, chest, and abdominal hair. Male-pattern baldness can also occur over time.

There is also an increase in insulin production, which encourages deposits into the fat cells, leading to rapid increases in weight during the teens and early twenties. At the same time, the hormonal imbalance stops ovulation, resulting in irregular or even absent menstrual periods and later infertility. Women who suffer from PCOS have an increased lifetime risk of diabetes as they become insensitive to insulin. High cholesterol levels lead to an increased risk of heart disease. PCOS is a serious condition, affecting nearly 10 percent of all women.[13]

Because the hallmark traits of this disease are weight gain, acne, facial hair, and irregular menstrual cycles, women with PCOS suffer from poor self-esteem and body image. They feel they have no control over their bodies and watch themselves gain weight while typically eating far less than their peers. The cosmetic changes these teens and young adults experience will typically be with them for life.

PCOS can be treated with birth control pills to put the ovaries at "rest" and stop the imbalance that is occurring. This will regulate the menstrual cycle and stop further unwanted hair growth. A brand that is specifically designed for PCOS is called *Yasmin*. It has a mild diuretic that daily flushes out the water retention and bloating commonly experienced by patients during their menstrual cycles. The progesterone component is unique in that it does not digest itself into any testosterone-like by-products, aiding acne and facial hair complaints.

The cosmetic changes in facial and body hair are more difficult to eliminate. Some dermatologists prescribe medication to stop hair growth. These take many months to work as each hair follicle has a long lifespan. For those wanting faster results, laser hair removal has become a popular alternative, but it is expensive for some and requires multiple treatments. We will discuss treatment of PCOS infertility in a later chapter.

# Chapter 3

# SEX AND TEENS

T HERE IS NOT ONE FEMALE WHO HAS NOT EXPERIENCED AND HAD TO DEAL with her sexuality. Sadly, sex has taken on such a negative connotation in the Christian community that most teen girls in the church will discuss sexual issues with their friends before they talk to a minister, priest, or Christian counselor—let alone their parents! Teen girls should be able to approach the mature women in their lives to openly discuss these issues before they give away their most valuable gift—their virginity—for a fleeting moment of passion.

*When Ann was eighteen, her mother brought her to the office for her first annual exam. Sensing her daughter felt uncomfortable, Ann's mom offered to leave the room during the examination. After she left, I (EAK) asked Ann if she had ever been sexually active. Tears began to well up in her eyes, and with a shaky voice she replied, "Sort of."*

*I asked, "What do you mean, 'sort of'?"*

*She began to cry. "I just broke up with my boyfriend. We had been dating for about a year. He kept trying to get me to have sex with him, but when I told him I wanted to wait until I was married, he said that we had been together for such a long time that he had waited long enough. Then he forced himself on me."*

*She felt degraded during the act but tried to convince herself that it was the right thing to do because, after all, he said he loved her. Shortly after that, they began having problems in their relationship. They were fighting more, and it seemed every time they were together, all he cared about was having sex with her. Finally, she decided to end the relationship.*

*"Ann, you shouldn't feel bad about what happened to you. It took a lot of strength and courage to get out of the relationship and not continue putting yourself in that situation. He had no right to force you to do anything against your will, even if you two were dating. What he did was a form of rape and should not be tolerated."*

*A year later, a confident Ann came to visit me, and she was smiling. When I asked her how things were going, she told me about her new boyfriend she had met at college. She said they were considering marriage after finishing college and planned to wait until they were married to have sexual intercourse. She said she had confided in him about her past, and he was supportive of her.*

# What to Expect

During puberty and adolescence, your hormones begin gearing your body up for what it is made to do—bear children. Reproduction is driven by desires placed in your heart by God to continue what He has created—life on Earth. However, these desires can become confusing when mixed with the hormonal signaling going on inside of your brain. It is important to realize that the desire to experience sex is normal at this time in your life. It takes considerable strength and control to overcome these urges.

One way to help avoid becoming overwhelmed by these urges is to not place yourself in a situation where you are able to express these thoughts. If you have a serious boyfriend, or even a friend you are becoming attracted to, make sure you hang out together in groups of people or with adults. If you do go out alone, make sure you are in a public setting, such as a restaurant or movie theater. Do not agree to go somewhere where the two of you will be alone.

Finding other ways to express your attraction is critical. Involve yourselves in activities you both enjoy when together. When you are alone, invest in the power of prayer, seeking strength from God during this challenging time in your life. Do not feel bad or dirty for thinking about sex or for desiring to explore another more fully. God has intended for you to share this special act and the bond it creates, but it is important that you find the right time and person in your life to do this with.

# Things to Watch Out For

## Sexual exploration

It is not uncommon for teens and college students to have periods of confusion regarding feelings of sexual attraction toward the same sex. Hormonal surges are hitting the brain, and sexual urges may become displaced, attaching themselves to close friends of the same sex. Acknowledging these feelings and realizing their temporary nature can diffuse the fears some teens have that they are homosexual. Once the root of these urges is known, most young people will find they are replaced with appropriate sexual attractions to the opposite sex.

There are some young people who find the sexual attractions to the same sex only intensifying with time. These are often those who have been sexually abused when they were young and have experienced sexual trauma that causes sexual confusion. The earlier these feelings are dealt with, the more likely that person can recover from their trauma and move to heterosexual sexual expression.

> (i)    Counseling centers now specialize in treating victims of sexual abuse and sexual confusion. A favorite resource of ours is Desert Stream Ministries (www.desertstream.org).

## Sexual abuse and incest

Sexual abuse, or molestation, is defined as forcing undesired sexual acts by one person on another. There are several ways sexual abuse can be carried out. One is nonconsensual, forced sexual contact, such as rape or sexual assault. Psychological abuse can occur verbally or by stalking. Using a position of power or authority for sex is also considered sexual abuse. Statutory rape is when a sexual act occurs with a minor who is under the age of consent determined by a particular state. It is different from other types of rape because force does not have to be present.

Young victims may not recognize that they are being sexually abused, and they are often reluctant to disclose the offense. They may feel like something is wrong with them or that the abuse is somehow their fault. Often, they fear that they may suffer consequences worse than the actual abuse. The victim may feel guilty that the perpetrator may suffer or be in fear of retaliation. Many victims are embarrassed by the abuse and are reluctant to answer questions about the abuse. In a study of 630 cases of alleged sexual abuse of children from 1985 to 1989, findings indicated that 79 percent of children initially denied the abuse or were tentative in disclosing. Of those who did disclose, most did so accidentally, and some recanted their statements.[1]

If you suspect that your daughter, sister, niece, granddaughter, or any female family member is a victim of sexual abuse, here are some of the telltale signs:

- Experiencing fear, anxiety, depression, anger, and hostility
- Difficulty with close relationships
- Problems with substance abuse and poor self-esteem
- May develop eating disorders, becoming either overweight or underweight so as not to feel sexually attractive

Incest is when sexual activity occurs between family members. Even if consensual, most cultures consider it to be wrong ethically and spiritually. Incest can lead to inbreeding, which is when people who are closely related reproduce, increasing genetic similarities. Parental incest can do severe psychological harm to a child, causing depression, post-traumatic stress disorder, and even suicide. Many children who are victims of this type of abuse go on to carry it out on their own children.

## IT'S IN THE WORD

Leviticus 18:6–18 discusses the prohibitions of sexual relations between family members. God instructs the people not to "uncover the nakedness" of family members, specifically, the father or mother, stepmother, sister or half-sister, grandchild, aunt, daughter-in-law, sister-in-law, and mother-in-law.

## Date rape

Date rape is sexual assault that occurs between two people who know each other. It is also referred to as acquaintance rape and accounts for approximately half of all cases of rape. Even if the two people involved were intimate or had previous sexual relations, *any* case of forced sexual contact is considered rape. *No one should be forced into a sexual act.* Rape does not come from passion or love; it is an act of violence. It does not ever occur because the victim brought it on herself.

Many cases of date rape occur in the presence of drugs or alcohol. Alcohol can lower inhibitions, impair common sense, and even incite aggression. There are drugs commonly referred to as "date rape drugs" that make a person black out and forget what happens. These drugs are often consumed when slipped into the drink of a young woman while she's not looking. It is estimated that over 80 percent of date rape occurs when one partner is under the influence of alcohol, and 50 percent of the time, both parties have used alcohol.[2] Date rape drugs are appealing to sexual predators because they are tasteless and odorless, they leave the body quickly, and they are not detected on routine drug screens. They leave the victim without any memory of what happened.

To protect yourself from becoming a victim of date rape, only go to parties or hang out with people you and your family know and trust. When drinking alcoholic or nonalcoholic drinks, only accept closed drinks at a party or drinks directly from the bartender. Never leave your unopened drink on the table. If people seem "too intoxicated" for the amount they are drinking, a date rape drug may be the cause. Get out of situations that make you uncomfortable and trust your gut instinct; God is telling you that you are not safe.

# SECTION 2
## THE HEALTHY WOMAN

# Chapter 4

# YOUR GYNECOLOGIST AND YOU

*Kim was our patient since her college years and has continued visiting us every year since then. Two years after getting married, she developed an abnormal Pap smear. This was the first abnormal examination, and she was very surprised by our call.*

*Her Pap smear showed that she had abnormal cells and the presence of high-risk HPV (human papillomavirus). She would need to undergo a colposcopy to better identify the extent of her abnormality. Sometimes during the screening process, Pap smears may be reported as "false positives" but in reality are completely normal. The colposcopy would help us determine the truth.*

*Two biopsies were taken of her cervix, and the pathologist's report showed "mild dysplasia, low-grade lesion." Kim was young and never missed an annual exam, so we gave Kim the option of waiting a few months to see if the cervix would heal.*

*After six months, Kim returned for another examination, which revealed she still had abnormal cells. She decided to undergo cryotherapy to freeze these cells, and after healing, Kim returned. The Pap smear was completely normal. Since then, we have kept track of her and she has had no recurrence.*

## The First Visit

Visiting the gynecologist for the first time can be a scary experience. Most women fear the pelvic exam, and many are embarrassed to be examined. But the gynecologist will be one of the most important physicians in a woman's life. He or she can be a confidant, a counselor, a trusted friend, an ally, and an instrument in healing. The gynecologist is there to offer advice in selecting birth control, planning for a baby, care during pregnancy, help through the changes of life, and treatment for any gynecological diseases that may come your way. But it all starts with the first visit.

Many mothers ask us when their daughters should see the gynecologist for the first time. This is an individual decision and is based on the need of that young woman. Anyone who is sexually active or planning to become sexually active needs a visit. Those who are already sexually active need screening for sexually transmitted diseases and cancerous changes of the cervix. If they do not desire pregnancy, counseling for birth control is given.

Many girls will transition from the pediatrician or family physician to the gynecologist in their teen years. We are seeing more teenagers since the HPV (human papillomavirus) vaccine was introduced because many mothers desire vaccination for their daughters before they become exposed to that STD. We will deal specifically with this topic in a later chapter. Mothers also bring in their daughters to discuss birth control. Our city has some of the highest rates of teenage pregnancy in the country. If a girl is planning on becoming sexually active, we certainly want the opportunity to discuss the options of birth control before she becomes pregnant.

Young women who are still virgins can also benefit from a visit to the gynecologist. They generally will not need a pelvic exam, and it can be a time to get to know one another. When she feels comfortable, a young woman is free to ask questions and receive valuable information.

Remember to ask your physician lots of questions. If your physician is going to treat you, then good communication is the key to discovering how to properly maintain your health. Here is a sample checklist of questions to ask:

- How do I do a proper breast exam?
- What is a Pap smear?
- How do I prevent STDs?
- Can you tell if I have an STD?
- What is a normal menstrual cycle?
- What are my options for birth control?

## What Is Checked at the Annual Exam

The annual examination includes several things. The first is a review of lifestyle issues that may need to be addressed. Personal habits such as smoking, alcohol and drug use, and sexual practices are addressed. Counseling in these areas is designed to prevent disease.

A physical exam includes height, weight, blood pressure measurement, and on some occasions a urine specimen. A BMI, or body mass index, can be calculated from the height and weight measurements to more accurately evaluate obesity than a simple weight alone. (See BMI chart on page 45.)

We generally palpate the neck to feel the thyroid gland and determine if it is enlarged. Women are five to nine times more likely to have thyroid disease than men, with most being undiagnosed.[1] A swollen thyroid gland can be a sign of disease.

Often the physician will listen to the heart to check for murmurs or abnormal rhythms.

A breast exam is then done to evaluate for lumps or other abnormalities. This is also a great opportunity to educate a woman on the technique of breast self-examination. This can be accomplished both standing and lying down. It has been suggested that it be done in the shower as a way of developing a routine. How, when, or where it is done is not nearly as important as simply doing a self-exam.

Breast self-examination is an important tool in the detection of breast cancer. If a woman does not become familiar with the feel and consistency of her own breasts, she will not be able to distinguish a change in them, which can be the first sign of disease. Many of our patients rely on their annual gynecologic exam to screen for breast disease. This leaves them vulnerable the rest of the year.

The woman who regularly examines herself is in much better position to notice a change compared to the physician who only sees her once a year. This applies not only to the breast exam but to other areas such as mole surveillance to prevent skin cancer.

The breast exam is done with two fingers pressing the breast tissue against the rib cage or gently squeezing between the fingers. This allows for the detection of irregular tissue or lumps. Most of these will be fibrous cysts or benign tumors, but it is important to enlist the patient to ensure there is no change in size between visits. Abnormalities detected during the breast exam may require evaluation with sonography or mammography to exclude breast cancer.

---

(i)  For more information on breast cancer and awareness, visit the Susan G. Komen for the Cure Web site at http://cms .komen.org/komen/index.htm.

---

Next, the abdomen is palpated for any tumors or hernias. An inspection of the vulva is done to evaluate for abnormalities or diseases, including herpes, genital warts, or cancer. An internal examination of the vagina and cervix is accomplished with a device called a *speculum*. The speculum is inserted into the vagina and opened to reveal the vaginal walls and the cervix. An inspection is done for the presence of vaginal discharge, which could indicate infection ranging from yeast or bacterial overgrowth to sexually transmitted diseases. If discharge is present, a sample may be taken for evaluation under a microscope or for laboratory analysis. Often a diagnosis is available by the end of the visit, but some laboratory assays and cultures make take two or three days.

Inspection of the cervix is followed by a Pap smear. This consists of a brush or swab that is twirled around the opening of the cervix to collect cells for evaluation. The primary goal is to identify cells that are precancerous. With regular Pap smears we hope to avoid the diagnosis of full-blown cancer. Once the smear is taken, the speculum is removed and one or two gloved fingers are inserted into the vagina while the other hand is pressed against the lower abdomen. This is called the *bimanual examination.* The uterus and ovaries are palpated between the two hands for any abnormalities in shape or size.

If necessary in younger women, and many times in those over fifty, the last component of the pelvic exam is the insertion of a gloved finger into the rectum. This is done to evaluate behind the uterus for nodules that could indicate endometriosis. In older women, a stool specimen is taken for evaluation for blood in the screening of colorectal cancer.

### The Pap smear

The Pap smear is probably the one item of the examination that is most closely associated with the yearly exam. Ask most women, and they will say they are going to get their yearly Pap smear. While family practitioners offer to do this test, it is most often done by a gynecologist who is specialized in diagnosing and treating female genital disorders.

Developed by Dr. George Papanicolaou in the 1930s, the procedure involves sampling the lining of the cervix at the opening of the birth canal called the *transformation zone,* or *T-Zone,* and examining the cells under a microscope. In the years since World War II, the Pap smear has become the most widely used cancer screening method in the world and the most successful cancer screening technique in medical history. Pap screening reduced cervical cancer death rates by 74 percent between 1955 and 1992, and the rate continues to decline by about 2 percent a year.[2]

It was common practice for technicians to view each slide themselves, but now an automated computer model can more accurately scan these slides. A liquid-based smear also allows for the detection of the human papillomavirus (HPV), which we will discuss in a later chapter.

### Menstrual cycles

A common component of the gynecologic history is the evaluation of the menstrual cycle. Every visit will record the last menstrual period and whether it was normal. One reason for an office visit, or for a referral from a family physician, is the evaluation and treatment of abnormal menstrual cycles. Every day in our offices, we see women who are unhappy with their menstrual cycles, and we can often bring them great relief.

In taking the menstrual history, it is important to determine if the patient could be pregnant, as we never want to treat someone with medications who might be pregnant. Your doctor may ask to do a urine pregnancy test as part of his or her evaluation. There may be blood work to check for hormone imbalance of the ovary, pituitary, or thyroid gland.

A bimanual pelvic examination will be done to feel for abnormalities in the size or shape of the uterus. A pelvic ultrasound may be offered either in the office or at a radiology facility to check for the presence of uterine fibroid tumors or polyps that could be causing abnormal bleeding patterns.

# When an Extra Visit Is Needed

There are times during the year when you may need to make an extra trip to the OB/GYN's office. The most common reasons are usually a follow-up visit after an abnormal Pap result, vaginal infections, and urinary tract infections. Let's begin with the most serious—an abnormal Pap.

### Evaluating and treating an abnormal Pap

When an abnormal Pap smear is detected, the current recommendation is to also screen it for high-risk HPV. If this is not present, there is no danger to the cervix and the smear is considered "normal." If a high-risk virus is detected, or if evidence of precancerous cells is seen, a more thorough inspection of the cervix is required for two reasons. First, each year millions of Pap smears are evaluated by computer and human microscopic inspection, which increases the chances of a "false positive." The second reason is that the Pap smear is a screening tool only. To truly gauge the extent of the disease and the risk of cervical cancer requires more than surface cells; a small biopsy of the full-thickness cervical tissue is needed so a pathologist can inspect it.

A procedure called *colposcopy* directly evaluates the cervix through a set of binoculars while a vinegar-like, topical solution is placed on the cervix. This solution changes the appearance of abnormal cervical cells so they can be detected through inspection using the colposcope. This inspection not only confirms if disease is present, but it also assesses the depth precancerous cells have penetrated. This information is critical in determining the treatment options available and their success in curing the condition.

### DID YOU KNOW?

Most cervical HPV infections will clear spontaneously, especially in women who are under the age of twenty-five.

The treatment options available depend upon whether it's a mild case or severe case. The mild, or low-grade, precancerous lesions of the cervix can be observed for several months to see if they clear on their own. Those that do not clear over time can be treated with freezing or cryotherapy. This involves placing a metal cone-shaped device onto the cervix and freezing the surface of the cervix through liquid nitrogen pumped into the device. It takes only minutes to achieve cell death and is generally well tolerated in an office setting with no anesthesia required. Most women experience some uterine cramping, so we advise our patients to take an over-the-counter pain reliever, such as ibuprofen or naproxen, about thirty minutes prior to their appointment. If you experience excessive bleeding or a high fever (101°F or higher), seek immediate medical attention.

If it is a more severe, or high-grade, form of dysplasia of the cervix, then that requires that the deeper layers of the cervix involved with disease be destroyed. It is preferable that they be removed as a specimen that can be evaluated to ensure complete removal and exclude an underlying undiagnosed cancer. This is done either in an office setting under local anesthesia or as an outpatient procedure with sedation. The LEEP (loop electrocautery excision procedure) is a common technique that uses laser or electrical cautery to remove these lesions.

For those who have had recurrent high-grade lesions and have completed their child-bearing phase, a hysterectomy is a final, but rarely used, option.

## Vaginal infections

Another common reason for visiting the gynecologist is evaluation and treatment of vaginal infections. Yeast infections are extremely common in women, with almost every woman suffering from this at some time in her life. The two most common complaints are a clumpy, white discharge and genital itching. The itching can be external, internal, or both, giving us clues to the origin of the problem.

We also ask the patient for a history of recent antibiotic use, especially for a sinus or upper respiratory infection, which is a common predecessor to the yeast infection. Antibiotics kill harmful bacteria, but they also tend to destroy the "good" bacteria that defend the vagina from invading yeast.

While there are effective over-the-counter (OTC) remedies for yeast infections, we would advise first-time sufferers to see a physician to ensure that it is not an STD. A sample can be obtained from a vaginal swab and immediate diagnosis can be made in the office.

## DID YOU KNOW?

Too many sweets or carbohydrates can contribute to recurrent yeast infections. Diabetes also raises the sugar content of the vagina and promotes the growth of yeast. If your diet is high in sugar, cut out refined sugars altogether, and you will see a dramatic improvement.

The second cause of vaginal infections is an overgrowth of abnormal bacteria, commonly called *bacterial vaginosis,* or BV. These infections may have some itching with them, but, unlike a yeast infection, the symptoms are a fishy odor and yellowish discharge. Most women try to treat this infection with an OTC yeast cream, only to discover that the relief was temporary. These infections require either a prescribed oral or vaginal antibiotic.

Some women come to the office thinking the external itching is an infection, but it is often a localized skin reaction. The vulvar skin is very sensitive to chemicals. Changing laundry detergent or fabric softener, soaking in bath products, or using synthetic materials like nylon can cause itching. Local steroid creams, changing to cotton underwear, and rewashing undergarments are often all that is needed to cure this problem.

Some women are allergic to latex, and exposure to condoms or medical exam gloves can cause vaginal irritation. But there are condoms and gloves that are made of polyurethane and, while more expensive, are designed for those allergic to latex.

### Urinary tract infection

Finally, another common reason for a gynecological visit is treatment of a urinary tract infection (UTI). From the urethra, it is a short journey to the bladder. If a woman is sexually active, bacteria from the vagina and rectum can be pushed into the urethra. Even girls or women who are not sexually active can have UTIs because bacteria from the rectum travels to the urethra. Common symptoms are an urge to urinate frequently, burning sensation when urinating, and pain. Some may experience severe symptoms such as back pain and fever, which may be an indication that the infection is affecting the kidneys.

## "MOM NEVER TOLD ME!"

Because yeast and bacteria come from the rectum, it is important to wipe from front to back after a bowel movement so the rectal contaminants are not brought forward to the vagina.

A sterile sample of urine is evaluated in the office for the presence of bacteria and white blood cells. Treatment with antibiotics may be given while a formal culture of the bacteria is done in the laboratory. Since this final result may take two or three days, the patient is often cured before the results are known. But a small percentage of infections are caused by bacteria that are resistant to the antibiotic your doctor may have prescribed, so it is important to have a culture for accuracy in treatment. Should a relapse of infection occur, it is also helpful to know if this is a new occurrence or an incomplete treatment of the prior infection.

# Chapter 5

# EMOTIONAL HEALTH

EVEN THE BRIGHTEST, MOST TALENTED, GODLY WOMEN CAN SUFFER IN the area of emotional health. There is tremendous stigma associated with mental health treatment, especially in the Christian community where many believe that prayer and meditation are the only avenues of treatment for anxiety, depression, or other disorders. We don't feel guilty if we need treatment for high blood pressure, diabetes, or thyroid conditions, but we feel tremendous shame if our brain chemicals and hormones are imbalanced. The brain is simply another organ of the body that sometimes needs help to function at its best. While we are strong proponents of prayer and meditating on the Bible, there are some medical circumstances that require medical intervention as well. We want to be there to lend a hand in a nonjudgmental way when medical treatment can be beneficial. Karen was one such case.

*Like many women, Karen was a wonderful wife and devoted mother. She placed her career on hold to meet the needs of her growing family. She was also a loyal and faithful friend, often called upon for her sound advice and wisdom.*

*But once a month, Karen would display explosive anger and biting sarcasm. Her husband and children received the brunt of her dramatic mood swings. Her husband noticed her mood swing from anger to depression in a single hour. She was like a female Jekyll and Hyde!*

*One day in the office, Karen told us of these uncontrollable mood swings. She noticed that during her period and the week after she was perfectly normal. But about ten days before she started her period, her emotions were irrational and she didn't feel like herself. Yet she felt powerless to stop the emotional changes she experienced.*

*We explained to Karen that it was not likely to be a major psychiatric disorder but a hormonal one caused by the changes in her menstrual cycle. She was most likely suffering from PMDD, or premenstrual dysphoric disorder, a variation of PMS.*

*We discussed various treatment options with her and recommended she stay away from caffeine and sugar during the last half of her cycle. It was also important that she reduce stress by not overloading herself with projects or commitments during that time.*

*We prescribed a low dose of an SSRI (selective serotonin reuptake inhibitor), a type of antidepressant medication, for those days of the month she felt were the most difficult to manage. She used about seven pills per month to raise her serotonin levels and maintain her emotional health. At our next visit, Karen related how she felt in control of her emotions for the first time in many years and no longer dreaded that "time of the month"—and neither did her family!*

## Things to Watch Out For

As OB/GYN specialists, perhaps the most common forms of emotional disorders we treat as related to hormonal imbalances in women are PMS, PMDD, depression, and generalized anxiety disorder (GAD). We are not specialized in the field of psychology or mental health, but we do work with these specialists to help patients regain their lives. Here are some things to watch out for in each of the four disorders.

### PMS

It is estimated that 75–85 percent of women experience some sign or symptom of premenstrual syndrome or PMS.[1] The common complaints include changes in mood such as anger, depression, irritability, and tearfulness; changes in attention such as forgetfulness, confusion, and difficulty staying on task; and physical changes of breast tenderness, bloating, headache, and decreased energy. These typically present in the second half of a woman's cycle, from ovulation to the beginning of menstruation, and are relieved when menstruation begins. A variation of PMS is called PMDD, which stands for *premenstrual dysphoric disorder*. This is a more severe form of PMS and affects 5 percent of women.[2]

Most women begin suffering PMS in their twenties and thirties, with symptoms actually worsening in the perimenopausal period. PMS usually fades after menopause is completed. While medical science has not identified the cause of PMS, it is no longer thought to be "only in their heads." Research has speculated that progesterone variations, endorphin changes, or prostaglandin levels interact at a particular time of the month to manifest dozens of signs and symptoms. No two women experience the exact same symptoms, and there is no set treatment that works for everyone.

Most households feel the effects of PMS each month, and many godly women struggle to control their thoughts and emotions during those critical days. A usually peaceful, organized, and happy woman can find herself transformed into someone she does not even recognize. This can be disruptive at work and home.

The good news is that there are remedies to alleviate this condition. A diet rich in complex carbohydrates and low in simple sugars seems to decrease the irritability of the nervous system. Similarly, decreasing alcohol and caffeine consumption during those two weeks also helps. Exercising several times a week releases endorphins that have a calming effect on the brain. Lessening salt intake can decrease bloating.

Additives like calcium and magnesium have been medically proven to aid PMS. Many of the symptoms of PMS are very similar to those seen with calcium deficiency. Some have wondered if a deficiency in calcium explains the development of PMS in some women. Calcium in doses of 1,200 mg per day is recommended for those who try this approach. Because calcium is needed to maintain good bone health, it is a helpful supplement regardless.

Magnesium is a mineral that has been shown to calm the nervous system. Obstetricians often administer it intravenously to stop premature labor or to protect women with toxemia from having seizures. Magnesium at 200 mg per day has been shown to lessen symptoms of PMS.[3]

## DID YOU KNOW?

Most women crave chocolate during their "time of the month." They tend to feel better after eating something "chocolatey." The reason they crave chocolate is because their bodies are deficient in magnesium, and chocolate is a source of magnesium.

Supplements of vitamins $B_6$ (no more than 100 mg per day) and E are also helpful, as are herbal remedies including evening primrose, chaste tree berry, and dong quai.[4]

Some women have found that simply understanding the variations of their bodies lessens the impact of PMS. Postponing difficult decisions for a few days may be the answer to the confusion and frustration some experience. If a family member or friend offends or angers you during that time of your cycle when you are vulnerable to irritation and anger, consider writing down your response and holding on to it for a few days. If, after your period begins, the feelings and thoughts on paper are still what you want to convey, you can be more confident with your response.

## PMDD

Like Karen at the beginning of this chapter, some women suffer from a more severe form of PMS known as PMDD. Prescription medications can be used and often begin with birth control pills to smooth the hormonal variations that occur in the second half of the menstrual cycle. These can lessen menstrual cramps and decrease irritability as well. There is even a birth control pill that includes a diuretic (or "water pill") to aid the physical symptoms of bloating and water retention. It is called Yaz and is the only FDA-approved oral contraceptive for the treatment of PMDD.

Many have found that a short course of medication that raises serotonin levels improves the mental as well as the physical symptoms. The feelings of depression, anger, irritability, and poor concentration are rapidly relieved in PMDD. This is very different from the psychiatric condition of depression, which takes at least two weeks to improve. The medications for PMDD are usually taken for the last seven to fourteen days of each cycle. It is unfortunate that these medications carry a pharmacology label of "antidepressants," conveying to the patients that we think they are "crazy." It is simply a category of drugs that we are discovering new uses for, such as weight loss, smoking cessation, and migraine control. Three of them are approved by the FDA for PMDD: Sarafem (a different name for Prozac), Paxil CR, and Zoloft. These also come in generic forms.

While we must live in this earthly vessel as we conduct our lives, knowledge of the body gives us tremendous power over it. Taking advantage of the natural, medical, and spiritual aids we have available can greatly improve our relationships at home, in the workplace, and with the body of Christ. We won't have to feel prisoner to "that time of the month" ever again!

## Depression

Depression and depressed mood seriously impair the quality of life of many women of all ages. In contrast to PMS and PMDD, these feelings persist throughout the month with little menstrual variation or relief. It is important to distinguish this from PMDD as the treatment is different.

Depression is thought to be the result of lowered serotonin and norepinephrine levels, brain chemicals that are necessary to the proper function of the brain. Heredity, life trauma, and gender also play a role. Over 32 million Americans will experience clinical depression at some time in their lives, with women being twice as likely to experience it as men. This may be due to hormonal changes with puberty, childbearing, and menopause.[5]

The diagnosis of clinical depression is more than just a brief period of sadness. Everyone feels sad when confronted with loss or unmet expectations. But these are temporary emotions that pass with time. Major depressive disorder, or clinical depression, is a set of symptoms that accompany sadness, persisting as a chronic state of mind. These symptoms include:

- Lack of interest in activities or hobbies you used to take pleasure in doing
- Loss of energy
- Change in appetite
- Change in sleep patterns (either too little or too much sleep)
- Difficulty concentrating or making decisions
- Feelings of worthlessness or hopelessness
- Thoughts of suicide or death[6]

There is also research to support an altering in the level of pain messages sent to the brain in those persons suffering with depression. Patients often report feeling overall body pain, similar to that experienced in fibromyalgia, a possible variant of depression. An estimated 65 percent of patients suffering from depression will exhibit symptoms of chronic pain.[7]

A wide variety of medications are on the market for the treatment of depression. The older class of drugs is called tricyclic antidepressants. These seem to work by indirectly affecting the balance of brain chemicals. One common side effect is sleepiness. These drugs may be given at bedtime to aid in both insomnia and depression. One of our favorites for use in treating insomnia is trazodone or Desyrel.

The newer classes of antidepressants are called selective serotonin reuptake inhibitors, or SSRIs. These medications work to increase the level of serotonin in the brain, a key chemical thought to be involved in depression.[8] These drugs are also used for anxiety, weight loss, smoking cessation, migraine control, and chronic pain therapy. Common brand names include Prozac, Paxil, Zoloft, Lexapro, and Celexa. Many come in a generic form. They generally take two to four weeks to begin working and peak at twelve weeks. Side effects include gastrointestinal upset, weight gain, decreased libido, and headache.

A variation of this class of drugs is called the selective serotonin-norepinephrine reuptake inhibitors, or SNRIs. In addition to providing relief for depression, these add the benefit of pain relief for those who need it. Two popular brands from this class are Cymbalta and Effexor.

⚠️ As with other medications, both SSRIs and SNRIs interact with other OTC remedies and other prescription medications. It is important to tell your physician about any other medications or herbal preparations you are taking to avoid potentially severe reactions.

## Anxiety disorder

Anxiety is another common psychiatric condition. A certain amount of anxiety can be a motivator to achieve at work or school. The feelings of dread may be warning signs of possible danger or risk. These are normal reactions.

Those who often feel anxious without reason and whose worries disrupt their daily life may have generalized anxiety disorder (GAD). This leads to excessive or unrealistic anxiety and worry about life circumstances, often without an identifiable cause. Other forms of the disease include phobias, panic attacks, and obsessive-compulsive disorder. Women are more likely than men to experience generalized anxiety disorder.[9]

There are prescription medications that help with the effects of generalized anxiety disorder. These fall into two classes, the antianxiety medications and the antidepressants. The antianxiety medications have the benefit of quick onset of action, able to treat the sudden and unexpected panic attack that can feel like a heart attack. Certain stressful situations may need only a short-term ability to relax, such as a plane flight or funeral.

Side effects of antianxiety medications include drowsiness, lack of muscle coordination, and problems with balance. For these reasons, it is not advised to drive or operate machinery when taking these drugs. They can also lead to dependency, using them daily to shield one from the normal stresses of work and family. For this reason, antianxiety medications are recommended for occasional and short-term use only. Commonly prescribed brands include Valium and Xanax.

The SSRIs are a useful class of medications for this condition that can be used long-term without the risk of dependency, and generally without the physical side effects noted above. Professional therapy is often useful in identifying root causes of anxiety and in guiding patients in the management of daily stress.

## IT'S IN THE WORD

There is no better source than the Word to replace negative thought patterns with the truth found in God's promises. As the Creator, God has intimate knowledge of how you were formed and for what purpose. When the world has knocked you down or told you lies about your abilities and strengths, turn to His Word for direction. The Book of Psalms is a great place to find encouragement.

Many are saying of me, "God will not deliver him." But you are a shield around me, O LORD; you bestow glory on me and lift up my head. To the LORD I cry aloud, and he answers me from his holy hill. I lie down and sleep; I wake again, because the Lord sustains me.

—Psalm 3:2–5

Why am I discouraged? Why is my heart so sad? I will put my hope in God! I will praise him again, my Savior and my God!

—Psalm 42:5–6, NLT


I will praise You, for I am fearfully and wonderfully made; marvelous are Your works, and that my soul knows very well.

—Psalm 139:14, NKJV

God's promises for you can be found throughout the Bible.

You will keep him in perfect peace, whose mind is stayed on You, because he trusts in You.

—Isaiah 26:3, NKJV

"For I know the plans I have for you," declares the LORD, "plans to prosper you and not to harm you, plans to give you hope and a future."

—Jeremiah 29:11

But the fruit of the Spirit is love, joy, peace, longsuffering, kindness, goodness, faithfulness, gentleness, and self-control.

—Galatians 5:22–23, NKJV

Be anxious for nothing, but in everything by prayer and supplication, with thanksgiving, let your requests be made known to God; and the peace of God, which surpasses all understanding, will guard your hearts and minds through Christ Jesus.

—Philippians 4:6–7, NKJV

# Chapter 6

# DIET AND EXERCISE

Having a healthy diet is one of the best things you can do for your overall health. Your diet, along with exercise, directly affects your weight, which affects your overall health. Many women have difficulty following a healthy eating plan. When you are constantly on the go and are focused on everyone but yourself, it is easy to skip meals or eat less than healthy fast food. Sometimes you may feel the need to reward your cravings, which are also often not healthy choices. Most of the time, planning and knowing what is good to eat can improve your diet and, therefore, your health dramatically.

*I (EAK) remember one forty-five-year-old woman who had moved to the area two years earlier. She came to see me for an annual exam. During the visit, she told me that she had not visited a doctor for several years. I knew she needed to have a Pap smear and a mammogram done soon. After her examination, I told her the importance of regular health screening and maintenance. She said she knew she needed to take care of herself, but after her father's death two years earlier, she didn't feel like doing anything. She had stopped exercising, was eating unhealthy foods, and had put on fifty pounds.*

*I talked with her about diet and exercise, emphasizing that in order to lose weight, she needed to consume fewer calories than she burned. We talked about healthy foods and ways to exercise. When she returned the following year, she had lost fifty pounds—down to her weight before her father's death. She had joined a cycling club and was looking forward to competing in a bike race the following month.*

## Nutrition

Proper nutrition is key to good health and is vital to the growth and development of children and adolescents. The Department of Health and Human Services publishes Dietary Guidelines for Americans every five years, most recently in 2005. Increase your intake of fruits, vegetables, low-fat dairy products, and whole grains to provide important health benefits. Choose healthy fats, such as extra-virgin olive oil, and lean protein, such as chicken and fish.

Avoid eating foods that are high in trans fats, saturated fats, and refined sugars. Alcohol provides calories but no nutrients; it should be used in moderation only. Pregnant women should avoid any amount of alcohol.

Women in particular have specific nutritional needs depending on age. Adolescent girls and women of childbearing age are frequently deficient in iron and should eat foods that are rich in iron. Folic acid is necessary for women who are or may become pregnant; these women should take a supplement of 400 mcg daily, which can be found in most multivitamins, in addition to eating foods high in folate. Calcium and vitamin D help protect against bone loss and are necessary supplements in increasing amounts as a woman ages. Postmenopausal women should take in 1,500 mg of calcium and 800 IU of vitamin D daily.

## Review of Popular Diet Plans

Just Google the word *diet*, and the search engine lists over 180 million Web sites. Each new year, millions of Americans make a resolution to lose weight and try all sorts of diets, but this chart focuses on the most popular plans.

| POPULAR DIET PLANS | | | |
|---|---|---|---|
| **Diet** | **Description** | **Pros** | **Cons** |
| Atkins | Restrict carbohydrates; eat more protein to use the bodies' fat reserves | Lose weight fast | Excess fats may lead to other health problems; limits the intake of healthy fruits and vegetables |
| South Beach | Similar to the Atkins plan, but instead of restricting carbohydrates, it limits the intake based on a glycemic index | Low-sugar carbs allowed; unhealthy fats restricted | Two-week induction phase where virtually all carbs are banned; while significant weight loss may occur, most of it is water weight. |
| Jenny Craig | Teaches people how to eat healthy and increase activity level | Prepackaged meals assist with portion controls; variety of foods; convenient; offers online support and individual counseling | Prepackaged foods are expensive; excludes the dieter's family members |

| | | | |
|---|---|---|---|
| Weight Watchers | Teaches people how to change their lifestyles by increasing activity level, learning portion control, and making healthier food choices | No special prepackaged foods needed; anyone can participate; offers choice of online support or weekly group meetings | Attending weekly meetings and membership can be expensive |
| Slim Fast | Portion control and limiting calories | Meal replacements and snacks take the guesswork out of what you should be eating; supportive Web site with an exercise program | Have to purchase Slim Fast products and like them for it to work |
| The Zone | 30 percent protein, 30 percent fat, and 40 percent carbohydrates | Will help you reduce risk of heart disease, high blood pressure, and diabetes; you lose weight and feel great; easy to follow, offering recommendations for foods as well as portion size | No scientific studies have been done to support these claims |

In the end, the only diets that are successful are ones in which you limit your caloric intake, make healthier choices, and increase your activity level.

## BMI: Body Mass Index and Health Risks

The number of Americans who are overweight or obese continues to increase in America. An estimated 97 million Americans are overweight or obese, with an annual cost of obesity-related disease approaching $100 billion in the United States. The latest data reports that 54.9 percent of adults aged twenty to seventy-four fall into one of these two categories.[1]

Body mass index, or BMI, is calculated by taking your weight (in pounds) and dividing it by your height squared (in inches), and then multiplying that by 703. The mathematical formula looks like this:

$$BMI = \frac{W \text{ (lbs)}}{H \text{ (in)} \times H \text{ (in)}} \times 703$$

## BMI Table

Height (inches)

| Weight (pounds) | 60 | 61 | 62 | 63 | 64 | 65 | 66 | 67 | 68 | 69 | 70 | 71 | 72 | 73 | 74 | 75 | 76 | 77 | 78 | 79 | 80 |
|---|---|---|---|---|---|---|---|---|---|---|---|---|---|---|---|---|---|---|---|---|---|
| 140 | 27 | 26 | 25 | 25 | 24 | 23 | 22 | 22 | 21 | 21 | 20 | | | | | | | | | | |
| 150 | 29 | 28 | 27 | 26 | 26 | 25 | 24 | 23 | 23 | 22 | 21 | | | | | | | | | | |
| 160 | 31 | 30 | 29 | 28 | 27 | 26 | 26 | 25 | 24 | 23 | 23 | 22 | 22 | 21 | 20 | 20 | | | | | |
| 170 | 33 | 32 | 31 | 30 | 29 | 28 | 27 | 26 | 26 | 25 | 24 | 24 | 23 | 22 | 22 | 21 | 21 | 20 | | | |
| 180 | 35 | 34 | 33 | 32 | 31 | 30 | 29 | 28 | 27 | 26 | 26 | 25 | 24 | 24 | 23 | 22 | 22 | 21 | 21 | 20 | 20 |
| 190 | 37 | 36 | 34 | 33 | 32 | 31 | 30 | 29 | 29 | 28 | 27 | 26 | 26 | 25 | 24 | 24 | 23 | 22 | 22 | 21 | 21 |
| 200 | 39 | 38 | 36 | 35 | 34 | 33 | 32 | 31 | 30 | 29 | 28 | 28 | 27 | 26 | 25 | 25 | 24 | 23 | 23 | 22 | 22 |
| 210 | 41 | 39 | 38 | 37 | 36 | 35 | 34 | 33 | 32 | 31 | 30 | 29 | 28 | 27 | 27 | 26 | 25 | 25 | 24 | 23 | 23 |
| 220 | 43 | 41 | 40 | 39 | 38 | 36 | 35 | 34 | 33 | 32 | 31 | 30 | 30 | 29 | 28 | 27 | 27 | 26 | 25 | 25 | 24 |
| 230 | 45 | 43 | 42 | 40 | 39 | 38 | 37 | 36 | 35 | 34 | 33 | 32 | 31 | 30 | 29 | 29 | 28 | 27 | 26 | 26 | 25 |
| 240 | 47 | 45 | 44 | 42 | 41 | 40 | 38 | 37 | 36 | 35 | 34 | 33 | 32 | 31 | 31 | 30 | 29 | 28 | 27 | 27 | 26 |
| 250 | 48 | 47 | 45 | 44 | 43 | 41 | 40 | 39 | 38 | 37 | 36 | 35 | 34 | 33 | 32 | 31 | 30 | 29 | 29 | 28 | 27 |
| 260 | 50 | 40 | 47 | 46 | 44 | 43 | 42 | 40 | 39 | 38 | 37 | 36 | 35 | 34 | 33 | 32 | 31 | 31 | 30 | 29 | 28 |
| 270 | 52 | 51 | 49 | 47 | 46 | 45 | 43 | 42 | 41 | 40 | 38 | 37 | 36 | 35 | 34 | 33 | 33 | 32 | 31 | 30 | 29 |
| 280 | 54 | 53 | 51 | 49 | 48 | 46 | 45 | 43 | 42 | 41 | 40 | 39 | 38 | 37 | 36 | 35 | 34 | 33 | 32 | 31 | 31 |
| 290 | 56 | 54 | 53 | 51 | 49 | 48 | 46 | 45 | 44 | 43 | 41 | 40 | 39 | 38 | 37 | 36 | 35 | 34 | 33 | 32 | 32 |
| 300 | 58 | 56 | 54 | 53 | 51 | 49 | 48 | 47 | 45 | 44 | 43 | 42 | 40 | 39 | 38 | 37 | 36 | 35 | 34 | 33 | 33 |
| 310 | 60 | 58 | 56 | 54 | 53 | 51 | 50 | 48 | 47 | 45 | 44 | 43 | 42 | 41 | 40 | 38 | 37 | 36 | 35 | 35 | 34 |
| 320 | 62 | 60 | 58 | 56 | 55 | 53 | 51 | 50 | 48 | 47 | 46 | 44 | 43 | 42 | 41 | 40 | 39 | 38 | 37 | 36 | 35 |
| 330 | 64 | 62 | 60 | 58 | 56 | 54 | 53 | 51 | 50 | 48 | 47 | 46 | 44 | 43 | 42 | 41 | 40 | 39 | 38 | 37 | 36 |
| 340 | 66 | 64 | 62 | 60 | 58 | 56 | 54 | 53 | 51 | 50 | 48 | 47 | 46 | 44 | 43 | 42 | 41 | 40 | 39 | 38 | 37 |
| 350 | 68 | 66 | 64 | 62 | 60 | 58 | 56 | 54 | 53 | 51 | 50 | 48 | 47 | 46 | 45 | 43 | 42 | 41 | 40 | 39 | 38 |
| 360 | 70 | 68 | 65 | 63 | 61 | 59 | 58 | 56 | 54 | 53 | 51 | 50 | 49 | 47 | 46 | 45 | 43 | 42 | 41 | 40 | 39 |
| 370 | 72 | 69 | 67 | 65 | 63 | 61 | 59 | 57 | 56 | 54 | 53 | 51 | 50 | 48 | 47 | 46 | 45 | 43 | 42 | 41 | 40 |
| 380 | 74 | 71 | 69 | 67 | 65 | 63 | 61 | 59 | 57 | 56 | 54 | 53 | 51 | 50 | 48 | 47 | 46 | 45 | 44 | 42 | 41 |
| 390 | 76 | 73 | 71 | 69 | 66 | 64 | 62 | 61 | 59 | 57 | 56 | 54 | 53 | 51 | 50 | 48 | 47 | 46 | 45 | 44 | 42 |
| 400 | 78 | 75 | 73 | 70 | 68 | 66 | 64 | 62 | 60 | 59 | 57 | 55 | 54 | 52 | 51 | 50 | 48 | 47 | 46 | 45 | 44 |
| 410 | 80 | 77 | 74 | 72 | 70 | 68 | 66 | 64 | 62 | 60 | 58 | 57 | 55 | 54 | 52 | 51 | 49 | 48 | 47 | 46 | 45 |
| 420 | 81 | 79 | 76 | 74 | 72 | 69 | 67 | 65 | 63 | 62 | 60 | 58 | 57 | 55 | 54 | 52 | 51 | 49 | 48 | 47 | 46 |
| 430 | 83 | 81 | 78 | 76 | 73 | 71 | 69 | 67 | 65 | 63 | 61 | 60 | 58 | 56 | 55 | 53 | 52 | 51 | 49 | 48 | 47 |
| 440 | 85 | 83 | 80 | 77 | 75 | 73 | 70 | 68 | 66 | 64 | 63 | 61 | 59 | 58 | 56 | 55 | 53 | 52 | 50 | 49 | 48 |
| 450 | | 84 | 82 | 79 | 77 | 74 | 72 | 70 | 68 | 66 | 64 | 62 | 61 | 59 | 57 | 56 | 54 | 53 | 52 | 50 | 49 |
| 460 | | | 83 | 81 | 78 | 76 | 74 | 71 | 69 | 67 | 66 | 64 | 62 | 60 | 59 | 57 | 55 | 54 | 53 | 51 | 50 |
| 470 | | | 85 | 83 | 80 | 77 | 75 | 73 | 71 | 69 | 67 | 65 | 63 | 61 | 60 | 58 | 57 | 55 | 54 | 52 | 51 |
| 480 | | | | 84 | 82 | 79 | 77 | 74 | 72 | 70 | 68 | 66 | 65 | 63 | 61 | 60 | 58 | 56 | 55 | 54 | 52 |
| 490 | | | | | 84 | 81 | 78 | 76 | 74 | 72 | 70 | 68 | 66 | 64 | 62 | 61 | 59 | 58 | 56 | 55 | 53 |
| 500 | | | | | 85 | 82 | 80 | 78 | 76 | 73 | 71 | 69 | 67 | 65 | 64 | 62 | 60 | 59 | 57 | 56 | 54 |

**Dark gray zone:** Your weight should not create any new medical problems or make existing problems worse.

**White zone:** Your weight is impairing your health. Even if you do not currently suffer from weight-related medical problems, at this weight you will predictably have medical problems earlier in life, and they will be more difficult to treat than at a weight in the dark gray zone. Diet and exercise have a reasonable chance of helping you get to a healthier weight, or may at least keep you from gaining more.

**Light gray zone:** Your weight is great enough to have a definite negative medical impact. Weight loss is a very important goal, and if diet and exercise aren't effective, then more extreme therapy may be appropriate, depending on your overall medical situation.

**Medium gray zone:** Your weight is the primary factor in your medical condition. If your weight is not brought to a lower level, then it is very likely to reduce the length and quality of your life. If diet and exercise are not successful, then extreme measures are probably appropriate from a risk/benefit standpoint.[2]

Being overweight or obese significantly increases your risk of developing heart disease, diabetes, stroke, gallbladder disease, arthritis, and respiratory problems such as sleep apnea, as well as endometrial, breast, prostate, and colon cancers. Mortality rates increase significantly as BMI increases, by 50 to 100 percent with a BMI over 30, compared to those with a BMI of 20 to 25. In women particularly, obesity is also associated with menstrual cycle irregularities, complications of pregnancy, male pattern hair growth, incontinence, and depression.

## Medical Weight Loss

When diet and exercise alone are not enough, there are several prescription drugs that can help you lose weight. One of these prescription medications was recently approved at a lower dose by the FDA as an OTC medication. *Alli*, otherwise known as *orlistat*, works by decreasing dietary fat absorption. It inhibits the enzyme lipase, which is responsible for breaking down fat for use. The prescription-strength orlistat is also known as *Xenical*, and it decreases dietary fat absorption by 30 percent. The main side effects are abdominal cramping and leakage of oily stool.

All of the other medications work by reducing your appetite. *Meridia* increases the brain chemicals responsible for suppressing appetite. Side effects include possibly increasing your blood pressure and heart rate. It should not be used by people with uncontrolled high blood pressure or a history of heart disease or stroke. It may also cause headache, dry mouth, constipation, and insomnia.

The other prescription drugs approved for weight loss are speed-like medications and should not be used for more than a few weeks. They should not be used by people with heart disease, high blood pressure, hyperthyroidism, or glaucoma. They have significant potential for addiction. These include Bontril, Desoxyn, Tenuate, and phentermine. The medications fenfluramine and dexfenfluramine were withdrawn from the market in 1997 due to an association with heart valve problems.

Maximum weight loss generally occurs over six months on weight-loss medications, after which it will begin to level off or decrease. If four pounds are not lost in four weeks, it is unlikely the medication will provide a benefit. A weight loss of 5 to 10 percent of body weight is significant in an obese person to improve their health. In general, weight-loss medications should not be used merely to improve appearance.

## Surgical Weight Loss

In people who are severely obese, with a BMI of 40 or more, or in those with a BMI of 31 or greater who also have medical problems such as diabetes, sleep apnea, or heart disease, surgical treatment for weight loss may be an option. For most women this means they are about eighty pounds overweight. Bariatric surgeries work by limiting the amount of food you can take in and digest. Most people who undergo these procedures lose weight quickly. Following a proper diet and exercise regimen after the surgery can help keep the weight off. There are risks associated with these surgeries, including the possibility of infections, hernias, or blood clots.

There are three main types of operations that can be performed: restrictive, malabsorptive, or a combination of the two. Restrictive operations limit food intake by reducing the amount of food the stomach can hold. Malabsorptive procedures are also known as *gastric bypass surgeries*; the food does not pass through the small intestine, so fewer calories are absorbed. This type of surgery results in severe nutritional deficiencies and is no longer recommended for that reason. Combined procedures use both stomach restriction as well as partial bypass of the small intestine.

The most common restrictive procedure performed is adjustable gastric banding. A rubber band is placed around the upper end of the stomach, creating a small pouch for food to enter. The band can be tightened or loosened by an access port under the skin. The outlet into the larger part of the stomach is small, delaying food from entering, and helps cause a feeling of fullness. At first the pouch can only hold about 1 ounce of food, but it can stretch to hold 2–3 ounces. Most people can only eat ½ cup to 1 cup of food at a time. The advantage of this procedure is that it is safer to perform than other surgeries and can be done laparoscopically. This means quicker healing and shorter hospitalization. However, patients who undergo this procedure lose less weight and are less likely to keep it off than those who have malabsorptive procedures performed. Sometimes the band can slip or break and another operation is required to repair it.

The Roux-en-Y gastric bypass is a combined malabsorptive and restrictive procedure; it is the most common weight-loss surgery performed in the United States. A small stomach pouch is first created. A Y-shaped segment of the small intestine is then attached to the pouch to bypass the lower stomach and small intestine. This reduces the amount of calories that can be absorbed. Most patients who undergo this procedure lose weight rapidly and are able to maintain it for ten years or more. These procedures are more difficult to perform than the banding and can result in nutritional deficiencies. Complications are also more common.

The most important thing to keep in mind is that the best way to lose weight and to keep it off is to expend more energy (burn more calories) than you take in, so exercise is also important.

## Guidelines for Exercise

The amount of exercise you need depends upon your situation. A good goal for most women to have is working out at least three times per week for thirty to sixty minutes. Any amount is better than none, and you need to start slowly. If you have not been exercising, you should consult your physician before beginning an exercise routine. Start with small changes such as taking the stairs, walking to work, or walking on your lunch break. Begin with ten minutes of moderate exercise, such as walking, each day, and then increase the amount of time and the intensity at which you exercise.

It is important to make exercise a habit so you are able to stick with it. Warm up with some light stretching for five to ten minutes to help prevent injuries. Stick to a regular time and keep a log of activities. Set goals, but don't get discouraged if you don't see changes immediately. Vary your routine so that you do not get bored. Find an activity you enjoy—you will be much more likely to stick with it if you are having fun.

Exercise is one of the most difficult things to get people to do. I always tell my patients the two hardest things to do are quitting smoking and losing weight. One of the best ways to lose weight and to keep it off is by doing regular exercise. There is a difference between being active and exercising.

While it is true that you will burn more calories by leading an active life than a sedentary one, to really burn fat, you have to get your heart rate up long enough to draw on fat stores.

In addition to weight loss, there are multiple health benefits that come from incorporating regular exercise into your life. It can reduce your risk of heart disease, diabetes, osteoporosis, and obesity. Exercise keeps you flexible and makes it easier for you to move. The effects of aging are reduced, and your outlook is improved. Stress and anxiety are reduced, as is depression. You will find that you have more energy and will sleep better. You also increase your metabolism and burn more calories even when resting.

## IT'S IN THE WORD

The bottom line: God gave you your body; take care of it and embrace what you have. God crafted you as a unique being in which He can dwell.

Do you not know that your body is a temple of the Holy Spirit, who is in you, whom you have received from God? You are not your own; you were bought at a price. Therefore honor God with your body.

—1 Corinthians 6:19–20

# SECTION 3

## SEX AND THE SINGLE WOMAN

# Chapter 7

# DATING AND SEX

IF THERE IS ONE AREA IN CHRISTIANITY THAT NEARLY EVERYONE STRUGGLES with at some time in their lives, it is the issue of dating, sex, and the single person. Each generation has tackled this issue differently, with progressively less sexual restraint placed on the single person. In today's society, it seems only the minority believe in abstinence until marriage.

*One patient, a beautiful young woman, would request STD testing at every annual visit. She had no stability in her dating relationships, and with each breakup, it left her with diminished self-esteem.*

*It all began after her high-school sweetheart broke up with her just before prom. She was devastated. He had told her that if she really loved him, she would sleep with him. She intended to remain a virgin until marriage, but she was afraid of losing him. He was her first real love and the man she was sure she would marry after graduation.*

*Because she feared she would lose him, she consented to having sex with him. For a while, they seemed to be closer than ever, and she was sure the relationship was going in the right direction. But talk of marriage after high school began to spook her boyfriend. He had earned a football scholarship to an out-of-state university, and he did not want to miss out on other "opportunities." Having a girlfriend to come home to during the college breaks was OK, but he wanted his freedom.*

*About five months after they became sexually active, he began dating someone else. When she discovered that he was sleeping with this girl behind her back, she became outraged. He quickly ended their relationship and continued dating his new girlfriend.*

*This patient was devastated. She had given her most precious gift—her virginity—believing it would show her love and commitment. When she realized she had been used for sexual pleasure alone, her heart hardened a bit.*

*With each subsequent sexual partner, she held out the hope of lifelong commitment, only to be used and abandoned once again. After a while, she gave up on the idea of marriage and moved in with her last boyfriend. But she suspected that he too was cheating on her, and she asked for STD testing. It was only a matter of time before he would move on to someone else.*

## Modern Life

Many now feel that abstinence until marriage is an outdated and unnecessary prohibition to a very pleasurable activity. Even the government assails attempts at abstinence-based education as ineffective and unrealistic despite the evidence that programs such as Worth the Wait, by Dr. Patricia Sulak, and materials by Dr. Joe McIlhaney of the Medical Institute for Sexual Health, have consistently led to a decline in teen sexual activity when they are used as curriculum in high school.[1]

So what is the Christian single person to do? Our culture prizes education and achievement more than any previous to it. Many young people are postponing marriage until their late twenties or thirties to pursue graduate degrees or job promotions, enjoying the freedom to achieve the American dream. Is it realistic to expect them to remain virgins until then?

Even biology seems pitted against abstinence in this new reality we live in. Young boys and girls enter puberty at earlier ages with each passing generation. In the 1800s, the average woman began menstruation at age seventeen.[2] By 1960, that age had fallen to thirteen. It is not uncommon to see full sexual development of girls in this country by age fourteen. Dramatic increases in sex hormones that accompany puberty also flood the mind with sexual thoughts and feelings.

Today's media are feeding the emerging sexuality of young people as never before. Marketing gurus have targeted the teen years with aggressive sexually oriented advertising. Clothing catalogs like Abercrombie & Fitch are filled with nude and half-nude young people, sending their sales to record highs.[3] Television channels aimed at tweens and younger have protagonists who explore sexuality on and off the camera, becoming another teenage pregnancy statistic. How can they be required to avoid sexual intercourse while they are peaking sexually? And what are the advantages of abstinence until marriage?

From a purely medical standpoint, abstinence outside of marriage has many advantages to the single woman. Unwanted pregnancy is a major concern of those contemplating intercourse. In generations past, the fear of pregnancy was a strong deterrent to premarital sex. The social taboos were much stronger and the consequences far steeper than they are today. But in today's culture, high schools have accommodated the all-too-common pregnant teenager with mainstream classes, childbirth and parenting instructions, and even home visitation, all in an attempt to reduce school dropout rates. It is no longer socially unacceptable to be pregnant in high school.

The government also plays a leading role in aiding unwed mothers with a variety of public assistance. Some have argued that a girl who is unhappy at home can get food stamps, an apartment, and free health care for the small price of getting pregnant outside of marriage.

Even the more financially established single female has motherhood celebrated in the media. Many successful Hollywood stars such as Jodie Foster and Calista Flockhart have abandoned their quest for the perfect mate and have purposely conceived a child to be raised alone. Today's carrier-oriented woman may find her biological clock ticking louder than her prospects for marriage. Many are seeking artificial insemination just to have a child before it is too late.

Against this backdrop, the single woman no longer finds unexpected pregnancy to be the deterrent it once was. And with readily available, private, and "safe" abortion as an alternative, it is even less feared than a generation ago. We are also experiencing a growth in contraceptive options that generations past could not access. Convenient daily, weekly, monthly, quarterly, three-year, five-year, and ten-year reversible birth control makes pregnancy much less likely for the "responsible" single adult.

If fear of pregnancy is no longer a roadblock to sexual intercourse outside of marriage, the prevalence of sexually transmitted diseases certainly should be. As we will detail in the next chapter, the scientific and statistical facts about STDs should restrain even the most daring in our society.

If premarital sex is not deterred by the risks of physical harm, the possibility of emotional pain may restrain us. Especially for women, the act of intercourse means something more than a mere release of sexual tension.[4] It signifies a new level of intimacy and the expectation of a deepening commitment to the relationship. While conventional wisdom rationalizes that intercourse will deepen a relationship and make it stronger, the reality is that intercourse more often than not divides the relationship. One or the other partner is not ready for the level of commitment expected from them once the relationship becomes sexual. Especially for women, an expectation that this relationship is heading toward marriage may frighten away the male partner who only wants to have fun and fulfill his sexual needs.

Both men and women may also use sex as a way to boost their self-esteem. The fact that someone finds them attractive and is willing to be joined with them sexually seems to validate their worth as a person. Like the woman in the story at the beginning of this chapter, a single woman may discover that her sexual partner was simply fulfilling a physical need and not looking for an ever-deepening relationship. This leaves the person more alone and degraded than before, ripe for the next person who will offer the promise of acceptance and love. A pattern of sexual addiction can develop from the basic need to be loved and understood at that most intimate level.

## The Case for Abstinence

If the fear of pregnancy, sexually transmitted diseases, or emotional pain does not deter premarital sex, the Bible offers its own cautions. The apostle Paul has more to say than anyone else on the subject of fornication (premarital sex, adultery, homosexuality). (See 1 Corinthians 7:2, 9; Ephesians 5:3; 1 Thessalonians 4:3–5.) Is Paul just a religious fanatic, out of step with today's culture? Or does he know something about sexual intercourse that lies beneath the surface act?

The key to God's prohibition of sexual intercourse outside of marriage lies in 1 Corinthians 6.

> The body is not meant for sexual immorality, but for the Lord, and the Lord for the body…Do you not know that your bodies are members of Christ himself? Shall I then take the members of Christ and unite them with a prostitute? Never! Do you not know that he who unites himself with a prostitute is one with her in body? For it is said, "The two will become one flesh."…Flee from sexual immorality. All other sins a man commits are outside his body, but he who sins sexually sins against his own body. Do you not know that your body is a temple of the Holy Spirit, who is in you, whom you have received from God? You are not your own; you were bought at a price. Therefore honor God with your body.
>
> —1 Corinthians 6:13, 15–16, 18–20

As Lewis Smedes writes in his book *Sex for Christians*, Paul's main problem with sexual intercourse outside of marriage is that it is a "life-uniting" act.[5] Just as in reality, the Holy Spirit lives inside of our bodies, our temples, so it is that the act of intercourse unites two people in a union with spiritual significance. Even if the people involved do not intend for it to carry such weight, the act of intercourse has changed them spiritually in ways that penetrate the many levels of the soul. Those two people will *never* be the same. God created sex, and it is a powerful spiritual bonding that God intended for the strengthening and deepening of the marriage covenant. But people outside of this covenant are playing with spiritual fire.

## Other Sexual Activity

Suppose you accept that premarital sex is not right. What about other sexual activity that falls short of vaginal penetration? Where do you draw the line between kissing and intercourse? The fear of pregnancy and sexually transmitted diseases has brought many "experts" who advise alternatives to release sexual energies. Among them is a practice called "outercourse," which involves mutual masturbation. It is foreplay taken to its extreme. But what are the motivations of the people involved? Will this activity leave the relationship stronger than it was, or will one of the parties feel used (especially the woman)? Will the couple feel the same pressures to move the relationship forward, even if one is not ready? Simply avoiding vaginal penetration is not what Paul was focusing on. Sexual activity has many pitfalls and dangers we may not realize until it is too late. Only the individual knows when he or she has gone "too far." If we are Christians, we carry Christ with us in all activities of life. Examine your motives and ask Him to guide you into appropriate intimacy and enjoyment during the dating years.

(i) A helpful resource is *I Kissed Dating Goodbye* by Joshua Harris.

## Masturbation

The final word is for those who are not in a relationship and who desire to remain sexually abstinent until marriage. I (SAF) am often asked what my views are regarding masturbation. The vast majority of Christians feel tremendous guilt over something the secular media treat with celebration. If a single person is sexually alive from puberty, what does she do for the decade or two that may pass before marriage? Is masturbation a legitimate option, and, if so, why does she feel so guilty about doing it?

I realize as I tackle this issue that people with far greater theological credentials may disagree with me. That is OK. This is just the opinion of one Christian physician who is willing to venture where few dare tread. There is little to go by in Scripture that is specific to the act. Genesis 38:8–10 is often used to condemn masturbation. In this story Onan is commanded to have sex with his brother's widow to produce an heir and continue the lineage of his brother. But Onan knew that if his brother died without an heir, the inheritance would come to him. So Onan "spilled his semen on the ground to keep from producing offspring for his brother" (v. 9). This was not sexual self-gratification but disobedience to the laws of that day and to his duty as a brother. It was not even masturbation but *coitus interruptus*, a method of birth control widely practiced.

Leviticus 15 gives a list of bodily discharges that causes a man to be "unclean" and unable to enter the presence of the Lord until cleansed. The Lord speaks to Moses about the ways to be made clean again. In verse 16, He states, "When a man has an emission of semen, he must bathe his whole body in water, and he will be unclean till evening." He adds in verse 18, "When a man lies with a woman and there is an emission of semen, both must bathe with water, and they will be unclean till evening." It appears that the Lord is listing two separate occasions when a discharge of semen would contaminate and render the man "unclean." If the second occasion is when the man has intercourse with a woman (presumably his wife), then what is happening in the first situation when he is alone? Is this masturbation? If so, there is no condemnation of this emission, simply instruction by God on how he was to be made "clean" again with respect to the worship.

Young children explore their bodies and masturbate with freedom before someone tells them it is "wrong." I have even seen male fetuses fondling their genitals during an ultrasonic examination, but they carry no moral or sexual baggage with it. Adults, however, may employ fantasies of past relationships or, more commonly, pornography to visualize an ideal sexual partner. In their minds, they are having intercourse with that person even if it is only on paper, television, or a computer screen. If one can masturbate without these entanglements, it is certainly preferable.

The other problem with masturbation is that it is often a form of stress relief and can become addictive. Just as alcohol, cigarette smoking, or pharmaceuticals can be used to relieve stress, so can the release brought on by orgasm or ejaculation. Paul writes, "'Everything is permissible for me'—but not everything is beneficial. 'Everything is permissible for me'—but I will not be mastered by anything" (1 Cor. 6:12). Of course, some people use food as stress relief with serious physical consequences. The bottom line is that addictive masturbation leads a person to see herself as the source of stress relief instead of the Father. "Cast all your anxiety on him because he cares for you" (1 Pet. 5:7). Masturbation is a shortcut that makes man the source instead of God, and in that regard it is sin.

Even in its "purest" form, masturbation will never feel completely right. That may be from needless self-condemnation, or it may reflect the reality that we are never really whole as sexual beings until we are united in marriage with that person who completes us and with whom the one-flesh union is all that God created it to be. Masturbation pales in comparison to that and is at best a temporary remedy for a soul that longs for union with another.

# Chapter 8

# SEXUALLY TRANSMITTED DISEASES

W E SEE CASES OF SEXUALLY TRANSMITTED DISEASES (STDs) IN OUR private practices almost every day. So many people live in a fantasy world when it comes to sexual activity that they are shattered when the reality of contracting an STD hits them. No one prepared them for the real world as it exists today—a world where STDs run rampant. Such was the case for one female patient.

*When we first met her, she was a single, thirty-five-year-old virgin. Being extremely careful in choosing a mate, she delayed marriage until she was sure she had found the right man. That's when she met her future spouse—a thirty-six-year-old man who had divorced his wife several years ago when he learned that she was having an affair. Although our patient wouldn't normally have dated a divorced man, she felt that he was every-thing she had been waiting for. She knew he was not a virgin, but he had been abstinent since his divorce and their moral beliefs were very similar. They did not have intercourse until their wedding night.*

*About a year after they married, she came to the office for her annual examination and Pap smear. A week later, we discovered through her Pap smear that she had contracted high-risk human papillomavirus (HPV) and had developed precancerous changes to her cervix. Since all of her previous Pap smears had been normal, and she was a virgin before marriage, it was easy to conclude that she contracted HPV from her husband.*

*She was devastated. She had kept herself pure trying to avoid STDs, and now she had acquired one. What would this mean to her chances for children? Would this plague her the rest of her life? Although she was deeply in love, she could not help but be angry with him. We met with both of them and explained that the HPV was most likely the result of his ex-wife's affair. He had just as innocently contracted an STD as his new wife had. And because HPV is often silent in men, he had no idea that he had been infected.*

*This knowledge seemed to heal their pain, and they were able to move on to the treatment phase. Our patient underwent colposcopy and cervical freezing. All of her subsequent Pap smears have been normal, and she has since given birth to two beautiful boys.*

## What Is the Likelihood of Contracting an STD?

From a purely medical standpoint, abstinence until marriage is sound advice because of the prevalence of so many STDs. They are among the most common infectious diseases in the United States, with experts estimating that at least 50 percent of the population will acquire an STD in their lifetime.[1] As of 2001, 65 million Americans were carrying a sexually transmitted disease.[2] The Centers for Disease Control and Prevention (CDC) estimates that 19 million new infections occur each year, almost half of them among young people ages fifteen to twenty. In addition to the physical and psychological consequences of STDs, medical costs associated with STDs in the United States are esti-mated at up to $14.1 billion annually, excluding the nearly $7 million spent for HIV/AIDS.[3]

The number of cases is believed to be rising due to an earlier age of sexual activity and a later age of marriage. This leads to more sexual partners in a lifetime than ever before. In addition, the nearly 50 percent divorce rate in this country means that many people will reenter the dating scene and add additional sexual partners to their life's experience.[4]

Because many STDs are asymptomatic (or silent), women often do not seek early treatment and suffer more frequent and more severe health problems than do men. Some STDs can spread into the pelvis and cause infections called PID (pelvic inflammatory disease), which can scar the fallopian tubes. These scarred tubes can lead to tubal (or ectopic) pregnancies, the leading cause of death in pregnant women. STDs are also the leading cause of cervical cancer and can lead to disability or even death in newborns who acquire them from their mothers at birth.

## Types of STDs

Sexually transmitted diseases can be divided into categories: bacterial or viral; acquired by skin contact or through bodily fluids. Bacterial infections can be eliminated with antibiotics; viral infections have no cure at the present time. Certain diseases can be transmitted simply through skin contact with another individual, which we will cover in this chapter. STDs acquired through bodily fluids are those that require transmission by blood, semen, or vaginal secretions.

## Chlamydia

Chlamydia is the most common bacterial STD in the United States, with nearly three million new cases each year.[5] The vast majority of cases occur in women ages fifteen to twenty-five. It is transmitted through oral, vaginal, or anal intercourse. Symptoms include pus or discharge from the penis or vagina and, in men, may result in painful urination. These symptoms present within one to three weeks after exposure to the bacteria.

If left untreated, chlamydia may develop into pelvic inflammatory disease, or PID, which is a serious infection of the reproductive organs. The infection spreads from the cervix to the uterus, through the fallopian tubes, and into the pelvic cavity where it circulates throughout the abdomen. Each year up to one million women in the United States develop PID, and 20 to 40 percent of women with chlamydial infections who are not adequately treated may develop PID.[6] This intense infection causes tremendous pain, fever, chills, nausea, and vomiting, requiring hospitalization for many to receive intravenous antibiotics and pain medication.

PID can cause scarring of the fallopian tubes, which can block the tubes and prevent fertilization from taking place. PID is the chief cause of ectopic pregnancy, where the embryo gets "stuck" in the fallopian tube. The placenta then penetrates the wall of the tube, causing it frequently to rupture. The hemorrhage caused by this rupture can be substantial, making ectopic pregnancy the leading cause of death in women due to pregnancy.[7]

Some women who develop PID in the first trimester of pregnancy will experience miscarriage because of this STD. Newborn babies born to women with chlamydia can contract it in their eyes, causing blindness, or in their lungs, leading to pneumonia. Some have recommended that every pregnant woman be tested for chlamydia at her first prenatal visit to eliminate this disease before she gives birth.

Men infected with chlamydia can experience inflammation of the testicles and prostate gland. The urethra can be a source of pain with urination, a symptom that often leads men to seek medical attention. Both sexes can acquire conjunctivitis, an infection of the lining of the eye often called "pinkeye," from touching their eyes after genital contact with themselves or an infected partner. Oral sex can lead to *pharyngitis*, or throat infections. People who believe they are practicing "safe sex" by mutually masturbating or by oral sex are quite surprised that contact with these bodily fluids can give them a sexually transmitted disease.

Unfortunately, 85 percent of women and 40 percent of men have no symptoms from chlamydial infection.[8] A study of military recruits published in the

*New England Journal of Medicine* found 10 to 12 percent had undiagnosed chlamydial infections at the time of enlistment.[9] In many areas of the country, chlamydia is present in 24 percent of sexually active girls ages fifteen to nineteen. The CDC estimates that 92 percent of all female chlamydial infections occur in those under the age of twenty-five. This has led them to recommend yearly screening for chlamydia in all sexually active patients under the age of twenty-five.[10] We have been amazed at the number of our patients who have tested positive for chlamydia at their yearly visit since this recommendation was put forth. These were all young women with no symptoms carrying a ticking time bomb for PID and infertility. While chlamydial infections can be cured with appropriate antibiotics, the damage done to the body may last a lifetime.

## Gonorrhea

Another bacterium that people commonly associate with sexually transmitted diseases is gonorrhea. It causes infections in the genital tract, mouth, and rectum—anywhere that bodily fluids are exchanged. Several years ago medical science was on the verge of eliminating gonorrhea, but it has rebounded, especially among teenagers. Since 2005, there are an estimated 600,000 cases in the United States each year.[11] It is often diagnosed in the same individual who has chlamydia, prompting laboratories to include gonorrhea testing whenever chlamydia is also sought.

Symptoms of the disease usually manifest within seven to ten days after exposure. For women, the disease can be silent or it can include bleeding after intercourse, painful urination, vaginal discharge, and PID. The most common and serious complication of gonorrhea in women is PID. Teenagers experience the highest rate of PID because the lining of the cervix is still immature and less able to protect them. Cervical mucus prevents the spread of sexually transmitted diseases (STDs) inward except during ovulation, when the organism may be carried on the backs of sperm, and menses, when the cervix opens to let menstrual blood escape. In fact, symptoms of PID often begin shortly after menstruation. Another factor implicated in PID is douching. STDs in the vagina can be pushed upward during the douching process. For that reason, among others, douching is not recommended by most gynecologists.

Approximately 50 percent of women experience very few symptoms of gonorrhea and miss the opportunity to prevent complications through aggressive use of antibiotics. The body is left to heal on its own, commonly with the creation of scar tissue as a way of trapping the offending organism. Scar tissue can form anywhere in the abdomen and pelvis. Some women may develop a condition called *Fitz-Hugh-Curtis syndrome*, where the normal circulation of abdominal fluids carries the bacteria upward, trapping it between the liver and diaphragm. The resulting scar tissue formed in this location sticks the liver and diaphragm together, causing upper abdominal pain under the right rib cage and transmitting pain sensations to the right shoulder.

Scar tissue in the pelvis can also cause pelvic pain on either side as various organs become stuck to each other or to the pelvic walls. There is a 20 percent chance of chronic, potentially lifelong pelvic pain with each episode of PID.

Men infected with gonorrhea experience pus draining from the urethra and painful urination. Infants exposed to gonorrhea at birth can develop eye infections, which are now routinely prevented by giving antibiotic ointments at birth in most states in this country. Prolonged exposure to gonorrhea can lead to arthritis, damage to heart valves, and inflammation of the brain.

## Syphilis

Syphilis, another bacterial STD, has been called the "great imitator" because it resembles so many other diseases. Syphilis is caused by a form of bacterium that infects through skin-to-skin contact and is poorly prevented by condom use.[12] It initially leaves an ulcer on the skin and then moves inside the body, eventually damaging internal organs if left untreated. While it is fairly easy to treat with antibiotics if caught early, it is often not diagnosed.

| STAGES OF SYPHILIS | | |
|---|---|---|
| THERE ARE THREE STAGES OF SYPHILIS:[13] | | |
| Stage | Time | Symptoms/Signs |
| First | 10 days to 3 months after exposure | Ulcer on the skin; may be painless and go unnoticed; disappears within a few weeks if untreated, only to return in Stage 2 |
| Second | 3 to 6 weeks after ulcer appeared | Brownish skin rash that covers the entire body or just certain areas; rash on the palms of the hands and soles of the feet; contact with this rash can spread the disease, even nonsexual contact; rash heals in time if not treated with antibiotics, a sign the person has moved into a dormant phase |
| Third | 7 weeks or more | Damage to internal organs begins, attacking the heart valves, bones, joints; can lead to blindness; affects the nervous system and brain |

Pregnancy is an especially vulnerable time to contract syphilis. Twenty-five percent of infected pregnant women will experience stillbirth or neonatal death shortly after birth. Of those babies who survive birth, 40 to 70 percent will be infected with syphilis. For this reason, most states mandate prenatal testing of all pregnant women for syphilis at their first office visit. Women are again tested when in labor to detect those who may have contracted the disease during the course of their pregnancies. These tests are run to quickly identify and treat those mothers in the hope of preventing complications to their newborns.

## Trichomonas

Another STD that can cause vaginal infections is trichomonas. Trichomonas is a parasite that is very easy to contract with sexual activity. An estimated 7.4 million people will be infected in the United States.[14] Women suffering from the infection may experience a variety of symptoms ranging from abdominal pain to severe irritation and discharge in the vaginal area. During pregnancy, infection may result in a number of neonatal problems, including premature rupture of the membrane, premature delivery, and low-birth-weight infants. Most men have no symptoms and appear to be able to clear their infections without treatment. This is not the case for women.

Women also run a greater risk of contracting HIV if infected with trichomonas and are more susceptible to cervical cancer and other STDs. It is thought that the inflammation of the vaginal tissues allows other STDs easier access and can affect the patient's own ability to fight other infections.

## Herpes

The most common viral STD is herpes, or HSV. There are two types of herpes—type 1 and type 2.

Type 1 is traditionally called "oral herpes" because it is associated with lesions around the mouth called "cold sores." Type 2 is the genital variety that has historically been called an STD. However, these distinctions are beginning to blur due to oral sex and the transmission of type 1 from mouth to genitals and type 2 from genitals to mouth. Herpes cannot be transmitted from a toilet seat or towel.

There are currently nearly fifty million Americans with herpes, with one million new cases diagnosed each year. One in five Americans over the age of twelve and one out of every four women in the United States has herpes! Blacks have a higher rate (46 percent) than whites (18 percent) and women (25 percent) than men (18 percent). These are certainly shocking and sobering statistics. It is estimated that only 10 percent of those infected know that they carry the virus. Most people who will acquire herpes do so by age forty.[15]

## What are the symptoms?

Herpes causes open sores or blisters in and around the vaginal opening, penis, anus, buttocks, and thighs. These are the locations that infected semen would touch as it spills out of the vagina. The sores can lead to burning and itching, often confused with yeast infections in women. Some women have misdiagnosed their HSV as a "heat rash" or hemorrhoids. With the ability to purchase OTC yeast remedies, it is quite possible that thousands of women are treating their herpes infections with the wrong medication and never being diagnosed with this STD. Herpes lesions also cause pain when urine touches them, causing people of both sexes to mistake this for a urinary tract infection. And as mentioned earlier, herpes can present as cold sores or as a throat infection mimicking strep throat.

For some women, the first outbreak of herpes can be very difficult. They can experience symptoms similar to a viral flu, with fever, chills, body aches, sensitivity to light, and swelling of the lymph nodes. If there are many blisters near the site of urination, the nerves can temporarily malfunction, causing inability to urinate or have a bowel movement. We have personally admitted women to the hospital who could not urinate and required a catheter for several days.

Symptoms are usually present within two to ten days after contracting the disease. The virus resides in the nerve cells that lead to the skin. The lesion begins as a bump on the skin that tingles and can last for two or three weeks at a time. The bump turns into a blister that becomes an open sore. This sore eventually crusts over as a scab and heals, occasionally leaving a scar. The lesion is infectious from the time the skin begins to tingle until the lesion has been covered with a scab. This is typically two days before a lesion appears and lasts about two weeks after lesions begin forming. The diagnosis is confirmed by a swab of the lesion for viral culture. Subsequent testing can differentiate type 1 from type 2. This can be helpful for prognosis as type 1 is much milder and recurs far less often than type 2 HSV.

Once healed, the virus travels into the inner nerve cell and becomes inactive until the next recurrence. Forty percent of patients will have six or more recurrences during the first two years after the initial infection; 20 percent have more than ten recurrences each year. The recurrences are almost always in the same location each time, unless new sites develop from autoinoculation, which is the process of transferring the virus from the fingernails to new skin sites during scratching of existing lesions. There they will reside for life, just like the original lesion.[16]

Often women can have HSV infections and show no symptoms because the virus resides inside the vagina or cervix. This is perhaps why HSV continues to be spread so frequently because women may not know they are infected.

### What are the long-term effects of HSV infections?

There have been reports of death due to herpes infections in women who have weakened immune systems. There have been at least twenty-five cases of women who contracted herpes during the last trimester of their pregnancy, causing the virus to spread throughout the body and to all the major organs. This condition carries a 50 percent mortality rate; 40 percent of the fetuses also died.[17] Acts of infidelity by a husband or boyfriend in the third trimester can result in the death of the mother and fetus.

The most devastating aspect of HSV is in its transmission to the newborn by an unsuspecting mother. Herpes acquired in the birth canal can be deadly in 50 percent of the newborns. Of those who do not die, serious and lifelong neurological difficulties are highly likely.[18] Because of this, women who are found to have a herpes lesion at the time of labor are strongly advised to undergo cesarean section to reduce the risk of this devastating disease to their newborn baby. We now commonly give antiviral medication in the last month of pregnancy to attempt to prevent an outbreak by the mother near the time of birth. Breast-feeding is not a source of transmission to the baby and is perfectly safe.

Long after the herpes lesions have cleared, the emotional and psychological stress of this STD can remain. We see many women in our offices for whom the diagnosis of HSV hangs like a scarlet letter around their necks. They wonder if they are obligated to disclose this history to future sexual partners and if this knowledge will hinder that new relationship. Once married, they bear the burden of preventing transmission to their newborns and struggle to explain why a cesarean section is needed but still hide their secret shame. Often the diagnosis of HSV reveals to many women that their husband or boyfriend has not been faithful to them, with all the emotional damage that revelation brings. There are even herpes support groups to help women deal with the stress this diagnosis has added to their lives.

### Is it possible to treat the infection?

Herpes can be treated with antiviral medications such as Valtrex, Famvir, and Zovirax or its generic, acyclovir. These are moderately effective in preventing recurrences if used daily or in shortening the duration of outbreaks when used for those occasions alone. But they are treatments; not cures. Herpes is a lifelong disease. The topical creams offer no benefit for HSV type 2 and are only useful for "cold sores" on the mouth.

## Human papillomavirus

One of the most common STDs in the world today is the human papillomavirus, or HPV. An estimated 20 million Americans are currently infected, with 6.2 million new cases diagnosed each year. At least 50 percent of sexually active men and women acquire genital HPV infection at some point in their lives. According to the CDC, by age fifty, at least 80 percent of women will have acquired genital HPV infection.[19]

There are one hundred types of this virus, with thirty of them responsible for the majority of the STDs associated with HPV. Certain high-risk types can cause cervical, vulvar, vaginal, and penile cancers. It is estimated that over 90 percent of all cervical cancer in the world is caused by HPV. HPV is the cause of genital warts, with approximately one million new cases each year.[20]

### How is genital HPV contracted?

Genital HPV is spread primarily through sexual contact, either skin to skin or through bodily fluid exchange. There is some debate whether the sharing of sex toys such as dildos or vibrators can transmit the virus. No evidence exists to date that the HPV virus can be acquired through tanning beds, toilet seats, or massage tables.

Risk factors include the number of sexual partners, age at first intercourse of sixteen or younger, number of sexual partners her male partner has had, and smoking.[21]

### What are the symptoms of HPV?

While visible genital warts are the most easily recognizable form of the disease, half of all women and the majority of men have no symptoms. Most women are diagnosed at their annual gynecologic examination when their Pap smear returns abnormal. HPV is highly contagious by oral, genital, or anal sex, and two-thirds of people exposed to it will develop the disease within three months of contact. Most teens and adults will clear their infections spontaneously, but the virus may remain dormant for years. This has made determining when and with whom the virus was contracted a nearly impossible task. For women, the common sites of HPV infection are the cervix, the vaginal opening, and the anus. Men can experience lesions at the penis, scrotum, and anus.[22]

### What are the possible complications?

Two main complications of HPV can occur. The first is cancer of the genital organs in both males and females. Precancerous lesions, formerly called dysplasia, can be detected in women by a Pap smear of the cells lining the cervix. This has been discussed in an earlier chapter. Other lesions may be diagnosed on the genitals of both men and women through biopsy of abnormal skin lesions. For women, a yearly Pap smear beginning at age twenty-one or with the onset of sexual activity, along with a visual inspection of the genital region by a health-care provider, is the best defense against genital cancers.

The other result of HPV infection is the development of genital warts, or *condyloma*, which are biologically and genetically similar to those often seen on the hand. It is the reaction to the virus in infected skin cells that causes them to pile up into a wart. Condyloma can be very small or quite large, making urination or defecation difficult. In pregnant women, the weakened immune system can allow these warts to grow to such an extent that the opening to the vagina is obstructed, blocking the passage of the baby at birth and requiring a cesarean delivery.

Infants born to women with genital warts may become infected themselves, most commonly from swallowing vaginal secretion during birth. This brings the virus in contact with the infant's throat, and the development of warts on the pharynx can occur. If these warts grow, they can obstruct the passage of air to the lungs and become life threatening. Repeated laser treatments may be needed to keep the airway open. The rarity of this condition does not require cesarean section for women who have genital warts.[23]

### What treatment options are available?

Genital warts may clear spontaneously, remain the same, or grow in size. These lesions can be treated with topical agents, freezing, electrocautery, or laser. Most of these treatments require medical application in either an office setting or an outpatient surgical suite, depending on the extent of the lesions. Smaller warts can be treated at home if the patient desires and can safely self-administer the topical solution available by prescription under the name Condylox or the gel under the prescribed name of Aldara.

Treatments can be painful and expensive. They are designed to rid the body of the visible warts but not the invisible virus. HPV can persist in the body for a lifetime with periodic recurrences. Unfortunately, even the best prevention strategies have fallen short. Research studies have been unable to confirm that condom use prevents the transmission of HPV, as we will discuss in the next chapter. In fact, many have been pressuring the government to require condom manufacturers to include warning labels alerting consumers that condom use may not protect them from acquiring HPV. A measure in the 2001 Health and Human Services appropriations bill approved by Congress requires the FDA to evaluate whether the labels on condoms are medically accurate in addressing their effectiveness in preventing STDs, including HPV.[24] We will discuss the option of HPV vaccines in the next chapter.

## Hepatitis

There are six known types of hepatitis virus, types A through E and G. Types B and C are those most commonly thought of as sexually transmitted diseases, although type A has been seen in the gay male population.

Hepatitis B is among the most common in the United States. In the 1980s, the number of new cases per year was nearly three hundred thousand, but in the new millennium that number has dropped to approximately sixty thousand. Most of these cases are in adults ages twenty to forty-nine. The greatest decline has been in children and adolescents due to a vaccine first developed in the 1980s. Over one million Americans are chronically infected with the virus.[25]

Hepatitis B is contracted through exposure to blood or blood products in about 50 percent of the cases. With the vigorous screening of the blood supply in the United States, most of the adult cases are from sharing needles during intravenous drug use and when tattoo needles or body-piercing devices are not properly sterilized. Children are susceptible to contracting the virus during birth from their infected mothers. Most states now require hepatitis B testing of all women during their prenatal care and upon admission to the hospital for delivery in an effort to identify those infants most at risk.

The remainder of the cases are from contact with bodily fluids. Those in the health-care field and family members of chronically infected patients are at risk. Virtually all health-care workers are vaccinated as a requirement of employment.

The last group is those exposed to fluids from intercourse, either hetero-sexual or homosexual contact. While it is thought that condom use may help prevent transmission, this has not been confirmed in scientific studies, as we will cover in the next chapter.

Another difficulty for sexual partners is that most people are unaware of their disease state. About 30 percent of persons with hepatitis B have no signs or symptoms. Signs and symptoms are less common in children than adults. Those symptoms include jaundice, fatigue, abdominal pain, loss of appetite, nausea, vomiting, and joint pain. The time from exposure to symptoms can be as long as sixty days.[26]

Ninety percent of adults and teens recover completely within six months and develop immunity. But 10 percent of adults, 25 to 50 percent of children between the ages of one and five, and up to 90 percent of infants develop chronic hepatitis for life. As many as 25 percent of these people die prema-turely from chronic liver disease. This is a common cause of liver failure, leading to the need for liver transplants.

Because of the higher risks placed on infants and children who contract this virus, hepatitis B vaccination is now offered for infants beginning at birth and for children who were not previously vaccinated as a part of their school vaccines. It is hoped that by vaccinating as many infants and children as possible, the next generation of Americans will be immune from this disease.

Adults who are at risk are also strongly encouraged to be vaccinated. For those who have contracted the disease and become chronically infected, there are several antiviral medications that can slow the progression to liver disease.

Hepatitis C is one of the most dangerous forms of the virus. It is transmitted in the same way as hepatitis B and is the most common blood-borne infection in the United States. Almost 80 percent of those infected have no symptoms at the time of the initial infection, and many do not develop signs of clinical disease for twenty years.[27]

Contact with infected blood or genital secretions can transmit the virus not only to adults but also to the infant at birth. Most cases occur in people between the ages of twenty-five and forty-six, with at least one hundred thousand new cases diagnosed in this country each year. Only 15 percent of patients clear the virus from their systems. The majority become chronically infected, comprising the three million carriers of this disease currently living in the United States. Of those with chronic infection, 70 percent will develop severe liver disease, leading to cirrhosis and liver cancer. Hepatitis C is the leading cause of liver transplants in the United States.[28]

There is currently no vaccine on the market for hepatitis C, although research is ongoing. Condoms offer the same limited protection as for hepatitis B. All blood products are now screened for the virus, but those who received transfusions before 1991 are encouraged to be tested for the disease.

## HIV

The STD that has received the most publicity is the *human immunodeficiency virus*, or HIV, the agent responsible for AIDS. HIV damages the immune system, rendering its victims unable to defend themselves against infectious diseases or cancer. There are currently 1.1 million people in the United States living with HIV. The CDC has estimated that approximately 40,000 persons become infected with HIV each year.[29] Half of all those who have been infected with HIV since its arrival to the United States in the early 1980s have already died. This represents 25 million Americans lost in the prime of their lives.[30] Even though less than 0.5 percent of our population is HIV-infected, it is still the leading cause of death in the United States for adults under age forty-five.[31]

While the largest population of individuals infected with HIV continues to be gay men, women now account for nearly 30 percent of all new cases. Of the HIV/AIDS diagnoses for women during 2001–2004, an estimated 15 percent were for women aged thirteen to twenty-four years.[32]

HIV is often acquired through needle-sharing by intravenous drug users, but the primary path to infection in women is from heterosexual transmission. Most women are not aware of their risks of HIV because they do not feel they are engaging in risky behavior. But many male partners are unaware of their disease state and may have been involved in IV drug use or bisexual practices that put their female partners at risk. It is estimated that 250,000 people in the United States are HIV positive and unaware of it. Up to 40 percent of those who are diagnosed have had the disease at least ten years and are responsible for nearly 70 percent of all new infections.[33]

In a recent study of HIV-infected people, 34 percent of African American men who have sex with men (MSM), 26 percent of Hispanic MSM, and 13 percent of white MSM reported having had sex with women. However, their female partners do not know of their bisexual activity: only 14 percent of white women, 6 percent of African American women, and 6 percent of Hispanic women in this study acknowledged having a bisexual partner.[34] In a recent CDC survey, 65 percent of the men who had ever had sex with men also had sex with women.[35]

African American women are especially affected by HIV infection and AIDS. In 2002 (the most recent year for which data are available), HIV infection was the leading cause of death for African American women aged twenty-five to thirty-four years. In the same year, HIV infection was the fifth leading cause of death among all women aged thirty-five to forty-four years and the sixth leading cause of death among all women aged twenty-five to thirty-four years. The only diseases causing more deaths of women were cancer and heart disease.[36]

It is believed that women are especially vulnerable to acquiring the HIV virus due to the amount of tissue exposed in the vagina compared to the penis. It is not uncommon for tiny tears in the skin to occur in women during intercourse that open pathways to the bloodstream similar to that experienced by men during anogenital sex with other men. The presence of other vaginal diseases such as gonorrhea or chlamydia increases the ability of the virus to infect women as well.

### How HIV spreads

The HIV virus is actually difficult to contract. Compared with the virus that causes the common cold, this virus dies when exposed to the air, cannot be left behind on toilet seats or telephone receivers, and cannot be passed by shaking hands with someone. It requires an almost immediate connection from the giver to the receiver, and it must travel inside bodily fluids such as semen, blood, vaginal secretions, and in some cases saliva. It is often not contracted by those exposed to it.

Then why is HIV so deadly? Unlike other deadly viruses, such as the Ebola virus, which act quickly and kill the host before he can make contact with many people, HIV acts slowly and silently. Many of its victims are without symptoms for months or even years, outwardly appearing completely normal to everyone else. Unaware themselves of their infectious state, and free to mingle with the uninfected, the virus is silently passed from one unsuspecting person to another.

Over the course of a person's lifetime, many people may contract the disease from a single individual. In every country where its origins have been traced, the virus is concentrated first in homosexual men and intravenous drug users. These people frequently share blood-tinged needles or have sex with multiple partners over a short period of time. It is not uncommon for homosexuals uneducated about the risks of HIV/AIDS to sleep with dozens of other men in a single day. As this occurs day after day in a particular segment of society, the concentration of infected people becomes higher. Soon, the girlfriend of the IV drug user contracts it from heterosexual sex or the bisexual male brings it home to his suburban wife, and the virus has entered a new arena.

## AIDS

AIDS, or *acquired immunodeficiency syndrome*, is a condition caused by HIV. The virus becomes incorporated into the genetic makeup of the human cell, preferring the white blood cells called lymphocytes. These cells are a major part of our immune system, protecting us against infection and cancer. The virus progressively destroys the immune system, leaving its victim vulnerable to unusual infections and rare cancers that a healthy person would not encounter. The infected person develops AIDS. The diagnosis is based on the development of certain infections in the presence of HIV that signals a critical loss of the immune system. A person does not die directly from HIV itself, but from the infections and tumors he cannot defend himself against.[37]

There are antiviral medications that can reduce the number of viral particles in the blood, or "viral load." The "load" is important because the higher the viral count, the more infectious the person. Also, the higher count usually reflects a poorer immune system. Drugs to decrease the viral load are not curative, but they have been crucial to the fight to make HIV/AIDS a chronic disease one lives with for decades, much like diabetes. It will eventually kill the individual, but not as rapidly as when first diagnosed in the 1980s.

These antiviral medications are critical to preventing the spread of HIV from a mother to her infant at birth, called perinatal transmission. Nearly all

HIV transmission to newborns and children in the United States could be prevented if the mother were diagnosed and treated early with these medications. Often cesarean section is recommended for women with high viral counts to decrease transmission to the baby. Breast-feeding is also discouraged as the virus can be transmitted through breast milk.[38]

### The AIDS epidemic

While HIV/AIDS has predominately been spread in this country through homosexual acts, the majority of cases worldwide are the result of heterosexual intercourse. As we attempt to remain "safe" in North America, the rest of the world is rapidly being consumed by a plague that seems unstoppable. In many ways, HIV/AIDS is changing human civilization on this planet, and the scope of these changes will affect the generations to come in a profound way.

The AIDS epidemic affects nearly every country on this planet. Worldwide, an estimated 39.5 million people are living with HIV, including 2.3 million children. In 2006 alone, 4.3 million people were newly infected and an estimated 2.8 million lost their lives to AIDS. According to the Joint United Nations Programme on HIV/AIDS, 95 percent of infected people reside in developing countries. There are currently 14 million children orphaned by the death of their parents to AIDS. It is estimated that in the next eight years, 45 million more people will become infected.[39]

A decade from now, nearly 100 million men, women, and children infected with the AIDS virus will be living on this planet. The cost to treat these people, the economic loss of productivity these adult workers would have brought to the world, and the missing generation of young people lost to AIDS will be staggering realities of the twenty-first century. Not since the bubonic plague pandemic of 1347–1351, when black death swept through Europe and killed 75 million, has the earth witnessed such devastation.[40]

## IT'S IN THE WORD

Many of the proverbs of Solomon warn of the dangers of pursuing sexual pleasures. They are as appropriate today as they were when he wrote them thousands of years ago.

"Come, let's drink deep of love till morning; let's enjoy ourselves with love!"...With persuasive words she led him astray; she seduced him with her smooth talk. All at once he followed her like an ox going to the slaughter, like a deer stepping into a noose till an arrow pierces his liver, like a bird darting into a snare, little knowing it will cost him his life.

—Proverbs 7:18–19

# Chapter 9

# STD PREVENTION

W HEN TALKING ABOUT DISEASE PREVENTION, IT IS IMPORTANT TO RECOG-
nize that there are many factors that determine whether a person who
comes in contact with an STD will actually contract it. Factors such as its
ability to infect, how it's transmitted from person to person, the person's
health, sexual behaviors, gender, age, and nutritional status also are important
considerations.

As we saw in the previous chapter, some STDs, like gonorrhea and chlamydia, are easily transmitted from one person to another. Others, such as
HIV or hepatitis, are fragile entities that require immediate transmission into
the receiving person. The route of transmission plays an important role as well.
Some infections are spread through direct skin-to-skin contact, such as HPV
and syphilis. Others, such as HIV and hepatitis, require body fluids to transport them. Such fluids can include blood, semen, and vaginal secretions.

The health of the infected individual, as well as the immune system of the
uninfected partner, will determine how aggressive his disease may be. Certain
sexual behaviors (vaginal versus anal intercourse, extended foreplay that tears
the skin, intercourse during menses) also affect transmission.

A person's gender, age, and nutritional status determines rate of infection as
well. Women are more vulnerable to STDs than men. The vagina is a sanctuary
protected from external forces such as the drying effect of air. This affords the
STD more time to infect before it dies. The greater surface area of the vulva
and vagina compared with the penis allows an STD more places of contact
in its quest to penetrate the defense system of the receiving person's skin. In
younger women, the cervix has not fully matured. The skin covering may only
be one-cell-layer thick in some areas that, with time, would be covered by
many layers. These areas are more vulnerable to infection.

In this chapter we will provide an overview of the common methods of
prevention: circumcision, condoms, and vaccines.

## Circumcision

An uncircumcised penis has a foreskin that covers the head, or glans, of the
penis. This covering can be an area that is protected from the air and even

from the normal cleansing agents. If the uncircumcised man does not regularly retract this foreskin to cleanse beneath it, bacteria and viruses can find protection there as well. It is felt that the lining under the foreskin is vulnerable to infection. Uncircumcised men have a higher rate of acquiring the HPV virus, which in turn leads to a higher rate of transmission. Female partners of uncircumcised men may be at higher risk of developing an STD than female partners of circumcised men.

While the subject remains controversial, recent reports suggest circumcision as an STD reduction strategy. In one recent study, men circumcised as infants were nearly 50 percent less likely to have acquired an STD than their uncircumcised counterparts.[1]

Another study showed that women whose male partners were circumcised had a much lower rate of cervical cancer than if their partners were uncircumcised.[2]

According to the Harvard School of Public Health, since 25 percent of men around the world are circumcised, the general adoption of circumcision might lead to a further reduction in the incidence of cancer of the cervix of 23 to 43 percent.[3]

New data also shows that circumcising adult men is an effective way to limit the transmission of HIV. The National Institutes of Health announced in December of 2006 that two clinical trials in Africa have been stopped early because an independent monitoring board determined the treatment was so effective that it would be unethical to continue the experiment. A drop in HIV infection of up to 60 percent was found in these recent studies.[4]

According to Dr. Anthony Fauci, director of the NIAID, "We now have confirmation—from large, carefully controlled, randomized clinical trials—showing definitively that medically performed circumcision can significantly lower the risk of adult males contracting HIV through heterosexual intercourse. While the initial benefit will be fewer HIV infections in men, ultimately adult male circumcision could lead to fewer infections in women in those areas of the world where HIV is spread primarily through heterosexual intercourse."[5]

## Condoms

In the past decade, the government has bombarded us almost daily about the use of condoms. Media celebrities and sports figures have been recruited to spread the "good news" that condoms save. What began as a response to the epidemic of HIV/AIDS seen in the homosexual community in this nation soon spread to the heterosexual community as well. Sports stars such as Arthur Ashe and Magic Johnson showed that HIV/AIDS was not confined to the homosexual community but could be acquired through blood transfusion or heterosexual sex.

While our nation has the safest blood supply in the world, the problem of sex is more difficult. Behaviors are very difficult to change. Multiplied millions of dollars have been spent trying to do that, but instead of teaching the public that sexual intercourse outside of marriage is dangerous, that anal intercourse between men is extremely risky, and that multiple sexual partners may infect you, the government has promised its own solution—the condom.

The government's message of "safe sex" is not monogamy in marriage, as God intended. It is the message of the condom, and virtually every child in the public school system will be taught "safe sex" and the virtues of condoms. The only debate is how early to begin teaching, with advocates reaching down into the elementary schools to place condoms on bananas, all with our tax dollars.

For those parents who believe in abstinence until marriage, and those religious institutions that support them, condom education in public schools threatens their ability to raise their young according to biblical standards. Many fear that condom education will encourage their children to become sexually active as peer pressure is magnified by the consent of the school system.

But those who have watched the skyrocketing teenage pregnancy, STD, and AIDS rates among teenagers believe abstinence is unrealistic and even dangerous. Those leaders look at statistics showing 60 percent of our nation's young people have become sexually active before they graduate high school.[6] They doubt that abstinence will change these behaviors and fear that, without condoms, these children will fail.

## HISTORY OF CONDOMS

As early as 1000 B.C., the ancient Egyptians used a linen sheath for protection against disease, while the Chinese are known to have used oiled silk paper. By the 1700s, condoms made out of animal intestines became widely available in Europe, but they were costly and often reused. The mass-production of "rubbers" began after 1844 with the invention of vulcanization, a process that turns crude rubber into a strong elastic material. These were as thick as inner tubes, had a seam, and deteriorated rapidly. Latex manufacturing processes improved sufficiently in the 1930s to produce single-use condoms almost as thin and inexpensive as the ones used today. Today, condoms come in a variety of colors, shapes, and sizes. There are "snug" condoms for smaller men and "extra-large" condoms for those who think they need it![7]

## How effective are condoms?

The bottom line is: do they work? Before the AIDS epidemic, the main focus of condom use was pregnancy prevention. As a contraceptive, studies have been done and statistics kept of the effectiveness of latex condoms. Those whose interests lie in family planning have calculated what they call "perfect use" and "typical use" in contraceptive effectiveness. The percentages of women who would become pregnant using a particular product over a one-year period of time is calculated for all available birth control on the market today. Perfect use is the number of pregnancies, or "failures," that would be expected to occur in one hundred women using that particular form of birth control, in the exact manner it was prescribed, for every single act of intercourse from beginning to end in the course of one year. Typical use is the percentage of pregnancies that occur in the general population using a particular product. This takes into account the additional human factors such as inconsistencies of use or improper techniques. The typical use is what will happen to the average couple who chooses that particular form of birth control.

For latex condoms, the percentage of couples who would get pregnant using this product perfectly for one year is 3 percent.[8] In typical use, of one hundred couples who use condoms for one year, twelve would become pregnant. To keep this in perspective, remember that pregnancy can only occur between three to five days per month due to the life span of sperm and egg. Of the one hundred couples per year studied, statistics show us that 10 percent are infertile and would not conceive even if no contraception were used. So of the ninety couples left, twelve would get pregnant using condoms. This raises the failure rate of condoms to over 13 percent for an event that can only occur a few times each month.

Why aren't condoms 100 percent effective? The truth lies in the inherent flaws of the material latex. Since 1976, the FDA has regulated condoms to ensure their safety and effectiveness. Each condom is electronically scanned for holes or other defects. The manufacturer tests condoms from each batch using a "water leak" test for holes and an "air burst" test for strength. The FDA specifies that no more than one in four hundred can fail these tests or the entire lot is discarded.[9]

But in real-life trials evaluated by Karen Davis and Susan Weller of the University of Texas, 1 to 6 percent of condoms will break. In an analysis of twenty-five studies of condom usage in heterosexual couples with one HIV-infected partner, they found that 1 percent of the previously uninfected partners became HIV positive each year when using condoms 100 percent of the time. If condoms were not used at all, 7 percent per year became infected. They concluded that condoms reduce the risk of contracting HIV by 85 percent.[10]

This has been widely touted as supportive evidence of condom efficacy and has prompted the FDA to allow condom manufacturers to put such a statement on the label. But is 85 percent a comforting statistic for a fatal disease? Has this statistic been shared with the American public? No. Most physicians do not even know these data exist.

In their discussion of these findings, Davis and Weller concluded, "Condom efficacy may be higher for pregnancy than for HIV....HIV particles are smaller than sperm cells and may actually leak through condoms."[11] Have you heard this on the nightly news? Is this what is being taught in our public schools as "safe sex"? Condom manufacturers have only recommended their product for penile-vaginal intercourse. It is not recommended for penile-anal intercourse due to the tightness of the anal opening. Condoms are among the least effective method of birth control available in the United States, yet this is our government's primary weapon against HIV/AIDS.

C. M. Roland and M. J. Schroeder of the U.S. Naval Academy tested samples of latex from two condom-manufacturing facilities. Latex condoms have intrinsic holes called "voids," which are very tiny. But the HIV virus is fifty times smaller than these holes. In one square centimeter of latex, one million particles the size of the HIV virus passed through the condom within thirty minutes. They went on to state, "The ability of a condom or surgical glove to prevent transmission of viral particles is problematic."[12] Problematic indeed!

## How do condoms fare against the more common STDs?

Four government agencies (U.S. Agency for International Development, FDA, CDC, and NIH) published a report—"Scientific Evidence on Condom Effectiveness for STD Prevention"—on the effectiveness of latex male condoms on STD prevention. A panel of experts looked at eight STDs: HIV, gonorrhea, chlamydia, syphilis, chancroid, trichomoniasis, genital herpes (HSV 1 and 2), and genital human papillomavirus (HPV). While trying to minimize this area of concern, they did admit, "For many STDs, risk of infection might not be proportional to exposure of a *volume* of semen" (emphasis theirs).[13]

The report detailed each STD studied and the effects of condom use on prevention of disease. The most infectious STD is gonorrhea. The report found no significant risk reduction of gonorrhea for women using condoms and no reduction in tubal infertility. There was some protective effect for men who used condoms.

Chlamydia, the most common bacterial STD, is also more easily passed to women, and again, condoms failed to protect women compared to those whose partners did not use them. But even men using condoms found no protection against chlamydia.

One of the most common viral STDs is herpes, which can be contracted by exposure to bodily fluids or skin-to-skin contact. The ability of the condom to protect against this virus is dependent not only on its intrinsic strength but also on its ability to cover all of the affected skin. Several studies on HSV and condoms found that condom use actually *increased* the spread of HSV.

Syphilis is another STD that can be contracted by skin-to-skin contact, a significant limitation of the condoms. It is easily acquired by contact with only a few organisms. The studies reviewed could show no statistically significant reduction in the transmission of syphilis with condom usage.

HPV infections can occur on the scrotum, inner thighs, and anal region, as well as be isolated on the hands and fingernails of infected persons. It was expected that condoms would only partially protect against transmission. After reviewing the available scientific literature, the panel concluded, "There was no evidence that condom use reduced the risk of HPV infection."

## Using a condom

So why do condoms fail? A significant reason is faulty usage. Many couples dislike condoms and feel they are disruptive to lovemaking. It is not as easy as it might seem to put a condom on correctly, which is why there has been such an emphasis on condom education in our public schools. The following information may help you understand what even the most motivated couple must overcome to achieve condom effectiveness. The product comes tightly rolled in a pouch with a shelf life of only three to five years. Latex is susceptible to heat, so it must be stored at room temperature and away from sunlight or heat. This makes the glove compartment of your car a poor choice!

Most condoms come with a reservoir at the tip designed to receive the semen. It must remain free and not pulled up against the head of the penis. Pinch off the head of the condom while placing it on the penis to ensure that the reservoir remains. The other benefit of pinching the end is that if the air is not kept out of the reservoir, the act of intercourse might push a pocket of air against the latex shell and cause breakage at the very place designed to collect the semen.

The condom must be unrolled correctly and not be placed inside out. It must also be slowly unrolled onto the penis and not pulled up after being unrolled ahead of time to prevent breakage. The condom must be placed on the fully erect penis to ensure fit and before the penis has any contact with the partner's skin. Upon erection, a small amount of lubricating fluid is released that not only contains a high concentration of sperm but also can harbor STDs. If vaginal penetration is begun and then the penis is withdrawn for condom application, the damage may have already been done.

Some of the failure of condoms can occur in breaks or tears that result because of friction during intercourse. It is recommended that commercial lubrication be added to help the condom glide freely. But it must be a water-based product, as oil-based lubricants such as massage oil, baby oil, lotions, or petroleum jelly will rapidly begin to decompose the latex. The most recommended lubricant is K-Y Jelly.[14]

Once ejaculation has occurred, the penis will immediately begin to soften and shrink. It is critical to condom effectiveness that the condom be held at its base and withdrawn immediately after ejaculation to prevent spill of semen out of the opening of the condom or leaving the condom behind in the vagina upon withdrawal.

One study of men who were experienced condom users showed that 13 percent of them were exposed to some risk during intercourse because of faulty condom usage. The most common error occurred because the condom was worn inside out, then flipped over and worn again, leading to increased risk of tears. Twelve percent of men lost their erections trying to use it. Almost 8 percent began intercourse without a condom, then stopped to put one on. Many others had their condoms break or completely fall off inside the vagina.[15] And these were the "experienced" users!

## THE POLITICS OF CONDOMS

Some leaders in health care have been bold enough to buck the politically correct emphasis on condom use.[16]

- Dr. Harold Jaffee, chief of epidemiology of the CDC, says, "You can't tell people it's all right to do whatever you want as long as you wear a condom. It (AIDS) is just too dangerous a disease to say that."

- In a statement by Dr. Robert Renfield, chief of retro-viral research at Walter Reed Army Institute, he makes the point that, "Simply put, condoms fail. And condoms fail at a rate unacceptable to me as a physician to endorse them as a strategy to be promoted as meaningful AIDS protection."

- A member of the U.S. Presidential AIDS Commission, Dr. Teresa Crenshaw, had this warning: "Saying that the use of condoms is 'safe sex' is in fact playing Russian roulette. A lot of people will die in this dangerous game."

Even the World Health Organization, far from being a bastion of conservative thought or moral values, issued this surprising statement during World AIDS Day: "The most effective way to prevent sexual transmission of HIV is to abstain, or for two people who are not infected to be faithful to one another."[17]

# Vaccines

Much of the hope of the medical community in the fight against STDs lies in the development of vaccines that can be distributed worldwide.

## Herpes vaccine

There is a tremendous amount of ongoing research to develop a herpes vaccine. The progress has been difficult, as the current experimental vaccine is only effective in women. It is still several years from being available to the public.[18]

> (i) The National Institute of Allergy and Infectious Diseases and GlaxoSmithKline Pharmaceuticals are supporting a large clinical trial in women of an experimental vaccine that may help prevent transmission of genital herpes. The trial is being conducted at more than thirty-five sites nationwide. For more information, visit the Herpevac Trial for Women Web site at http://herpesvaccine.nih.gov.

Despite numerous vaccine trials proposed over the past thirty years, none have proven to be effective. The medical community is almost no closer to an HSV vaccine than when we started.

## Chlamydia vaccine

Scientists are getting closer to a vaccine against chlamydia, one of the world's leading causes of blindness and a common STD. Research into the vaccine has been stalled for twenty-five years until recent advances in DNA knowledge have led to a better understanding of the disease. Antibodies to one protein of the bacterium may prevent infection by all fifteen strains of chlamydia. The research so far has been conducted in test tubes, where it has been effective in killing the bacterium. It will soon move on to animal testing. Testing will soon be complete, and clinical trials in humans could begin in a few years.[19]

## HPV vaccine

At the time of this publication there is one HPV vaccine on the market and one that will be released shortly. This is the beginning of what may be a series of modifications to produce the best vaccine possible. The first vaccine to be approved by the FDA and CDC is called *Gardasil*. It is made from inactive pieces of four of the most common HPV viruses that cause the disease. Out of the one hundred strains of HPV that have been detected, types 16 and 18 cause the majority (70 percent) of cervical precancerous and cancerous changes of the cervix, vulva, vagina, penis, and anus. The two others included in the vaccine, types 6 and 11, cause 90 percent of all genital warts.[20]

Ideally, the vaccine will be offered to young girls between the ages of nine and twelve so they can develop immunity to these HPV types before they become sexually active. Gardasil is also recommended for women ages thirteen to twenty-six, even if they are already sexually active. The vaccine will not protect women who already have a particular HPV infection, but it will prevent infection in the future from other strains in the vaccine that the woman has not yet encountered. The HPV vaccine will not treat or cure any current genital lesions, whether they are condyloma or dysplasia.

While the vaccine, given in a series of three injections over six months, is nearly 100 percent effective in preventing infection from the four most common viral types, 30 percent of cervical cancers and 10 percent of genital warts will not be prevented. For this reason, it is critical that vaccinated women maintain their yearly cancer screenings.[21]

At the present time, the vaccine is not recommended for men or women over the age of twenty-six. This is primarily because these groups were not studied in the original clinical trials. Young teens and women are the most susceptible to genital warts and cancer, so the focus of prevention has been on them. There is also no "Pap smear" for men, so clinical trials are unable to judge the vaccine's effectiveness on men.

## Trichomonas vaccine

Trichomonas is usually cured with an antibiotic such as metronidazole or tinidazole, but it can be misdiagnosed by the woman as a yeast infection. The availability of OTC yeast remedies can lead to a delay in treatment. A woman may attempt to relieve her symptoms at home, only to find those symptoms returning as the soothing properties of the cream fades.

In our hometown of San Antonio, at the University of Texas Health Science Center Department of Microbiology, John Alderete, PhD, is moving closer to developing a vaccine against trichomonas. He states:

> We know what nutrients it needs and how it evades the immune system. You really need this fundamental knowledge base to learn how the organism survives before you can begin to develop strategies to interfere with the infection.[22]

Various animal models are being used to test possible vaccines, but trials in humans are still years away.

## AIDS vaccine

The hope for a "savior" for AIDS is being placed on the development of an HIV vaccine. Millions of dollars are being spent by Western governments and pharmaceutical companies searching for the still elusive vaccine. NIH funding more than doubled from $232 million in FY (fiscal year) 2000 to $602 million in 2006. Since 1987, investigators supported by the National Institute of Allergy and Infectious Diseases (NIAID) have enrolled more than twenty-three thousand volunteers in ninety-six HIV vaccine clinical trials that have tested at least fifty-eight different vaccine candidates. As of this writing, an effective vaccine still eludes us.[23]

But former surgeon general C. Everett Koop believes there will never be a vaccine.[24] And the reason is very simple: there is more than one type of HIV virus.

In the United States, HIV-1 is the predominant variety, but in Africa, there are many types. HIV-2 was discovered in 1986. Because it is so rare in the States, the CDC does not recommend HIV-2 testing, although most blood banks test for type 1 and 2 simultaneously. Those people currently asking to be tested for HIV are tested only for type 1.[25] It is possible that with the influx of immigrants from other nations who carry HIV-2, the spread of this variety could remain undetected in the United States for some time. Not only is HIV-2 resistant to the available medication we have to fight it, but it is also not the focus of any vaccine strategy at this time.

## IT'S IN THE WORD

Science is proving what God the Father knew along. The only way to prevent serious, lifelong disease and death is for both partners to be virgins at marriage and to remain faithful to one another for life. It is not some outdated and archaic moral position. As Moses proclaimed to the children of Israel, "This day I call heaven and earth as witnesses against you that I have set before you life and death, blessings and curses. Now choose life, so that you and your children may live" (Deut. 30:19). It is literally a matter of life and death.

# Chapter 10

# ABORTION

PROBABLY ONE OF THE MOST CONTROVERSIAL, DIVISIVE ISSUES IN POLITICS and religion that has polarized our nation is the subject of abortion. It is one of the most common medical procedures in the United States. An estimated half of all pregnancies among American women are unintended, and four in ten of these are terminated by abortion.[1]

*I (SAF) will never forget a night I spent working in the University Hospital Emergency Department as a medical student doing a rotation on the GYN service. The resident to whom I was assigned received a call of a young woman who was miscarrying. We arrived in her room to the sounds of deep sobbing and distress. I assumed she was troubled over the loss of her pregnancy, but as the resident began to interview her, we discovered that she had visited a local abortion clinic earlier that day. Because she was so advanced in her pregnancy (at about four and a half months), medical therapy was not possible. But she wanted an abortion, so the doctor at the clinic dilated her cervix and physically had to remove the fetus.*

*At that stage in pregnancy, the fetus was very fragile. The doctor did not dilate her cervix far enough to be able to retrieve the entire fetus in one piece, and he had failed to count the body parts at the end of the procedure. She was discharged to go home, believing that everything was complete. Several hours later, she felt something coming through her vagina. When she went to the restroom to investigate, the tiny left leg of her unborn baby came out of her underwear.*

*She was hysterical. She had no idea the baby would look so well formed. She always thought it was "just a bunch of cells." The moment she saw that perfectly formed leg with its miniature foot and toes, reality set in quickly, and she knew she had killed her baby. The resident checked to make sure other fetal parts were not still retained inside her uterus and began a course of antibiotics to prevent infection. She physically healed from her ordeal, but she left the hospital a different woman. I would never see her again.*

# What Is Abortion?

Medically speaking, an abortion is the removal or expulsion of an embryo or fetus from the uterus. Abortion can be divided into several categories that have different meanings in the medical world.

Spontaneous abortion is also called "miscarriage." This is an abortion due to natural causes, accident, or trauma. Most are the result of chromosomal abnormalities that come about when the egg and sperm mix together. If chromosomal material is lost, duplicated, or damaged along the way, the necessary information to create a normal human being is compromised. These pregnancies often end spontaneously in miscarriage.

It is estimated that 10 to 50 percent of all pregnancies end in miscarriage, depending on the age of the mother. More than 50 percent of these have been found to be genetically abnormal.[2] Spontaneous abortion can also be caused by environmental factors such as toxins in food or the environment as well as radiation. Further discussion of pregnancy loss is found in chapter 11.

Induced abortion is deliberate removal of the fetus. It can be further subcategorized into therapeutic and elective. Therapeutic abortions are those done to save the life of the mother or to preserve the woman's physical or mental health. It can also mean the termination of a pregnancy that would result in a child born with a congenital disorder that would be fatal or associated with significant complications. In the infertility world, where multiple fetuses are often created during in vitro fertilization, therapeutic abortion can reduce the number of fetuses to lessen health risks that come from the premature delivery of triplets, quads, or even greater numbers. This is also called "selective embryo reduction."

Elective abortions are those performed for any other reason. This includes the desire to delay childbearing until some later date, concerns regarding career or education, financial or relationship instability, or the perception that they are either too young or too old for children.[3] The term *abortion* as used by the public covers both subtypes of induced abortion.

## THE FACTS ON ABORTION STATS

Statistics for induced abortion vary depending upon stage of pregnancy. In the United States, 86.7 percent of abortions occur at or prior to twelve weeks of pregnancy, 9.9 percent from thirteen to twenty weeks, and 1.4 percent at or after twenty-one weeks.[4]

A study done in 2002 concluded that 54 percent of women who had an abortion were using some form of contraception at the time they became pregnant, while 46 percent were not. Problems with inconsistent use were reported by 49 percent of those using condoms and 76 percent of those using oral contraception; 42 percent of those using condoms reported some failure through slipping or breakage.[5]

Efforts to restrict legal abortion almost always allow the clause "except in cases of rape or incest." It is important to know just how small a role this plays in abortion. Statistics indicate that only 1 percent of women who obtain abortions became pregnant as a result of rape and 0.5 percent as a result of incest.[6]

# Methods of Abortion

A pregnancy can be intentionally aborted in a variety of ways. These include medical (by means of medication), surgical, and nonmedical (those not performed by trained medical personnel). The manner selected depends upon the gestational age of the fetus. How far the pregnancy has advanced is a key factor, in addition to the skill of the physician who will perform the procedure. Other considerations include the availability of services in that particular region of the country as well as any state or federal laws that pertain to the performance of the abortion. Patient preference is always a factor, as is the financial cost involved.

## Medical abortion

In September 2000, the U.S. Food and Drug Administration approved the abortion drug *mifepristone,* or Mifeprex, to be marketed in the United States. It is commonly referred to by its original name of RU-486. The drug works by counteracting the effects of progesterone on the lining of the uterus that holds the pregnancy, leading it to degenerate. It also makes the uterus more susceptible to agents that can cause contractions. The drug is FDA-approved in the United States to terminate pregnancy up to forty-nine days after the beginning of the latest menstrual cycle. Under the approved regimen, a 600 mg tablet is administered by a physician following a counseling session. Two days later, the patient returns for a 400 mg dose of another medicine, misoprostol, to induce contractions. This method terminates pregnancy in about 92 percent of cases.[7] In cases of failure of medical abortion, vacuum or manual aspiration is used to complete the abortion surgically.

Medical abortion has the advantage of more discreet use in a doctor's office as opposed to the more public setting of a traditional abortion clinic. It is accomplished in the privacy of one's home and currently comprises 10 percent of all abortions in the United States. With greater physician awareness and training, the percentage of medical abortions is expected to increase. Because of the ease of receiving these medications, accurate statistics will probably never be compiled.

Medical abortion in its simplest form causes the patient to experience a miscarriage at home, with the attendant risks of blood loss, painful cramping, and infection. Between 4.5 and 7.9 percent of women in clinical trials required surgical intervention to complete the abortion.[8]

Since the approval of mifepristone in September 2000, the FDA has received reports of six deaths in the United States following medical abortion with mifepristone (Mifeprex) and misoprostol.[9] According to a House Subcommittee on Criminal Justice, Drug Policy, and Human Resources document, the number of patient fatalities in the United States related to mifepristone abortions is estimated at 1.39 in 100,000, almost fourteen times the rate for the more traditional surgical method.[10] This has led a variety of organizations, both pro-life and medical, to demand its removal from the market. The FDA has issued a "black box" warning, its highest form of warning, about the dangers of infection and death from use of this pill.

## Surgical abortion

In the first twelve weeks, suction-aspiration or vacuum abortion is the most commonly used procedure.[11] This is likely to change as medical abortion becomes more widely accepted. The first type is a manual extraction, where a thin tube is inserted into the uterus after minimal dilation and a syringe is attached to manually apply suction to remove the developing embryo. This procedure can only remove a small amount of tissue and must be done in the very first two weeks of pregnancy.

The second, and more common, procedure is vacuum abortion (commonly referred to as a D&C, or dilation and curettage), usually done between seven and thirteen weeks of pregnancy. It involves dilating the cervix and inserting a hollow plastic tube called a *cannula* into the uterus. Suction is applied by a machine that removes the pregnancy, including the fetus and placenta. This same technique is used for patients who are miscarrying. Most elective abortions are done with a local nerve block and possibly some intravenous sedation. Most abortions are done in a hospital or surgery center under general anesthesia for comfort and patient preference.

## Second trimester

To accomplish an abortion in the second trimester, suction cannulas are too small, and so delivery of a preterm pregnancy is an option. This can be done by injecting the uterus with a salt or urea solution, which acts as a poison when swallowed by the fetus. Other drugs such as prostaglandins are given to promote labor and the fetus is delivered. One complication is that sometimes the babies live through the procedure and are born alive, often with significant medical problems from both the chemicals and prematurity.[12] There have also been reports of coagulation disorders that can cause maternal death due to an inability to clot blood after a saline abortion.[13]

More commonly, a D&E, or dilation and evacuation, procedure is the one of choice. Since this involves stretching the cervix far wider than dilators can accomplish, a two-step procedure is usually done. The first step involves inserting a dilating device made from compressed seaweed or synthetic material into the cervix and gradually dilating the cervix overnight by absorbing fluid from the mother's cervix. After the dilation has occurred, the patient is brought back into the clinic to have the fetus extracted by forceps.[14]

After the fetus is extracted, a suction device is used to remove the placenta and any other tissue that may remain. The procedure becomes increasingly more difficult and dangerous as the pregnancy progresses. There are fewer practitioners who are trained in these techniques, and the cost is much greater. Because of this, only 9 percent of abortions are D&E procedures.[15]

### Third trimester

Similar techniques are used to induce abortion in the third trimester. Premature delivery can be induced with prostaglandins; this can be coupled with injecting the amniotic fluid with caustic solutions containing saline or urea to ensure that the fetus is not born alive. Very late abortions can be induced by intact dilation and extraction (intact D&X), known as "partial-birth abortion." This requires that the fetus be delivered feet first up to the level of the head. Then a suction cannula is inserted to remove the brain and decompress the fetal head before delivery. Usually the fetus has already died from either trauma of birth or previous chemical solutions injected into the uterus or directly into the fetus. Most commonly, this procedure is reserved for a late diagnosis of severe congenital abnormalities. The legality of the procedure for everyday use was called into question by a congressional law banning the procedure. This was recently upheld by the Supreme Court in *Gonzalez v. Planned Parenthood*, reversing the earlier positions of appeals courts.[16] Unless this changes, "partial-birth abortion" is illegal at this time.

### Fetal pain

The presence or absence of fetal pain during abortion is a matter of medical, ethical, and public interest. The evidence is conflicting, with some authorities believing that the fetus is capable of feeling pain from the first trimester,[17] and others maintaining that the development needed to experience such pain does not exist until the second or third trimester.[18] We know that pain receptors begin to appear in the seventh week of pregnancy. The thalamus starts to form in the fifth week of pregnancy. This is the part of the brain that receives signals from the nervous system and sends it to the conscious part of the brain.

## IT'S IN THE WORD

Although the word *abortion* is never mentioned in the Bible, there are enough supporting verses to inform us of what God thinks about this procedure. Read for yourself.

They shed innocent blood, the blood of their sons and daughters, whom they sacrificed to the idols of Canaan, and the land was desecrated by their blood.

—Psalm 106:38

There are six things the LORD hates, seven that are detestable to him... hands that shed innocent blood.

—Proverbs 6:16–17

Surely the arm of the LORD is not too short to save, nor his ear too dull to hear. But your iniquities have separated you from your God; your sins have hidden his face from you, so that he will not hear. For your hands are stained with blood, your fingers with guilt....Their deeds are evil deeds, and acts of violence are in their hands. Their feet rush into sin; they are swift to shed innocent blood. Their thoughts are evil thoughts; ruin and destruction mark their ways. The way of peace they do not know; there is no justice in their paths. They have turned them into crooked roads; no one who walks in them will know peace.

—Isaiah 59:1–3, 6–8

# Chapter 11

# POST-ABORTION RECOVERY

Each year, three million women become pregnant "accidentally."[1] Of these unplanned pregnancies, one million women will choose abortion. Since abortion became legal in 1973, over forty million procedures have been done in this country.[2] In fact, by age forty-five, one out of every three women in the United States has had at least one abortion.[3] That means many women sitting in church pews have had an abortion in the past. Many Christian men have also participated in these decisions, often with women who are not their current partners. Whenever an abortion is performed, the post-abortion recovery is not just the body but also the mind and soul, because God created us to be triune beings. Depending upon what happened to the patient, the ramifications can last a lifetime. The good news is that God still heals and forgives.

*We met a young couple who loved each other very much. They had been married for three years when he discussed his desire for children. Although apprehensive about the idea, the wife agreed to stop her birth control and attempt pregnancy. Within three months, she was pregnant.*

*When they came for their first obstetrical visit, we discovered that while there was evidence of a small eight-week-old fetus in the womb, there was no fetal heartbeat. The pregnancy was in the beginning stages of miscarriage.*

*The couple was disheartened, as anyone would expect. After a brief discussion of the risks and benefits of allowing spontaneous miscarriage at home versus an outpatient D&C, they decided to have the procedure. Two weeks later, she came in for a postoperative evaluation. She was doing well physically but not emotionally. At first we reassured her that grieving is a normal process after a miscarriage and that she would most likely be able to get pregnant again soon. The odds were very high that the next pregnancy would be fine.*

*But then she revealed something she had not disclosed on her medical history form—when she was eighteen years old, she had an abortion. She was convinced that God was punishing her for killing her first child by taking away the child she now wanted with her husband. He had no knowledge of her past abortion, and she was sure he would leave her if he knew. How could he forgive her when her sin had cost them their baby?*

*We tried to reassure her by telling her that no scientific studies had shown an increased risk in miscarriage after only one abortion, especially if there were no surgical complications, and miscarriages were more common than she thought. But she never accepted God's forgiveness for the abortion. She felt free from all other sins from the past but this one. Murdering an innocent child was unthinkable in her mind, and if God could not forgive her, her husband certainly would not.*

*What she did not know was that during his teen years he had a sexual relationship that resulted in an unwanted pregnancy. He was not ready to be a father and convinced his girlfriend at the time to have an abortion. Soon after, they broke up, and she moved away. Since he became a Christian, the guilt of this decision haunted him when he realized that abortion was morally wrong. Now, he too was convinced they had miscarried because of his past sin.*

*When she finally got the courage to confess her past to her husband, he was free to share his story as well, and the healing began. A new level of intimacy came to their marriage, and they felt free to share their deepest secrets and fears. The sins of the past became a bridge to greater communication and love than they had ever known.*

*At the same time, through counseling at their local church, they began to see that God did not put different sins into categories. There was no such thing as "little" sin or "big" sin. It was all sin. And there was no sin that Christ could not, or would not, forgive if He was asked. Just as they forgave themselves, so did they receive His forgiveness. Eventually she had a healthy pregnancy and delivered a beautiful, healthy baby boy—the fulfillment of God's promise.*

## Risks of Surgical Abortion

Like any surgical procedure, abortion carries potential risks to the patient. These can range from minor to potentially serious complications. The minor risks include infection, especially if the abortion is done in the presence of an undiagnosed STD, which can lead to infertility.[4] For this reason, many clinics prescribe oral antibiotics after an abortion. Dilation of the cervix can cause trauma, which predisposes the woman to future pregnancy complications such as premature rupture of the membranes, premature birth, and incompetent cervix with loss of the pregnancy.[5]

Incomplete emptying of the uterus can cause hemorrhage and infection. Many abortion centers will use ultrasound to verify the location and gestational age of the pregnancy prior to proceeding with the abortion. Immediate follow-up of patients who continue to report pregnancy symptoms after the procedure or who have unusual bleeding and cramping can reduce the risk of permanent injury or death.

Other serious and potentially life-threatening risks of abortion come from infection and trauma caused by the instruments placed into the uterus to do the abortion. These complications include a perforated uterus,[6] perforated bowel or bladder,[7] septic shock, and death.[8] The risk of complications increase depending on how far pregnancy has progressed.[9]

There is also a chance that the pregnancy was never in the uterus but was a tubal or ectopic pregnancy. Because most abortion providers do not send pathology on their specimens to cut the cost of the procedure, some women have suffered serious complications such as emergency surgery, blood transfusions, and death from ruptured ectopic pregnancies that were not diagnosed.

The risk of induced abortion depends on a number of factors. There is a wide variation in the quality of health services in different societies and among different socio-economic groups. This can result in poor patient follow-up and aftercare, which leads to delays in treatment of complications. The degree of risk is also dependent upon the skill and experience of the practitioner, the age and health of the pregnant woman,[10] and the stage of pregnancy she is in when the abortion is performed. For example, the risk of death from second trimester abortion is one hundred times greater than it is in the first trimester.[11]

There is a lack of uniformity in reporting data on abortions, so the actual risks of the procedure will likely never be known. Personally, we see patients in our office who have had an abortion somewhere in town and suffered a complication. Even though the aftercare is included in the price of the procedure, the patient is unwilling to return to the place of her abortion, either from regret or fear that the personnel were not competent. Since we are not an abortion provider, those complications are never counted.

There have been cases of teenagers dying after an abortion in our own city that were never reported because they died in a hospital under the care of a different physician. In a year where only four deaths were reported in the entire United States, our town would have been responsible for 25 percent of the complications.[12] This is highly unlikely. That is why it is easy for abortion providers such as Planned Parenthood to profess that abortion is safer than childbirth.

Uncommonly, abortion will be unsuccessful and pregnancy will continue. This is termed a "failed abortion" and can result in the delivery of a live infant.[13] Depending on the circumstances, the fetus can be damaged from the attempted abortion and a disabled baby may result.

# Other Complications

Great controversy exists in the medical community over a number of proposed risks and effects of abortion. The evidence is most certainly influenced by the political and religious aspects of abortion. Given the more than forty million abortions that have taken place since the 1970s, it should be easy to determine if there were other complications not originally thought to occur from abortion. Again, the studies tend to be based on self-reporting of patients about their abortion history, something many women are reluctant to do. It also depends on women remembering their past health history, which may introduce some bias in the reporting process. The following are proposed complications that have yet to be confirmed.

## Breast cancer

The abortion–breast cancer (ABC) theory deals with the relationship between induced abortion and an increased risk of developing breast cancer. In early pregnancy the level of estrogen increases, leading to breast growth in preparation for lactation. The ABC theory suggests that this process is interrupted with abortion before full development of breast structures is completed, usually in the third trimester. This leaves the breasts with more vulnerable cells that have not finished developing, resulting in greater potential risk of breast cancer. The hypothesis has not been scientifically verified, and abortion is not considered a breast cancer risk by any major cancer organization.

In 2004, a reanalysis of fifty-three epidemiological studies concluded that abortion does "not increase a woman's risk of developing breast cancer."[14] But an expert at the National Cancer Institute workshop, Dr. Joel Brind, filed a dissenting opinion criticizing these conclusions.[15] Brind argues that the majority of interview-based studies have indicated a link, and some are statistically significant.[16] There remains debate in the medical community with the ABC issue seen by some as merely a part of the pro-life strategy against abortion. Nevertheless, the subject continues to be one of both political and scientific contention.

## Mental health

Post-abortion syndrome (PAS) or post-abortion stress syndrome (PASS) is a term used to describe a set of mental health characteristics that have been observed in women following an abortion. Symptoms are similar to those of post-traumatic stress disorder (PTSD), but they have also included repeated and persistent dreams and nightmares related to the abortion, intense feelings of guilt, and the "need to repair."[17]

Researchers in 2002 reported that the risk of clinical depression was higher for women who chose to have an abortion compared to those who carried their babies to term, even if the pregnancy was unwanted.[18]

Recently, data gathered over a twenty-five-year period found an increased risk of depression, anxiety, suicidal behavior, and substance abuse among women who had previously had an abortion.[19] In 2008, the Royal College of Psychiatrists in England recommended that "women should not be allowed to have an abortion until they are counseled on the possible risks to their mental health." This reverses the previous thought that unwanted pregnancies were more risky to mental health than any later regrets over having an abortion.[20]

Despite these studies, most mainstream medical organizations do not recognize PASS as an official mental disorder. Those that do recognize it believe it is extremely rare, considering that over forty million abortions have taken place. It is doubtful that any substantive research will ever be done to answer this question. Neither the pro-life nor pro-choice camps are willing to risk an answer that does not support their position. And Congress has failed in multiple attempts to pass legislation to study this syndrome.[21] The religious and political factions make this aspect of medicine difficult indeed.

According to a leading aftercare group, PASS can be defined as a syndrome where the reactions and feelings in the first three months following an abortion are severe, causing such problems as:[22]

- Self-harm, strong suicidal thoughts, or suicide attempts

- Increase in dangerous and/or unhealthy activities (alcohol/drug abuse, anorexia/bulimia, compulsive overeating, cutting, casual and indifferent sex, and other inappropriate risk-taking behaviors)

- Depression that is stronger than just "a little sadness or the blues"

- Inability to perform normal self-care activities

- Inability to function normally in her job or in school

- Inability to take care of or relate to her existing children or function normally in her other relationships (i.e., with a spouse, partner, other family members, or friends)

- A desire to immediately get pregnant and "replace" the baby that was aborted, even when all the circumstances that led her to "choose abortion" the first time are still in place.

For more information on symptoms of PASS, visit the Web site www.afterabortion.com.

## IT'S IN THE WORD

Most Christians are convinced that God will not forgive them for past abortions, so they cannot forgive themselves. Just like the story at the beginning of this chapter, I (SAF) regularly counsel with women in my office about past abortion. Most fear the Christian community will reject them and be repulsed if their past sins were discovered.

Forgiveness is the key to spiritual and emotional healing from abortion. A woman must forgive herself and let go of the past. She must accept God's unconditional pardon, realizing His promise to her.

> I, even I, am he who blots out your transgressions, for my own sake, and remembers your sins no more.
>
> —Isaiah 43:25

> For I will forgive their wickedness and will remember their sins no more.
>
> —Jeremiah 31:34

> For as the heavens are high above the earth, so great is His mercy toward those who fear Him. As far as the east is from the west, so far has He removed our transgressions from us. As a father pities his children, so the LORD pities those who fear Him.
>
> —Psalm 103:11–13, NKJV

You *do* deserve to be happy and fulfilled, no matter what is in your past, because of what Christ has done for you on the cross. To refuse to forgive yourself is to make Jesus's death less than sufficient for you. That is a lie you cannot afford to believe if you want to live in the unmerited favor of God's grace and be the helpmate the Lord intended your spouse to have.

Once I have guided the woman in accepting God's forgiveness and forgiving herself, I encourage her to tell her husband. We have all sinned in our lives, and the men are no exception. A wife's confession gives her husband permission to share his own past with her. It takes courage to trust God and your spouse, but the rewards are far greater than you can imagine.

# SECTION 4
## THE MARRIED WOMAN

# Chapter 12

# THE WEDDING NIGHT

FROM TIME TO TIME, VIRGINS ASK FOR ADVICE REGARDING THEIR WEDDING night. We wish this situation was more common, but on those occasions when both partners have saved their virginity until marriage, one or both may be nervous about their first sexual experience.

For women, the greatest fear (besides pregnancy) is that intercourse will hurt. Most women are familiar with the hymen, a band of skin that encircles the opening to the vagina. It is a seal upon virginity that, once opened, will never be resealed. In the Old Testament, the breaking of the hymen, along with the resultant bleeding that occurred, was proof that a husband had been given a virgin as a bride. The bed sheets were inspected for the presence of blood the following morning. A bride who was found not to be a virgin could be stoned to death (Deut. 22:13–21). So proving one's virginity by bleeding on the wedding night was a major event in the culture of the Bible, one that held life-and-death consequences.

But in our day, the rupturing of the hymen (and bleeding) is not a celebrated event. In fact, the thought of it causes fear among many a virgin bride. Since such evidence is not necessary in the New Testament, it is preferable to many of the couples we counsel to avoid such physical trauma. Men, on the other hand, may be concerned that they don't know the anatomy very well and might appear clumsy and feeble.

## What to Expect

Ask any couple who has been married awhile, and they will tell you that sex gets better over time. Honeymoon sex is often not that great, and much of it is "hype." Sex is a rite of passage, but it is not the benchmark to measure all encounters.

Generally, the bride and groom will be exhausted from the activities of rehearsal, wedding, reception, and so on. By the time the happy couple arrives at their hotel room that night, neither will be in peak physical condition. Both will have worn uncomfortable clothing and shoes, smiled endlessly until their cheeks hurt, and ate sporadically, if at all. This is not the foundation for a night of great sex! All we are suggesting is to be realistic and not have expectations that you can't fulfill and that were based on fantasy in the first place.

Hopefully before the wedding night, you have both talked about contraception and whether or not you wanted to use any. If you chose hormonal birth control (pill, patch, ring, or injectable), you would have needed to be on your second month to have adequate protection for your wedding night. If you were fitted for a diaphragm or decided upon condoms, these need to be brought with you. It is a good idea to have any barrier methods you are going to use readily accessible before initiating intercourse so that the flow will not be interrupted. As will be mentioned in the chapter on contraception, a diaphragm must be inserted ahead of time, while a condom can be placed as part of foreplay. Review in your mind the proper technique for whichever method you choose, if you are going to use contraception at all.

## Preparing for Lovemaking

There are great resources available with diagrams and drawings as well as instruction on sexual techniques that may be of great value. Sitting down before the wedding and reviewing these materials together can be a way to open up a dialogue about whatever fears or reservations each person might have. Gaining knowledge about the male and female anatomy can give the opposite partner more confidence when approaching intercourse for the first time.

(i) There are books that are biblically based and offer good advice: *Intimate and Unashamed* by Scott Farhart, MD; *Intended for Pleasure* by Ed Wheat, MD, and Gaye Wheat; *The Honeymoon of Your Dreams* by Walt Larimore, MD, and Susan Crockett, MD.

Part of the counsel to betrothed virgins is about the stretching of the hymen before the wedding night. If they have been tampon users, some stretching of the hymen has undoubtedly occurred. If it has not, we instruct the women to take a lubricant, such as K-Y Jelly, and place it on their index finger. Gently inserting it to the second knuckle will begin the process of stretching the hymen. The next step is the insertion of two fingers crossed over each other. The goal is to eventually be able to comfortably insert two lubricated fingers side by side into the vagina. While the erect penis is still wider than this, it will be a good starting point for the evening.

Some women will not want to do these things and prefer to experience their wedding night without any prior preparation. That is, of course, completely acceptable. These suggestions are for those who fear the tearing of the hymen and would like to reduce that risk, providing for a more pleasant beginning to their sexual life.

Of course, the conduct of the groom is equally important if this preparation is to be successful. While the hymen is a bridge of skin that can be stretched, the vagina is a tunnel of circular muscle that can be contracted to a very small opening prior to childbearing. A frightened bride can squeeze the opening so tightly that the groom cannot gain access. So the conduct of the man must be slow, gentle, and as relaxed as possible.

We suggest wine or champagne for both partners, either during the reception or at the hotel. The goal is to be as relaxed as possible but not drunk! Both should change into clothing that is appropriate for the evening and is easy to remove. Try to avoid complicated bra fasteners or belts that can interfere with romance and cause the other person embarrassment or feelings of insecurity from struggling to remove an article of clothing. Save those daring maneuvers for a later time. The point is to have everything go as smoothly and as confidently as possible.

When both are ready, slowly undress each other, taking time to admire how God has created the other. Don't be in a rush to reach the genitals. Take time to explore other things and build excitement. This will increase the woman's natural lubricating fluids and prepare the vagina for later entry. After several minutes of foreplay, and when both partners feel ready, it is up to the groom to enter his bride. She can facilitate this by taking the penis and guiding it slowly into herself.

This accomplishes two things. First, it relieves a common fear (and mistake) that men have of missing the vaginal opening and ending up at the anus. It is an easy thing to do since the two openings are only an inch apart. Secondly, by guiding the penis, the woman can feel in control of the speed of entry and give herself time to get accustomed to the stretching as the penis is progressively inserted.

As mentioned in an earlier chapter, every vagina can accommodate a penis. But the penis does come in different lengths and widths when erect. The bride and groom will form a perfect fit no matter what the size if they are both gentle and patient. Sometimes the addition of a lubricant, such as K-Y Jelly, is helpful, especially if the woman does not feel she is well lubricated on her own. This will reduce friction as a source of tearing of the vaginal skin.

Some couples have discovered that when the woman is positioned on top of the man, she is better able to control the speed of entry of the penis and does not have to fear his generally larger body on top of her. Once insertion has comfortably been achieved, the couples can change to any position they desire.

Most of the discussion so far has centered on the hymen, which is an issue of width or girth of the penis. The topic of length comes to bear in the back of the vagina. Once penetration has been achieved and the bride is comfortable with the penis fully inside of her, the groom will begin to withdraw it partially and thrust it back in again in a rhythmic motion. This is the basis of intercourse and what is necessary for the male to achieve ejaculation. Several facts mentioned in earlier chapters now come into play.

If the woman is sufficiently aroused, the muscles of the deep vagina will pull the cervix inward and cause the vagina to elongate, accommodating almost any length of penis. But this is not universal. Sometimes the arousal phase will not be complete, either from pain or fear, and the vagina will not reach its maximum elongation. Some men have longer penises than others and are able to reach the back of the vagina, hitting the cervix. Since the cervix is attached to the uterus, which is attached to the ovaries, rhythmically bumping the cervix can transmit pressure waves to the ovaries. This can be an unpleasant sensation for the woman, akin to slapping the testicles repeatedly.

If during deep penetration the bride is uncomfortable, she should say so, because the groom has no way of knowing otherwise. He should press inward to the depth that she finds comfortable; she should let him know if he is going too deeply. Since the majority of the pleasure sensations for the penis are located in the upper third of the organ, the depth of entry makes no difference in the ability to achieve ejaculation. And since the clitoris is on the outside, pushing into the vagina too deeply can only cause pain. Communication is the key. A couple will discover the right "fit" both in the vertical and horizontal dimensions of the vagina.

If after ejaculation the woman has not achieved orgasm (and roughly 70 percent will not), then the groom should begin to directly stimulate the clitoris to bring this about.[1] Again, communication is the key. The bride must tell her husband where to rub, how hard or soft, how quickly or slowly, depending on what she needs to achieve orgasm. It takes far longer for women to achieve this experience than the man, especially in the beginning when neither is experienced. And the woman is capable of several orgasms in a row if allowed to continue to the end. In general, the female orgasm is a process of many minutes, while the male orgasm can be measured in seconds![2]

This reminds us to caution those who may be disappointed with their first sexual experience. Intercourse, like most things in life, gets better with practice. We often feel that because it is "natural," we should automatically be good at it. But no activity we do in life is excellent without instruction and practice. Several years into your marriage you should be able to look back on those first few months of lovemaking and see the great progress you have made. This comes from "knowing" each other in all the ways God intended when He created marriage. The more we get to know one another, the greater the intimacy and the sweeter the lovemaking.

## What Is "Honeymoon Cystitis"?

One final note of instruction for newlyweds: there is a medical condition nicknamed "honeymoon cystitis." It is a bladder infection that is caused by intercourse, especially in virgins or those remarrying after several years of abstinence. The female urethra is short, and bacteria from the vagina can be pushed into the urethra by the thrusting penis, especially if the vagina is not well lubricated. Within twenty-four to forty-eight hours, the woman will experience burning with urination and a tremendous urge to void, even though there is no urine there. Antibiotics are the cure, but if one is on a honeymoon far away from the family physician, antibiotics can be difficult to procure.

### HONEYMOON CYSTITIS QUICK TIP

If you don't have a prescription and are unable to see a physician soon, here are some things you can do to ease discomfort:

- Empty your bladder before and after sex.
- Drink lots of water.
- Drink cranberry juice (not a sugary version, but a 100 percent juice version).

One preventative measure is for the woman to void after she is finished with lovemaking. This will flush the urethra of any bacteria that may have entered during intercourse. The other is to ask your family physician or gynecologist for a prescription of antibiotics that treat urinary tract infections and to fill the prescription before the wedding.

If the bride is taking birth control pills, some antibiotics can interfere with the absorption of these hormones and reduce the effectiveness of the contraception. Ask for one specifically designed for the bladder. Nitrofurantoin is an excellent choice, as it will not kill the normal vaginal bacteria that are necessary to prevent yeast infections. Take one tablet at bedtime each night of the honeymoon. In about a week, the woman's body should have adapted and it will no longer be necessary.

**DID YOU KNOW?**

Common brand names for nitrofurantoin are Furadantin, Macrobid, and Macrodantin.

These are merely suggestions to help make your wedding night a pleasant experience and lay a foundation for a lifetime of marital happiness. Only time, communication, and attention will fill in the details of each other's likes and dislikes. You have the rest of your lives to discover one another; take the time to enjoy each moment together.

# Chapter 13

# METHODS OF BIRTH CONTROL

*Like so many couples, Tim and Julie were thrilled to be the parents of two small boys. Yet Julie, who had had the two boys in the past fourteen months, felt she needed a break from childbearing and was reluctant to resume intercourse with her husband. She was afraid of getting pregnant again, and although her youngest child was six months old, they had not resumed intercourse since his birth.*

*They had attempted to do natural family planning according to the teachings of their previous church, but Julie was irregular in her cycles. They could not reliably determine when she was ovulating.*

*With the pressures of raising two small children and a recent job relocation, some decrease in sexual activity was to be expected. But Tim was beginning to become impatient with Julie and secretly bore a mild resentment toward his children for the impact they had had on his sex life. Although he knew they were not to blame, he could not help but remember what life was like before children.*

*Julie was desperate for a better form of birth control but wanted one that was consistent with their faith. Because Julie was irregular in her menstrual cycles, we suggested oral contraception. It would give her a regular and predictable period. Julie had heard from her former church that oral contraception was abortifacient, meaning that it could cause abortion. She and Tim were pro-life and could never use such a product.*

*We explained the way traditional birth control pills work and the difference between them and the "morning after" pill. Julie felt more comfortable with this as an option and took some samples home along with a prescription.*

*We saw her three months later to evaluate her experience with them. Julie was very pleased with the regularity in her cycles. In the midst of a very hectic life, predictable menstrual cycles had a definite advantage. She noticed some additional benefits she was not expecting. Her cycles were shorter and lighter, with less cramping. Her skin was clearer, and she had less PMS than before.*

*As a benefit for Tim, their sex life improved dramatically. While it was still a challenge to find time for intimacy with small children, Julie was*

*free of her fears of an unplanned pregnancy. She was much more receptive
to Tim's advances, and their relationship became even stronger.*

# Understanding Contraception

Contraception is an extremely sensitive issue among believers of differing
doctrines. While we realize that some reading this may be offended, our
objective is only to help readers. Just as marriage takes two people, the choice
for contraception and having children should also be a mutual decision. For
those who desire instruction on contraceptive options, we will examine the
advantages and disadvantages of each method, letting the reader decide which
method is best suited for her life.

In our discussion of condoms in chapter 9, we explained that researchers
use two methods to measure effectiveness.[1] The first is called "perfect use."
This is the number of pregnancies per one hundred women during one year
of using the product exactly as prescribed for every act of intercourse. This
statistic is what is presented to the FDA to win approval as a contraceptive
device. The second measure is called "typical use" and is the percentage of
women getting pregnant in one year who use the product as a typical couple
would in real life. This combines the difficulty in using the product correctly,
the motivation of the couple to use it every time, and the failure that occurs
even when the couple uses it correctly. Typical use is the statistic that is most
important when counseling a couple about failure rates.

As an example, the average typical use for barrier methods shows a success
rate of between 64 to 88 percent. In other words, twelve to thirty-six couples
out of one hundred will get pregnant using these products each year. The perfect
use has a success rate in the 90 percent range, but this is rarely achieved in real
life except by the most diligent and motivated couples.[2] As we describe each
method, you will be able to see where the typical couple falls into trouble.

## Natural family planning

A popular form of birth control that many Christian couples are comfortable using is natural family planning (NFP). Also called "the rhythm method,"
it was widely used by past generations when other contraceptives were not yet
an option. It is the exact opposite of the method used to enhance fertility. To
use NFP, a woman attempts to discover the most fertile times of her cycle and
avoids having intercourse on those days of the month.

This method requires no drugs or devices and is absolutely free. It does not
interfere with the body's own reproductive cycle; it is merely an attempt to
avoid having intercourse on days when conception is more likely to occur. In

this way, a measure of abstinence is included in every menstrual cycle. Discipline is involved if one is to effectively use NFP. It may well require denying the marital rights of intercourse for ten to fourteen days each month. That is not an easy task for many people, especially the newly married.

The principles of NFP are rooted in reproductive science. A woman will ovulate one egg every twenty-eight days on average. This generally occurs fourteen days from the beginning of the menstrual period if the woman has menses every four weeks. If her cycle is longer or shorter than twenty-eight days from the start of one period to the beginning of another, modification of this rule must be done.

The egg can be fertilized for only eighteen to twenty-four hours after ovulation. This seems like a narrow window of opportunity, and it is, except for one thing. God, in His wisdom, gave sperm the ability to live for three to seven days after ejaculation. In some women, the cervix has glands that form small inlets where sperm can be stored and nourished, gradually being released for up to one week. In practicality, then, the fertile period is not the one day that the human egg can survive but the seven days that the sperm can still fertilize after intercourse.

The cervix also secretes mucus that enables the sperm to leave the vagina and enter the uterus. Once the egg has died, the mucus shrinks rapidly, and the pathway to further sperm migration is closed. The ovary begins producing progesterone to prepare the uterine lining to accept an embryo. Progesterone thickens the mucus and raises the body temperature. These two signs signal the end of the fertile portion of the cycle.

One way to enhance the efficacy of NFP is to monitor the changes in cervical mucus production throughout the menstrual cycle. As menstruation comes to a conclusion, the vagina is dry. After a few days, thick mucus will develop. As a woman gets closer to ovulating, the mucus will become more abundant and thinner. At its peak, the woman will notice a large amount of thin, sticky mucus that signals impending ovulation. For those trying to conceive, this is a helpful sign. After the days when fertilization of the egg should have occurred, the production of progesterone thickens the mucus again and another "dry" spell will occur, leading to menstruation. For those practicing periodic abstinence using cervical mucus, the days from the start of mucus production until it dries up again would be considered the nonintercourse period.

The second addition to NFP involves measuring the basal body temperature (BBT). This is a person's body temperature upon awakening. It requires measuring a woman's temperature as she awakens, before any bodily activity can raise the temperature level. A graph is made, and one can see that after ovulation has occurred, the BBT is about one degree warmer until menstruation, when it returns again to a lower level. (See sample chart on page 154.) Those practicing abstinence using the BBT do not have intercourse from the menstrual period until after the temperature has risen to its higher level.[3]

In using either of these methods, a significant number of days per month are off-limits to intercourse. This method requires diligence and self-sacrifice to be successful. Many do not achieve perfection with this method due to their lack of self-control, and it has a failure rate (or pregnancy rate) of 25 percent per year.[4] In other words, one in four couples who choose this method of birth control will get pregnant each year.

Because of the measure of abstinence required in NFP, a variation that is also "natural" is often used either in conjunction with NFP or by itself. It is the "withdrawal method," or *coitus interruptus.* This is the withdrawing of the penis during intercourse just before ejaculation occurs and experiencing ejaculation outside of the woman's body. It is the same method that Onan used to avoid fathering Tamar's child (Gen. 38:6–10).

The withdrawal method allows for intercourse whenever a couple desires in the menstrual cycle, but it demands of the man that he have the discipline to pull out of the vagina at the very moment he is experiencing the greatest pleasure. Again, because of the lack of self-control, this method will fail 20 percent per year.[5] There is also a small amount of sperm concentrated in the lubricant or pre-ejaculate that is made at the beginning of the erection and is available to fertilize before ejaculation ever occurs.

### Barrier methods

The next class of birth control is called the "barrier method." It involves blocking the entrance of sperm into the cervical canal to prevent fertilization of the egg. There are four types of products used in this method: spermicides, diaphragm, cervical cap, and condoms.

The first group is the spermicides. These include jellies, creams, foams, films, and suppositories. They can be purchased without prescription and are inexpensive. The spermicide used in all of these products is nonoxynol 9, which can cause irritation in up to 25 percent of women. The spermicide kills sperm and must be placed in the back of the vagina before each act of intercourse. Some preparations must be inserted ten to thirty minutes prior to intercourse to be fully effective.

Two barrier products that require the addition of spermicidal jelly are the diaphragm and the cervical cap. The diaphragm is a round piece of rubber that covers the cervix and comes in a variety of sizes. It requires a prescription from trained medical staff who fit the woman with the appropriate size. It is roughly seven centimeters in diameter and is flexible, so that it is folded in half for insertion, opening up as it enters the back of the vagina.

At the patient's initial appointment for diaphragm fitting, the appropriate size is selected that will cover the cervix while lodging behind the pubic bone for support. If it is too large, pressure against the urethra can cause bladder infections. If it is too small, it may fall forward, allowing semen to pass around it. When properly fitted and placed in the vagina, neither the woman nor her partner will be able to feel the diaphragm during intercourse.

It does require some practice to insert it correctly. The outer ring of the diaphragm is coated with spermicidal jelly in the event that sperm try to pass around it. Squeezing this lubricated dome in half and pushing it into the vagina can be initially challenging. The diaphragm has been known to shoot across the bathroom during insertion! It must be placed before intercourse, and if this has not been done prior to the husband initiating sex, the wife must get up, find the diaphragm and the jelly, lubricate it, and put it in. This is usually done in the privacy of the bathroom while the husband waits and can be disruptive to the flow of intimacy.

Great discipline is required on the part of both partners, and it is not uncommon for the man to discourage his wife from using it "just this one time" rather than interrupt the flow and possibly his erection. Once intercourse is over, the diaphragm must remain in the vagina for at least six hours to allow all of the sperm to die.

Diaphragms should be replaced every two years to prevent holes from occurring in the rubber. If the woman has gained or lost significant weight, had vaginal surgery, or delivered a baby since the diaphragm was prescribed, a new fitting should be done to ensure the size is still appropriate.

The cervical cap is similar in concept to the diaphragm, only smaller. It is also made of rubber and fits over the cervix with a tight seal. It also requires a small amount of spermicide. While it may be easier to insert, some women find it difficult to manipulate the cap over the cervix to make a tight fit. One may feel like a contortionist, attempting to reach around and find the cervix while maintaining the sexual passion for lovemaking. The cap also must remain at least six hours after intercourse but can stay in place for up to thirty-six hours, allowing multiple acts of intercourse with one application. The longer it remains, however, the greater the chance of vaginal irritation or odor. It too requires a prescription after the correct size has been determined by a trained medical professional.

The final barrier method, and the most popular, is the male condom, which has already been discussed in great detail in chapter 9. A newer variation is the female condom, which appeals to women whose partners refuse to use the male condom. This is a pouch that has a front and back section. It is inserted into the vagina by squeezing the inner ring between the fingers. When properly inserted, about one inch of the condom remains outside of the vagina and is held in place by the woman during intercourse. Some women have complained that the condom makes noises during intercourse, and lubrication may be necessary to reduce friction. Just as with any latex product, the lubricant must be water-based and not a petroleum product to prevent melting the latex. After ejaculation, the outer ring is twisted closed and the condom removed. Most patients have found this product to be the least appealing of the barrier methods available. Sales of the female condom have been minimal.[6]

# Controversial, but Effective, Methods of Contraception

The remainder of the contraceptives discussed in this chapter have typical use rates between 95 and 99 percent, but they are also the most controversial within the Christian community.[7] There has even been conflicting safety data in the medical literature on most of these products. They all have some expense to them and require the expertise of medical personnel. We will discuss their mode of action, letting you and your spouse decide which, if any, of these methods may be the right choice for you.

### Birth control pills

A breakthrough in contraception occurred in the 1960s with the development and widespread distribution of the birth control pill. It has been credited with spawning the "sexual revolution" of the same decade, as women were "freed" from the fear of unwanted pregnancy. The "pill," as it is referred to, is a combination of estrogen and progesterone that mimics pregnancy, preventing ovulation of the egg through signals sent to the brain. If there is no egg present, pregnancy cannot occur. To keep the ovaries in a dormant state, at least twenty-one consecutive days of hormone ingestion are required.

Most birth control pills come in four-week packets that contain three consecutive weeks of hormones, followed by one week of placebo or "sugar" pills that signal the uterus to menstruate. When that menstrual week is over, a new round of pills begins again. The effectiveness of the pill depends upon maintaining a consistent level of female hormones in the bloodstream. If the woman forgets to take them at the same time each day, variations in blood levels could allow natural ovulation to occur and opens the possibility of conception.

Two secondary mechanisms of action are known to take place in addition to preventing ovulation. The progesterone component of the pill simulates the "dry" part of the cycle and tightens the cervical mucus, preventing migration of the sperm into the cervix. The lining of the uterus is also thinned, making it more difficult for implantation to occur should fertilization take place.

It is the latter property of the pill that has some concerned that this is an abortifacient, a product that causes abortion of an embryo. We can tell you from both a scientific and medical perspective that this is not the case when the pill is used in the standard fashion. If the pill has not stopped ovulation, it is highly unlikely it will stop implantation at the doses commonly prescribed. In fact, we see dozens of pregnancies each year that occurred despite patients faithfully taking their pills, even through the first two months of an unsuspected pregnancy, with no ill effects to the baby.

There is a form of birth control that is called the "morning after pill" (or emergency contraception in the medical community). It is specifically designed for cases where the condom breaks or a woman has not used contraception prior to intercourse and desires pregnancy prevention after the fact. One form is a two-pill dose-pack, which is marketed under the name *Plan B,* but contains only progesterone. Plan B can postpone ovulation by a few days, allowing any sperm that exists time to die. It also shrinks the lining of the uterus dramatically to prevent implantation if ovulation has already occurred.

Plan B must be taken within three days of unplanned or unprotected intercourse. If taken as prescribed, it is 89 percent effective in preventing pregnancy. If the woman is already pregnant, it will not cause abortion. Even if taken correctly, 11 percent of women will still conceive. The earlier the pill is taken following intercourse, the better it will work. This is why the FDA has recently allowed it to be sold by pharmacists without a doctor's prescription if the women is eighteen years of age or older. A prescription is required for those younger than eighteen.

This product could be considered an abortifacient if a person believes that life begins at conception. If a person believes that life begins with implantation into the mother's womb, then it is not. From a medical perspective, "pregnancy" is not conception but attachment of the embryo to the mother's uterine lining and the development of a placental connection between the two. It is only then that pregnancy hormone is made and a woman can be diagnosed as pregnant by blood or urine tests.

The union of egg and sperm is done every day in fertility clinics around the world, but these unions can be frozen for years awaiting implantation into the woman. Life begins for the embryo when it is accepted by the uterus and nourished. As many as 50 percent of all conceptions that occur naturally fail to develop into pregnancies because the embryo does not attach to the lining and is washed out of the womb.[8]

There are also numerous biblical passages that speak to the shedding of innocent blood, commonly applied to the abortion debate. The medical facts are that the embryo makes no blood until it implants in the womb approximately one week after conception and becomes a fetus. We are discussing this issue because it is an important consideration when it comes to choosing contraception, if one even chooses it at all. We have great respect for those who believe that life begins at conception, and they may struggle with the issue of the birth control pill if indeed it prevents implantation.

Our medical opinion is that at the lower doses used in 99 percent of all the birth control pills on the market today, conception is not occurring very often. If it does, implantation seems to happen at the rate it would normally, as evidenced by the thousands of babies born each year in the United States to women taking the pill for contraception. The morning-after pill is a separate issue, and one can make the case that its goal is to prevent implantation after fertilization has already occurred. This may or may not be a morally sound choice for you.

From a medical standpoint, the pill is not without its potential dangers. Women older than thirty-five who smoke and take the pill are at greater risk of heart attack and stroke. There is a small risk of high blood pressure, blood clots in the legs, gallbladder disease, and liver tumors in some women who take the pill, although these are rare complications. The jury is still out on whether taking the pill increases the risks of breast cancer. There are some benefits to taking the pill besides preventing pregnancy, which has a long list of potentially life-threatening complications of its own. Women who use birth control pills have fewer ovarian cysts and a reduced risk of ovarian and uterine cancers. There is less uterine bleeding and cramping, with less anemia as a result. Some pills reduce acne and facial hair, as well as control PMS.[9]

Since the introduction of the pill some forty years ago, the doses have been progressively reduced and the safety concerns have greatly diminished. In fact, current doses are just one-fourth what they were when the pill was first introduced. A variation of the pill is the "minipill," a progesterone-only product that is used as contraception by breast-feeding women. Other patients may wish to use it who, for medical reasons, need to avoid estrogen. It does not cause a regular menstrual cycle and, unlike traditional pills, is taken without a placebo week. Many women stop menstruating on this formula, but it is weaker and has a higher failure rate when not used as a supplement to breast-feeding.

## Other avenues of hormonal contraception

Because the pill must be taken daily, some women find it difficult to maintain consistency, and pregnancy does occur. It can also interact with other oral medications that reduce its absorption into the bloodstream. A couple of formulations have been introduced that combine estrogen and progesterone into a vehicle that delivers it directly into the bloodstream. All of these variations still contain similar hormones as the pill, so the same benefits and risks apply. It is hoped that the newer delivery systems will make compliance easier and improve the typical use statistics.

One such contraception is Ortho Evra, a patch that is worn once a week for three weeks followed by one week off to allow menstruation. It was very popular when first introduced, but it had some decline in usage after a study showed a doubling of the risk of blood clots in the legs and lungs compared to conventional birth control pills. The amount of hormone in the bloodstream is about 60 percent greater than in the standard pill regimens, which is believed to be the reason for the increased risk. Women who are healthy and do not smoke can still use the patch with very little real-life risk.

Another form of contraception is the NuvaRing, which contains both hormones in a flexible plastic ring the size of a fifty-cent piece. It is inserted by the woman into the vagina and left there for three weeks. It is removed in the fourth week to allow menstruation. Neither the woman nor her partner can feel the ring when it is properly placed.

There are two other hormonal contraceptives available at the present time that contain only progesterone and are delivered directly into the bloodstream. These are also suitable for breast-feeding patients. The first is the Norplant, a series of six small rods that are inserted under the skin of the upper arm and release progesterone over a five-year period. It is a highly effective contraceptive, but complications of irregular bleeding and ovarian cysts occur regularly. There has also been difficulty in training personnel to insert and remove the rods correctly. Together, these complications have resulted in a class-action lawsuit that has caused the product to no longer be sold in the United States.

Out of that experience, a new contraceptive rod called Implanon has recently been introduced. It is a single flexible rod inserted under the skin of the arm to release progesterone for up to three years. It is much simpler to insert and remove, but it must be done in the hands of trained practitioners only. Side effects are similar to Norplant, but it remains a very effective method of birth control that is easily reversible. Not every doctor has received the necessary training, so check with your doctor before having one either implanted or removed. For more information on this contraceptive rod, visit the Web site available from the company at www.implanon-usa.com.

The other product is Depo-Provera. It is an injection of progesterone that is given every three months in the doctor's office. It has been especially popular in family planning clinics that see young women who are less likely to take the pill correctly. The Depo-Provera injection usually results in a cessation of menses after a few months and can be of great benefit to those women who suffer from heavy monthly bleeding, severe menstrual cramping, or PMS.

The side effects of Depo-Provera are irregular bleeding in the first few months and weight gain that averages ten to fifteen pounds over a year. It is slightly less effective in the severely overweight woman. In general, it provides some of the most effective contraception available that is still reversible.[10] Because the injections last for up to six months but must be overlapped every three months, there are at least six to nine months from the last injection before a woman can conceive. This must be accounted for in any contraceptive strategy a woman makes with her physician.

## Continuous birth control

As more women discover that a monthly menstrual cycle is not mandatory for gynecologic health, many are seeking ways to use hormonal contraception to their advantage by either delaying menses for particular events in life or by skipping menses completely. Many of the birth control products we have mentioned can accomplish this, but we would like to highlight some of the more popular.

A product called *Seasonique* is a thirteen-week pill pack that contains twelve weeks of birth control pills followed by one week of placebo pills. This pattern will give a period every three months, or four times a year. A similar product called *Lybrel* is a monthly pack with no placebo week that is taken daily throughout the year to completely avoid periods. In theory, these products are very attractive, but about 25 percent of women will have breakthrough bleeding on these regimens and find the unpredictability of this kind of bleeding undesirable. In general, the average yearly bleeding is the same whether done monthly or seasonally, but for some, this pill regimen has been a great benefit.

Any of the standard birth control pills can be similarly pieced together simply by skipping the placebo week and proceeding directly to the next pill pack. This can be done for only one cycle, in the case of a wedding or vacation, or for the three months as does Seasonique. The Ortho Evra patch can also be extended for as many weeks as desired. The NuvaRing actually has four weeks built into the product. This allows it to be used sequentially by removing and replacing a ring for up to three consecutive months. After twelve weeks it is recommended that the patient allow one week off to menstruate.

As mentioned earlier, the Depo-Provera almost always results in absent menses for long periods of time. The "minipill" generally will not bring on menstruation as long as the woman is still breast-feeding.

## The IUD

For those women who do not want to take, or cannot take, hormonal preparations and who find the barriers methods undesirable, there is a final form of reversible contraception. It is the intrauterine device, or IUD. The IUD has had a difficult history and is a choice that must be evaluated carefully. In its early development, several designs caused problems with infection and later infertility. Because it is a device that is inserted into the uterus, STDs such as gonorrhea and chlamydia can migrate up the IUD and enter the fallopian tubes, causing infertility. For this reason, an STD test is often done prior to insertion; antibiotics may be given with it also. The IUD must be inserted by a trained health-care professional, as improper insertion of the IUD can lead to perforation of the uterus.

One other controversy of the IUD is whether it is an abortifacient. There are two types of IUDs in the United States: the ParaGard and the Mirena. The Mirena is a progesterone-containing device that releases the hormone locally. It does not cross into the bloodstream. The device causes the uterine lining to become thin and does impede implantation. Because the lining is thin, many women will cease menstruating; the Mirena may be a choice for women who have excessive periods as an alternative to hysterectomy. This gives similar results as the Depo-Provera injection but without the side effects of weight gain. The Mirena is inserted through the cervix by a trained health-care professional and can last for up to five years.

The second IUD on the market is the ParaGard. It is a T-shaped device that contains copper, a naturally occurring spermicide designed to kill any sperm that enter the uterus. It is effective for up to ten years. It does not change the uterine lining, but should the sperm live in spite of the spermicidal effect of the copper, implantation may be prevented by the T-shaped design blocking entrance of the embryo into the uterus.

If pregnancy does occur, it is more likely to be ectopic. This is a serious situation that demands immediate attention. Fortunately it is very uncommon. Should pregnancy occur in the womb, the IUD must be removed if one hopes to prevent damage to the developing fetus. Removal of the IUD can carry a 25 percent miscarriage rate, depending on the proximity of the fetus to the IUD.[11] The IUD is used in our practice primarily for married couples who think they may be finished with childbearing but do not want to make a permanent commitment to sterilization.

## Permanent sterilization

Finally, there are those who have completed the number of children they desire to have. While some do not feel Christians should choose how many children they should have, there are couples who have agreed upon the number they feel that they can raise. Sterilization may be an option for them to consider. It is the most widely used method of birth control in the United States, but it is meant to be permanent. Attempts at reversal are expensive and often unsuccessful. This is a weighty decision that a couple must make after much discussion and, hopefully, prayer.

For those who have made that choice, the options are tubal ligation for the woman or vasectomy for the man. From a purely medical standpoint, vasectomy is simpler and safer. It involves cutting the vas deferens and sealing off the ends, preventing the migration of sperm from the testes to the urethra. The procedure is done under local anesthesia in the doctor's office. The skin of the scrotum is numbed, and a small incision is made on each side to locate the vas deferens, tying off and removing a small piece. It is mildly uncomfortable but requires only a weekend to recover at home.

One word of caution: a vasectomy does not become effective for several weeks. The sperm are like troops marching down the road. A vasectomy blows up the bridge so no further sperm can cross. But all of the "troops" who made it across before the vasectomy are still marching on. It takes a certain number of ejaculations to clear these sperm from the system.

Some men are fearful of the pain of vasectomy. It is a region of the body that men guard carefully. To voluntarily ask someone to operate there is a psychological leap for some. Others fear that sex will be different, that they will be "shooting blanks" and ejaculation will not feel the same. In truth, the sperm are a very small part of the ejaculate. The semen is mostly fluid from the seminal vesicles and prostate gland. Ejaculation will be exactly the same with the same volume of semen as before.

But because of these fears, and because women are the ones who get pregnant, tubal ligation is more popular in the United States than vasectomy. Tubal ligation involves interrupting each fallopian tube and preventing the union of egg and sperm. The procedure can be done immediately after delivery and is called a postpartum tubal ligation. A small incision is made in the navel, and the tubes are pulled through the hole. A segment of each tube is cut out and the remaining ends tied off. It requires some form of anesthesia such as an epidural, spinal, or general.

Another form of tubal ligation that is popular is the laparoscopic version. This can be done anytime after a four-week postpartum period. It involves inserting a laparoscope, which contains a small camera, through a navel incision and either burning, clipping, or banding the tubes. This is an outpatient procedure done in a hospital setting and requires general anesthesia. If done correctly, only one out of two hundred women will get pregnant after tubal ligation.[12] Those who do get pregnant after a tubal ligation have a high risk of tubal pregnancy and must seek immediate medical attention.

There is a final technique for tubal ligation called hysteroscopic ligation with the Essure system. Using a hysteroscope, which is a small camera that looks through the cervix into the uterus, an Essure insert is placed into each fallopian tube opening. The insert then expands, anchoring itself in the fallopian tube. Over time, the insert causes scarring of the opening of the fallopian tube and completely closes off the tube so no sperm can enter.

The Essure system was 99.8 percent effective after four years of follow-up and 99.7 percent effective after five years of follow-up. The main advantage of this system is that there are no incisions and the procedure does not take much time. One disadvantage is that success is achieved in one operative setting only 86 percent of time and only 90 percent with a second attempt due to difficulties in technique. This means that between 10 and 14 percent of women who desire Essure will find they are unable to have it completed successfully. Another disadvantage is that a tubal X-ray called an HSG must be done three months later to confirm that complete scarring of the tubes did indeed occur. Unlike the other methods of tubal ligation already discussed, alternate methods of birth control are needed for those first three months.[13]

## IT'S IN THE WORD

There are those who believe that contraception is against the Word of God and support their belief with verses such as, "Be fruitful and increase in number" (Gen. 1:28). Or, "Like arrows in the hands of a warrior are sons born in one's youth. Blessed is the man whose quiver is full of them" (Ps. 127:4–5). They believe that the Lord will control how many children they should have and that they should not hinder conception.

But there are those who feel that they can only afford to take care of a certain number of children with the expenses of college and so on. They see scriptural truths about being able to support one's family and rule over them in a way that brings God glory: "But if any provide not for his own, and specially for those of his own house, he hath denied the faith, and is worse than an infidel" (1 Tim. 5:8, KJV); "If anyone does not know how to manage his own family, how can he take care of God's church?" (1 Tim 3:5).

What glory does it bring God if a man cannot take care of what he has brought into this world and must depend upon the government to assist him? There are many in the body of Christ who feel that they can only handle a certain number of children. Others want to postpone having children for various reasons. Whatever the reason, they need to weigh all the options for contraception and choose which one aligns with their spiritual convictions.

# Which birth control method is right for me?

There are many birth control options available today, and the choices can seem confusing. This list can help you decide which method would best fit your lifestyle.

**HORMONAL CONTRACEPTIVES**

Hormonal contraceptives work by preventing release of an egg from your ovaries into the uterus, and may also make the uterus an "unfriendly" environment for sperm. While most women know about the birth control pill, there are other hormonal birth control methods that are now available.

| | HOW EFFECTIVE IS THIS METHOD?* | HOW MANY OPTIONS ARE AVAILABLE? | HOW OFTEN DO I NEED TO USE IT? | ARE THERE INTERRUPTIONS WITH THIS METHOD? | HOW QUICKLY CAN I GET PREGNANT IF I STOP USING IT? | DO I NEED A PRESCRIPTION OR WILL I RECEIVE IT FROM MY HEALTHCARE PROFESSIONAL? | DO I NEED TO SEE MY HEALTHCARE PROFESSIONAL TO START? | DOES THIS PROTECT AGAINST† HIV AND STDs?† |
|---|---|---|---|---|---|---|---|---|
| The Patch | Greater than 99% effective | There is only 1 contraceptive patch | The Patch is applied once a week for 3 weeks. During Week 4, no patch is used | There are no interruptions with this method | Once stopped, it may take a few cycles before you can become pregnant | Prescription needed | You need to learn how to apply the Patch correctly | No |
| Oral Contraceptive (The Pill) | Greater than 99% effective | There are a variety of pills available depending on dose and desired frequency of period | You should take your pill every day, at approximately the same time each day | There are no interruptions with this method | Once stopped, it may take a few cycles before you can become pregnant | Prescription needed | You may need instruction on the correct way to take your pills | No |
| Implantable Contraceptive | Greater than 99% effective | There is 1 implantable contraceptive | The implant is inserted on the underside of the upper arm for a 3-year period | There are no interruptions with this method | Once removed, fertility can occur within 1 week | Receive from healthcare professional | Your healthcare professional inserts and removes the implant | No |
| Contraceptive Injection | Greater than 99% effective | There is 1 contraceptive injection currently available | You receive an injection every 3 months | There are no interruptions with this method | Ovulation may be delayed up to a year | Receive from healthcare professional | A healthcare professional administers the injection | No |
| Progestin-Releasing Intrauterine Device (IUD) | Greater than 99% effective | There is 1 hormone-releasing IUD currently available | The suggested length of use is 5 years or less | There are no interruptions with this method | Once removed, fertility can return within a year | Receive from healthcare professional | Your healthcare professional inserts and removes the IUD | No |

## NONHORMONAL CONTRACEPTIVES

Nonhormonal contraceptives prevent pregnancy by providing a barrier against sperm by interfering with sperm movement, or by creating an "unfriendly" environment for sperm. These methods do not use hormones, so they do not interfere with your natural reproductive cycle.

| Method | Effectiveness | Description | Usage | Interruptions | After stopping | Prescription needed | What you need to do | STD protection |
|---|---|---|---|---|---|---|---|---|
| Vaginal Ring | Greater than 99% effective | There is only 1 vaginal ring | Each month, the vaginal ring is inserted into the vagina and left in place for 3 weeks. During Week 4, you do not wear the ring | There are no interruptions with this method | Once stopped, it may take a few cycles before you can become pregnant | Prescription needed | You need to learn how to insert and remove the vaginal ring | No |
| Male Condom | 98% effective | There are a variety of styles, sizes, colors, materials, and textures | A new one must be used every time you have sex | Must be applied when the penis is erect. May cause a slight interruption before sex | Without this device, there is no protection against pregnancy | No | Tell your health-care professional that you plan to use condoms | Yes |
| Female Condom | 95% effective | There is 1 female condom currently available | A new one must be used every time you have sex | A female condom can be inserted up to 8 hours before sex | Without this device, there is no protection against pregnancy | No | Tell your health-care professional that you plan to use a female condom | Unless the female condom slips out of place or is torn, it should provide protection against STD exposure comparable to that of male condoms |
| Intrauterine Device (IUD) | Greater than 99% effective | There is 1 copper-T IUD currently available | Once inserted in the uterus, it can be left in place for up to 10 years | There are no interruptions with this method | Once removed, fertility can return within about 1 month | Receive from healthcare professional | Your healthcare professional inserts and removes the IUD | No |
| Spermicides | 82% effective —use with a barrier method increases effectiveness | There are a variety of spermicides available in foams, jellies, creams, and vaginal suppositories | Must be used every time you have sex | Must be inserted no more than 1 hour before sex | Without this device, there is no protection against pregnancy | No | Tell your healthcare professional. You may be advised to use an additional contraceptive method | No. As per the FDA, the chemical Nonoxynol 9 in stand-alone vaginal contraceptives and spermicides can irritate the vagina and rectum, which may increase the risk of contracting HIV/AIDS from an infected partner |
| **VAGINAL BARRIERS** Diaphragm | 94% effective | There are a variety of sizes available | Must be used every time you have sex (and fresh spermicide must be applied each time) | The diaphragm can be inserted up to 6 hours before sex | Without this device, there is no protection against pregnancy | Prescription needed | You need to be fitted and must learn how to use the diaphragm | Diaphragms do not protect against HIV (AIDS). There is a mild reduction in the risk of some STDs |

| | HOW EFFECTIVE IS THIS METHOD?* | HOW MANY OPTIONS ARE AVAILABLE? | HOW OFTEN DO I NEED TO USE IT? | ARE THERE INTERRUPTIONS WITH THIS METHOD? | HOW QUICKLY CAN I GET PREGNANT IF I STOP USING IT? | DO I NEED A PRESCRIPTION OR WILL RECEIVE IT FROM MY HEALTHCARE PROFESSIONAL? | DO I NEED TO SEE MY HEALTHCARE PROFESSIONAL TO START? | DOES THIS PROTECT AGAINST HIV AND STDs?† |
|---|---|---|---|---|---|---|---|---|
| **VAGINAL BARRIERS** Diaphragm | 94% effective | There are a variety of sizes available | Must be used every time you have sex (and fresh spermicide must be applied each time) | The diaphragm can be inserted up to 6 hours before sex | Without this device, there is no protection against pregnancy | Prescription needed | You need to be fitted and must learn how to use the diaphragm | Diaphragms do not protect against HIV (AIDS). There is a mild reduction in the risk of some STDs |
| Cervical Cap | 74% effective in women who have had a child (91% in those who have not) | There are a variety of sizes available | Must be used every time you have sex (and spermicide must be applied when inserted) | The cervical cap provides continuous protection for up to 48 hours | Without this device, there is no protection against pregnancy | Prescription needed | You need to be fitted and must learn how to use the cervical cap | No |
| **PERMANENT METHODS** Surgical Sterilization | Greater than 99% effective | For women, there is tubal ligation (having your tubes "tied"); for men, there is vasectomy | These procedures are considered permanent and irreversible | There are no interruptions with this method | You will no longer be able to get pregnant | Physician recommended | These surgical procedures are performed by a healthcare professional | No |
| Tubal Implant Sterilization | Greater than 99% effective | There is 1 tubal implant currently available | This procedure is considered permanent and irreversible | You must continue to use alternative birth control methods for the first 3 months after having the procedure. After the success of the procedure has been confirmed, there are no interruptions | You will no longer be able to get pregnant after the success of the procedure has been confirmed | Receive from healthcare professional | This is a nonsurgical procedure performed by a physician | No |

*When used perfectly (both consistently and correctly).
†STDs = sexually transmitted diseases.

# Chapter 14

# SACRED SEX

*Each year our church sponsors a "Women of God" conference, at which I (SAF) am a regular speaker. At the beginning of my workshop, I have the women write down any questions about sex that they want answered. The questions are submitted with total anonymity with the knowledge that they give me permission to speak about such topics in a church setting.*

*I am asked a variety of questions, such as:*

- *What does God think about sex?*

- *Is it OK to have oral sex?*

- *Is it wrong to use sex toys or a vibrator?*

- *Are there any sexual positions that are unpleasing to God?*

- *The Bible says, "The marriage bed is undefiled," so does that mean having sex anywhere else but the bed is sinful?*

- *By the end of the day, I am so exhausted that the last thing I want to do, much less think about, is having sex. What's wrong with having sex in the morning or afternoon?*

- *Is role-playing acceptable in a Christian marriage?*

- *Does God say it's sinful for me to wear sexy lingerie for my husband?*

- *Is fantasizing wrong?*

- *We have been married for over thirty years, and our sex life is boring. Can we use sexual images (movies, photos) to "spice up" our sex life?*

*The questions seem to be the same with each group that attends.*

*After addressing about five hundred women at one conference, I retreated to the resource center for a book signing. A woman was in line and waited patiently until the last woman had gone by. I always know that when someone lingers, it is because she has a personal question she wants answered.*

*Like so many women, Tracy wanted to know, "What does God think* about sex?" Tracy and her husband had been married for several years before becoming Christians. They were unclear what "Christian" sex was like, and they had settled for a very routine and sterile sex life, believing this was what God wanted. When she heard me speak about sexual boundaries in marriage, Tracy realized that perhaps they had given up too much.

While she had already decided that pornography was wrong, she and her husband both missed giving and receiving oral sex. Secretly they were jealous of their secular friends who seemed to have great sex lives even though they knew that in other areas, these couples' lives were a mess. She felt there must be a trade-off between eroticism and a Christian marriage. Could it really be that God would allow her and her husband to enjoy many of their "old" ways?

I explained to Tracy that the motivations and intentions of the sexual experience were key to evaluating whether they enhanced her marital relationship or not. Everything should be mutually agreeable. If something was unpleasant, degrading, shaming, or unwanted by either party, it did not further their intimacy in a godly way. There must also be no participation by outsiders, be it live persons or pornography.

With those guidelines, Tracy left more free to explore her sexual relationship with her husband. She no longer had to be jealous of the world. With God as their foundation, sexual intimacy could be better than anything their old lives had to offer.

## What Does God Say About Sex?

Over the years, many of our patients have had the courage to ask us, as Christian gynecologists, questions about sex that we have answered one-on-one in our offices under strict confidentiality. We realize that for most of the church, questions about sex and sexuality are pressing issues that are sparsely addressed from the pulpit. Most Christians have nowhere to turn, other than the secular media, to base their sexual relations upon.

The majority of the women we've encountered have struggled with sexual issues in a spiritual vacuum. Deep down they wondered how their faith in Christ and their human sexuality could peacefully coexist. They sensed there must be more to their sexual lives than they were experiencing, but they wondered if God really wanted them to have it. Was sex the "forbidden fruit" in all but the most plain and sterile variety?

These women struggled to be "holy" and "righteous" while their flesh flooded them with feelings and desires they didn't think Christians should have. They were aware that this battle over sex might be the one area of their lives that threatened their personal relationship with God more than any other.

If you are like these women, you know what we are talking about. Your thought life intrudes into your quiet time with God, and it seems you are bombarded with messages about sex from the secular world that cause you to doubt yourself. But who can you turn to with these fears and frustrations? Will your pastor think you are less spiritual and holy than he once believed? Will your friends understand your struggles, or will they share their concerns about you with others? Could you ever pray to a holy God about the struggles you are having being the woman you are supposed to be? Fearing all of this, you have kept quiet, thinking this is your "thorn in the flesh," your cross to bear.

## The Big Question

Of the many hundreds of questions we have been asked, the main theme is this: Is God really interested in my sexual life? What does He think about sex? The answer is: It's God's idea! He created the sexes and sexual intercourse. He instilled the sexual drives into our bodies, knowing they would work their way into our thoughts and minds. He is not ashamed of our sexuality, nor does He regret creating it. From the second chapter of Genesis, God weaves His plan for our sexuality throughout the pages of Scripture.

He has an intense desire to have intimacy with us, to know us, and for us to know Him at the deepest level. But the invisible God shows us a glimpse of the intimacy that is possible when He made man and woman as intimate creatures. His hope is that we will see the power of such a union between two people and grasp the power of a spiritual union with Him. If our spouse can bring us comfort, peace, and solace, how much more can the perfect Creator give to us what we lack? And ultimately, the true power of sexual intimacy reveals just that.

No one would ever question that just because God placed the forbidden fruit off-limits to Adam and Eve, the rest of the garden ceased to be paradise to them. The beautiful flowers and majestic creatures the Lord had created still filled Adam and Eve with wonder as they discovered each day a new aspect of creation and began to take dominion over all the Lord had given them. Had this not been so, being banished from this garden would not have caused them such sorrow. But many Christians mistake the few hedges of protection placed by God around our sexuality to mean that God is against sex, that it represents our "forbidden fruit."

While few areas of our lives have been as distorted since the Fall as our sexuality, it is still God's desire for us to experience all that He had in mind when He created us. He hasn't changed His mind, nor does He secretly wish we were never introduced to sex. It is still His gift to us, not just for reproduction, as many in the church seem to believe, but for intimacy and pleasure. And yes, He knows how much fun it is. He made it feel that way! But for so long, the church has looked at the way the secular world has expressed itself sexually and closed its doors to all discussions of sex, fearing that worldly influences would corrupt the holiness of the church.

That is why Satan tries to distort the church's perception of sex. If the pressures of life melt away in the loving and nurturing haven of our spouse's embrace, the world might be drawn to this God who provides all of that in the midst of so much chaos. The marital bed is a powerful agent of healing, restoration, fulfillment, and joy that most of us rarely enjoy to its fullest.

## IT'S IN THE WORD

Can you name Adam and Eve's first assignment from God as a couple? God's first command to them in Genesis 1:28 was, "Be fruitful and increase in number." In other words, God told them to have intercourse.

As the two perfectly formed beings explored the different parts of the other's body, they discovered sensitive areas created by God for their pleasure, and they freely enjoyed themselves whenever they wanted, not afraid God would "catch" them or that what they were doing was "wrong" or "filthy." Sin had not yet entered the garden, and there were no limits placed on them but the tree.

Yet we struggle fiercely with the idea that a holy God could want anything to do with our sex lives. We somehow pretend that He and all the angels flee to the backside of heaven whenever we make love. There is no consciousness of a loving Father standing by to give us wisdom and knowledge about how He created this body we live in or how to please the partner with whom He has joined us in holy unity. The very idea of God in our bedrooms is a shocking thought, yet it is very real. Do we leave the Holy Spirit waiting in the bathroom while we have intercourse? Do we ask the Son, who said He would never leave us or forsake us, to stay downstairs and watch TV while we make love? Do we somehow think God would be offended by what He saw, the uniting of two people into one, just as His Word says?

Man's fall has brought sin into every aspect of our lives, but it has never changed God's original intention for us: that we have the very best in intimacy and sexual pleasure in our marriages. Scriptures written after Genesis support the fact that God intends for sex to be more than reproduction. He intends for His children to view themselves as sexual beings, filled with desires for one another and possessing the need for those desires to be fulfilled. He created the marriage bed for that very purpose.

## Sex and the Christian

Many of us became Christians after we had already begun our sexual lives. With the "new creation" we experienced in so many other areas, it is easy to assume the "old man" died sexually as well. To some extent that is true. Our old way of *looking* at sex simply to fulfill a sexual need or drive has been replaced. But with what? What does the Bible say about sex?

How does one honor God with her body, be a temple for the Holy Spirit, be holy before God, and yet experience the joys and delights of sexual union? It seems for many of us that when the Bible says to present our bodies as living sacrifices, it really means sacrificing a fulfilling and exciting sex life. We envy those "role models" on television and movie screens who seem to enjoy sex with great abandon. We escape into the fantasy world of romance novels, soap operas, or pornographic videos to become spectators of a life we may never enjoy as Christians. This is especially difficult for those of us who carry memories of a pre-conversion sexual life that was fulfilling.

While the secular world has pushed the envelope of sexual exploration to the extremes, we as a church have been robbed of our inheritance in Christ of a mutually satisfying intimacy with our spouse.

Jesus teaches, "But at the beginning of creation God 'made them male and female.' 'For this reason a man will leave his father and mother and be united to his wife, and the two will become one flesh.' So they are no longer two, but one. Therefore what God has joined together, let man not separate" (Mark 10:6–9). Jesus reminds us that from the very beginning it was God's intention that man and woman come together sexually and be "one flesh," a condition that only occurs in intercourse. This drive to unite is so strong that a man will leave the comforts of home and all he has known to begin a new life with his wife. This bond is so important to God that man must not separate it.

We are, of course, aware of the teachings of Paul recommending celibacy, preferring a devotion to the work of the Lord instead of marriage. Most of us are not called with this "gift" of celibacy, a fact Paul readily admits in 1 Corinthians 7. Since you are reading this chapter, we can safely assume that you too are not called to a life of celibacy!

So we accept that God is interested in our sex lives, but what are the boundaries? It can be difficult to picture God approving of intercourse itself, let alone any deviation from the "missionary position." Because intercourse is necessary for procreation, many Christians accept that God wants them to have *that* kind of sex. But what about all the other things?

# Boundaries

There are really very few boundaries in marriage regarding sexual activity in the Bible. Obviously, adultery is forbidden (Exod. 20:14). But Jesus expanded the definition of adultery to include what you see with your eyes: "But I tell you that anyone who looks at a woman lustfully has already committed adultery with her in his heart" (Matt. 5:28).

What we focus on with our eyes, we take in through our imagination. We begin to fantasize about what it would be like to have sex with that person, that image. If that person is not our spouse, then it becomes adultery. Some couples wonder if pornographic magazines or videos can be used as marital enhancements to "spice up" their sex lives. According to Matthew 5:28, I would say no. You are inviting those people into your bedroom when you do that. The focus then shifts from intimacy with your spouse to a "shared" intimacy with them. This is adultery. Even when the material is not physically present in the bedroom, if you bring it back to your mind and think about a particular image or person when you are making love, it is adultery.

You are missing the whole point of intercourse. It is to "know" your spouse in the most intimate fashion God could create. If your mind is somewhere else, you are simply performing a sexual act; you are not "making love." Soon even that will become old and stale because it lacks the power that a godly union would bring to the relationship and is thus ultimately disappointing. Your spiritual man knows that there is more and will be dissatisfied with the mediocre.

The only other boundaries, besides premarital sex (to which we have devoted considerable attention), are found in Leviticus 18. A quick perusal will reveal a prohibition against incest, sexual relations with a variety of relatives, homosexuality, and bestiality (or sex with animals).

# Oral Sex

So what about oral sex? This is the most common question asked by both men and women at the seminars we hold. A close second behind vaginal intercourse, oral sex, or *fellatio*, is a highly desired sexual activity for men. Many men also like to give orally to their wives, stimulating the clitoris with their tongues instead of their fingers or a vibrator. But more often when the question is asked, it is about the wife giving oral sex to her husband. This involves taking the penis into the mouth and simulating intercourse there, often with a light suction. It may lead to orgasm in the mouth or outside of the mouth.

You may think, "Surely there is some Bible verse for this one," but there is not. It is not listed as being prohibited, and God is never caught off guard.

It falls within the broad freedoms we possess within marriage to explore each other and discover what pleases the other (1 Tim. 4:4). One reason that oral sex is so desired by men is that it feels good! The other reason lies in the fact that the penis is the symbol of manhood. When a woman acknowledges that organ and gives special attention to it, she is letting her man know that she appreciates him as a man. Many a man secretly struggles with insecurity regarding his ability to please a woman, wondering how he compares to any other man she could have had (or has had). Oral sex tells him that he is man enough for her and that she likes what he has to give. It can be an incredible gift that a wife can give to her husband.

Some women do not enjoy oral sex for fear of the ejaculate; it does not have to continue to climax, but can be a part of foreplay alone.

## Freedoms

This brings up a major theme of sexual exploration. *Nothing* should be asked for or done that is demeaning, painful, humiliating, or brings shame upon the other party. Everything must be *mutually acceptable*, or it will not further love and intimacy, which is the goal of sex.

Many Christians are surprised that God did not give specific instructions regarding sexual technique, positions, or attire. He did not even confine sexual relations to one particular room of the house, or say it must be inside the house at all! If sex is discreet and private, it can be done anywhere and at anytime. A private beach or picnic spot can be an exciting departure from the same bedroom walls you've seen for years. Adam and Eve didn't have a bedroom but made love under the stars, or wherever else the urge struck them.

No one even says you have to wait until the evening to have sex. Sometimes a brief interlude in the afternoon when the kids are napping or otherwise preoccupied with a video can be helpful for the wives who may be more tired in the evening than they are in the daytime. Sneaking home for a lunchtime rendezvous can be very exciting and romantic. People having affairs seem to master these concepts better than those who are faithfully married.

Some people ask us about vibrators and other sex toys. Vibrators can be used to help a woman reach orgasm and may be something that is acceptable to each party. Other things that are novelty items may also add some fun to the encounter. Bondage items such as leashes, handcuffs, and whips may demean and demote the other person, but if it is honestly mutually acceptable to both spouses, it is allowed. There are those who even find various foods such as chocolate, whipped cream, or strawberries an exciting addition to love-making. It might make a great excuse for you to break your diet!

Some couples ask if there is a role for fantasy in sexual intercourse. As long as it involves just those two people, they can pretend to be whatever role they wish. A man can pretend to be a fireman rescuing a woman in distress, as long as he is not pretending to be a specific man that they know. He must still be himself, playing a role. A woman can pretend to be a nurse, giving her "patient" a sponge bath. You get the idea. A word of warning concerning role-playing: each person must stay true to his gender. The man should never dress up or pretend to be a woman and vice versa.

God knew that in the fifty or sixty years we might be married to the same person, there would be a lot to learn. Part of the excitement of marriage is the discovery of what makes the other person happy and what pleases them. As our bodies are constantly changing, we will never come to the end of our quest for knowledge, if we will only continue to pursue it.

In general, we find men more willing to experiment than women. A certain Puritan ideal is prevalent in many Christian circles that convey a false modesty, even into the bedroom. Many women would never dream of wearing a Victoria's Secret garment to bed because it reflects the world's view of sex and women. The problem with Victoria's Secret is that it is has left the bedroom and now appears on billboards and television sets across America. But it is not wrong in the bedroom if the message you are trying to convey is an invitation to explore the sweet gift God has given your husband when He gave you to him.

## Erotic Love

Probably one of the least read or quoted books of the Bible is the Song of Solomon, which paints an intimate portrait of a wife who knows how to use the resources God had given her to both arouse and capture her man's attention. Most Christians seem embarrassed that it is even in their Bibles, and most clergy avoid all reference to it. And yet it is exactly what we need to hear—the truth. We are created as sensual beings with God-given sexual needs that are powerful. The most complicated of all the created beings on the earth is programmed by God to experience His creation through the five senses, and sex is no exception. Each of the senses is used by the lovers in the Song of Solomon as a biblical reminder of the gift of our bodies for one another.

> Why should I be like a veiled woman beside the flocks of your friends?... While the king was at his table, my perfume spread its fragrance. My lover is to me a sachet of myrrh resting between my breasts.
> —Song of Solomon 1:7, 12–13

This is the portrait of a sensual woman who has perfumed herself and worn garments that are pleasing to her lover. It is not the image of a beleaguered housewife in flannel pajamas with curlers in her hair and creams on her face! It is difficult to understand those women who go to bed with all that stuff so they will look good in the daytime. Look good for whom? If you can't look good for him in the bedroom, what benefit is that to your marriage?

The man replies:

> You have stolen my heart, my sister, my bride; you have stolen my heart with one glance of your eyes, with one jewel of your necklace. How delightful is your love, my sister, my bride! How much more pleasing is your love than wine, and the fragrance of your perfume than any spice!...The fragrance of your garments is like that of Lebanon.
> —Song of Solomon 4:9–11

In the fifth chapter, the woman describes the object of her intense desire in very powerful terms. We are going to quote it here since many of you are too afraid to read it in your own Bibles!

> My lover is radiant and ruddy, outstanding among ten thousand. His head is purest gold; his hair is wavy and black as a raven. His eyes are like doves....His lips are like lilies dripping with myrrh. His arms are rods of gold set with chrysolite. His body is like polished ivory decorated with sapphires. His legs are pillars of marble...His mouth is sweetness itself; he is altogether lovely.
> —Song of Solomon 5:10–16

In modern terms, she's saying, "My man is a hunk!" She does not describe his intelligence, his social standing, or his wealth. There is no talk of his wit, wisdom, gentleness, kindness, or any other virtue. In fact, his spiritual nature is never even mentioned. She longs for his *body*, the object of her desire. Only he can satisfy the burning passion that has been awakened. There is no shame or secrecy about this. She tells her friends openly about her husband and extols his beauty to all who will listen to her.

When was the last time you thought about the different parts of your husband's body and felt so powerfully drawn to him that you could not eat or sleep until he was again in your arms? For so many, the passion of the early years has faded to talk about what a good father he is, what a faithful provider he is, how well he is doing at the office.

The man's description of his wife in the seventh chapter is even more graphic!

> Your graceful legs are like jewels....Your navel is a rounded goblet that never lacks blended wine. Your waist is a mound of wheat encircled by lilies.

> Your breasts are like two fawns, twins of a gazelle. Your neck is like an ivory tower.... How beautiful you are and how pleasing, O love, with your delights!
>
> —Song of Solomon 7:1–4, 6

He even goes on to describe his intentions toward her:

> Your stature is like that of the palm, and your breasts like clusters of fruit. I said, "I will climb the palm tree; I will take hold of its fruit."
>
> —Song of Solomon 7:7–8

Why did God put this in the Bible? It is because He wanted His people to know that the desires and drives they feel are part of what it means to be men and women. They are not something to be ashamed of or to hide from God. They are to be experienced in all their richness within the protective hedge of marriage.

There are countless other examples we could give of questions we have been asked. The bottom line is that sex is an invitation God extends to a husband and wife. He invites them to know one other person on this planet at a level and a depth that will not be found anywhere else this side of heaven.

In the union of man and wife, of two differing yet complementary strengths, God reveals Himself in His creation. As we experience the riches of marital love and intimacy, we are drawn to the One who is the source of it all. Through our union, we reflect to the world His character, His love, and His heart.

# Chapter 15

# FEMALE SEXUAL DRIVE

*In seminar after seminar, almost all the men ask me (SAF) the same question: "Why won't my wife have sex more often?" The flip side of that question from women is, "Why is my sexual drive so low compared to my husband's?"*

*Most married women are juggling multiple responsibilities daily. The average woman works fifty-plus hours a week, helps the children with homework, bathes and puts the kids to bed, cooks dinner, cleans the house, pays the bills, and is supposed to have energy left over to take care of her husband's sexual needs. It's not gonna happen! With everyone taking away pieces of her, it is easy to find there is nothing left to give. And if there is anything left, she is reluctant to give it up.*

*A wise husband shares the duties at home to relieve some of the burden off his wife's shoulders. If the wife works full-time outside of the home, there must be some sharing of the domestic responsibilities. Even if she's a stay-at-home mom, he should still shoulder some of the household duties. It is ultimately in the husband's best interest if he wants his wife to have any energy left for sex.*

*Some women have come to the office thinking they have a physiological problem when it comes to sex. They sometimes equate low sexual desire with a possible hormonal imbalance, and most of the time it has nothing to do with a hormonal imbalance; it's just physical exhaustion. While the hormone testosterone in men is the primary sex hormone, it plays a small part in fueling a woman's sexual drive.*

*One study revealed that one in three women complain of low sexual desire.[1] This is a complex issue involving many factors, but it is vital to couples struggling in their sexual relationship. We will examine factors that influence a female's sexual drive and possible treatment options available.*

## Initiators and Receivers

In *Pursuing Sexual Wholeness,* Andrew Comiskey explains these differences.[2] Men are formed in the image of God the Creator: the ability to initiate, to effect change, to push through to victory against all resistance, to act on one's deeply held convictions, to protect and defend, to pursue a goal until it is achieved. Even the masculine sex organ, the penis, symbolizes the ability to go forward into unknown territory and take charge.

Women are created to be receivers, able to simply "be": in relationships, before the Lord, with themselves. They are not consumed with "becoming" something; they can just be themselves. They are able to listen and hear from God and man before acting. They can yield and follow, just as Jesus did with His Father, without feeling inferior.

Women don't define themselves by what they do but by who they are. They are the nurturers, the comforters, and the restorers. When the husband or children come home bruised and bleeding from the hostile world they live in, it is the woman who holds them and makes everything all right. She listens to their war stories and calmly builds them back up, ready to face the challenges of another day.

The female sexual organs are, in turn, receptive. They take in the penis and receive life within the womb. They are "receivers."

Together, men and women share everything we see demonstrated between the Father and the Son: different characteristics but equal position. The problem comes when men want women to think and act as a man would, and women expect their husbands to respond as a woman does.

## "MOM NEVER TOLD ME!"

Much of the discrepancy in sexual drive is in perception: what *you* think you should be doing versus what your *spouse* thinks you should do.

Most Christian women play down their natural, God-given sexual desires because the media have fed them the lie that it's every man's sexual fantasy for a woman to seduce him and be sexually aggressive. God's Word gives us the truth in the Song of Solomon (Song of Sol. 1:7, 12-13; 5:10–16). It's not "wrong," or sinful, for a woman to have strong sexual feelings and desires toward her husband and *only* her husband.

While men are routinely taught that their sex drive is a strong aspect of what it is to be a man, the Christian community has conditioned women to misinterpret "submissiveness" and wrongly interpret a desire to have intercourse with their spouse as outside their rights. But the apostle Paul commands the husband to fulfill his marital duty to his wife and says the husband's body belongs to her (1 Cor. 7:2–5). In other words, she has a right to have sex. Just discovering this truth can increase a woman's desire because she now realizes she has a right to it.

The bottom line is that God created men and women with drastically different sexual drives. If we accept this fact, we will have a much healthier idea of what "normal" really is.

## The Way It Used to Be

Many women express frustration because their sexual desire is lower than it used to be. They compare themselves to the way they used to be and sense a problem. This too can be for several reasons. The first is hormonal. Depending on the woman's age, many have noticed that as they approach or proceed through menopause, their sexual desire declines. The ovaries begin to decrease production of all the sex hormones, particularly estrogen, and several things occur. The lining that covers the vagina and clitoris thins, making it more fragile and easier to traumatize. The amount of natural lubrication lessens, increasing the friction in intercourse and the likelihood of tearing the lining. This makes the act of intercourse painful, and anything painful is avoided. Why would your body release a desire for something that it knows will hurt you? As a protective mechanism, a woman's desire will decline if she perceives that the act will be painful. Each time intercourse is uncomfortable, it only reinforces this response, and the cycle of ever-lowering sexual drive continues.

In addition to estrogen, the hormone testosterone plays a role in sexual arousal and libido. This hormone begins to decline after age thirty and more rapidly so with menopause. Women who undergo hysterectomy with removal of the ovaries have a sudden decline in both estrogen and testosterone. Nearly 50 percent will experience some form of sexual dysfunction, even if they begin estrogen therapy after surgery.[3] This is one reason there has been a gradual shift away from routinely removing ovaries at the time of hysterectomy unless medically necessary.

## Medications

Even younger women can find themselves with lower testosterone levels than they used to have due to the effects of birth control pills. As we discussed earlier, the birth control pill suppresses the ovary's natural production of hormones and replaces it with its own formula. This is often accompanied by a decrease in previous testosterone levels. It is one of the reasons the pill is used to treat female acne, a testosterone-driven condition. But many women complain about loss of sexual drive after initiating hormonal birth control. Often changing to a brand with a different formula will alleviate this, and she will find her sexual drive returning to more acceptable levels. On the positive side, the fear of pregnancy can be a powerful deterrent to intercourse, and effective birth control can be of great relief.

Other medications can decrease the sexual drive. The most common medications include those used to treat high blood pressure, depression, and other psychiatric conditions. These can inhibit not only sexual desire but also the ability to achieve an orgasm. Antihypertensive medications such as diuretics and beta blockers seem to have more sexual side effects than newer drugs of the angiotensin class. Interestingly, untreated women with hypertension are twice as likely to have sexual dysfunction as properly treated patients. Drugs that dilate blood vessels appear to improve sexual function.[4]

The common antidepressant medications are the serotonin drugs, or SSRIs. Brands such as Prozac, Paxil, and Zoloft (along with their generic equivalents) tend to decrease libido, while Lexapro can lead to delayed orgasm. The one SSRI touted for having the least sexual side effects is Wellbutrin, or bupropion. Consultation with your physician can determine if a change in prescription might benefit your sexual drive without compromising your health.

In one study of the herb ginkgo biloba, an extract derived from the leaf of the Chinese ginkgo tree, 84 percent of participants found it effective in treating antidepressant-induced sexual dysfunction. Women were more responsive to the sexually enhancing effects of ginkgo biloba than men, with a success rate of 91 percent versus 76 percent. Dosages of ginkgo biloba extract ranged from 60 mg daily to 240 mg twice a day. The main attribute of increasing blood flow to the pelvis was also responsible for the side effect of increased menstrual flow in some women.[5]

## Decreased Energy

Decreased energy is another area that causes women to lose their sexual desire. As we shared at the beginning of this chapter, women today have more roles and responsibilities than God ever meant for them to handle.

Speaking of energy, a physically active woman has much more stamina than a more sedentary one. She is in a much better position to handle the rigors of wife and motherhood if her body is strong. So often people complain that they are too tired to exercise, but exercise builds strength and stamina and will leave you less tired at the end of the day. If you could in faith begin to exercise even when you feel tired, within a few short weeks, you would be surprised at how much more energy you had. And the sexual benefits have been well documented.[6]

Three aspects of exercise are key to lovemaking. Flexibility reduces the risks of injury and can increase blood flow to the pelvis, making the nerve endings more sensitive. Whatever one may feel about the spiritual philosophies of yoga, the pelvic stretches that are incorporated in the practice of yoga are very beneficial. The ability to relax and decrease stress is another benefit.

Strength training improves tone and the ability of the body to hold certain positions in lovemaking without cramping or collapsing from fatigue. This can be accomplished with weight training at a gym. Both upper and lower body weight training are important.

Endurance is essential to libido and healthy sexual function. A good cardio-vascular workout that includes twenty to thirty minutes of exercise three to five days a week will increase stamina and improve blood flow to the pelvis, leading to better arousal. One hour after exercising, there is a measurable increase in blood testosterone levels in both males and females, leading to a higher sexual drive.[7]

## Marital Harmony

One aspect of sexual drive in women that men too often ignore is in their relationship. Women need commitments of time, intimacy, and caring from their husbands. They need to know that their views have been heard and that they have shared their lives with the person with whom they will be uniting themselves in intercourse. This doesn't happen over the brim of a newspaper or while channel-surfing.

For a woman to desire to be "known" sexually by her husband, she also desires to be known in all other aspects of herself. Lack of communication, lack of attention, and marital discord poison the well of sexual desire for women. Women want to be treated to the same intensity of relationship as when they were being courted. Pressures of job, money, children, and even ministry can take us away from our first love for our spouses. A woman is less willing to give of herself sexually to someone who has not first given of himself the consideration of time and attention.

If a husband and wife are fighting, a woman's sexual drive will be decreased as well. The ability to have "make-up" sex only occurs when the differences between the couple are resolved to some level of satisfaction for the woman. Men are capable of having pleasurable sex when they are not even on speaking terms with their spouse, but this is rarely the case for women.

## Pleasure or Pain

Another factor in sexual desire for women involves pleasure. Was intercourse a pleasurable or painful experience for her? If her partner rushed into penile penetration before she had adequate foreplay to be well lubricated, the process of intercourse could be painful for her. Arousal in women causes the vagina to lengthen by 30 percent and pulls the internal organs away from penile contact.[8] Entering the vagina before arousal is fully developed can lead to bumping of the internal organs. The equivalent in men would be if the testicles were bumped repeatedly! As we stated earlier, anything that is consistently painful will be avoided. Gynecologic conditions such as endometriosis, uterine fibroids, or pelvic scar tissue can also be painful and should be discussed with a knowledgeable physician.

After childbirth, discomfort from episiotomy sites or lack of estrogen from breast-feeding can lead to vaginal pain with intercourse. Menopause often brings thinning of the vaginal tissues and more frequent tearing of the skin, leading to pain as well.

### Scars from the past

Pain need not be physical to cause decreases in sexual drive. Emotional pain is just as vigorously avoided as physical pain. It is estimated that 25 percent of women have been either physically or sexually abused during their lives.[9] This may cause them to unconsciously separate themselves from the sexual experience as a defense. Even in a relationship that is now free from danger and harm, the body may respond to sexual advances with avoidance behavior.

As mentioned in the sections on STDs and abortion, the past can influence the present. When past sexual relationships have had negative physical and emotional consequences, it is difficult to separate them from the desire for sexual intimacy in the present. They linger in the subconscious as an unseen barrier to sexual pleasure. Counseling is often needed to be able to recapture what has been stolen and enjoy the intimate pleasures God had in store from the beginning.

# The Sexual Experience

Even without a history of abuse, a wife may experience emotional hurt. If the experience of intercourse does not leave her feeling better about herself or her relationship with her husband, the desire to experience that activity again will diminish. And her perception of the event will color the reality of it. If she feels she did not perform well or is no longer satisfying to her husband, her sexual drive will diminish. She could wrongly interpret his erectile dysfunction as a reflection on her ability to arouse desire, when it may have nothing to do with her. It could be a medical condition her husband needs help with.

If the sexual experience is always one-sided, she will grow frustrated or resentful. Many women do not know they have a right to orgasm or don't know what it takes to achieve one. Misconceptions, often fueled by Hollywood or romance novels, lead women to believe that orgasm should be achieved automatically during vaginal intercourse alone: "Everyone else seems to experience simultaneous and mutually satisfying orgasm in this way. What's wrong with me?"

But scientific studies document that only 30 percent of women will achieve orgasm solely on the basis of vaginal intercourse.[10] Most women need more direct clitoral stimulation to achieve orgasm, but both they and their spouse are ignorant of what it takes to achieve this. Consequently, women often leave the experience of intercourse feeling that it was rather one-sided. And while it is nice to please one's husband, that alone will wear thin over time, and the desire to initiate such activity will be low.

## Body Image

Perhaps the final hindrance to female sexual drive is body image. Increased weight gain, poor muscle tone, and other anatomic changes wrought by aging and pregnancy factor into low sexual desire. While men are not nearly as preoccupied with their own body image when it comes to sexual desire, many women are reluctant to face the scrutiny they fear will happen during sex. In later chapters, we will discuss the changes that occur over time or with pregnancy, and how to recapture what has been lost. We will also discuss whether plastic surgery has a role in the life of a Christian woman.

## Treatment

The medical community has struggled to identify truly effective treatments to female sexual problems. The issues are so complex and intertwining that it has been difficult to prove which therapies or interventions are any better than a placebo. There is ample evidence that simply acknowledging a problem exists is the first step toward healing.

Realizing you are not alone is another helpful factor. Many of our patients are relieved to know they are not the only ones who struggle with low sexual desire. Giving them insight into the possible causes in their lives brings validation and acceptance. Simply realizing they are not supposed to feel the same as men is a very freeing concept.

We encourage the exploration of issues at home that might be causing unspoken resentments. Sharing household duties, having "date nights," and improved communication are all beneficial in improving sexual desire.

Issues from the past such as sexual abuse, STDs, or abortion must be overcome. Fear of pregnancy can be calmed with birth control counseling, and medication side effects can be lessened with appropriate substitutions.

Gynecologic pain can often be successfully treated and body image issues addressed with appropriate interventions. Estrogen deficiency is treatable, as is low testosterone. For those seeking herbal remedies, DHEA (dehydro-epiandrosterone) and ginkgo are options. A mixture of several herbs in a blend called ArginMax has shown a 73 percent improvement in overall sexual function after four weeks. Areas of improvement included sexual desire, reduction of vaginal dryness, frequency of sexual intercourse and orgasm, and clitoral sensation. No significant side effects were noted.11

There is no "magic" pill to improve sexual desire, but there are usually areas that can lead to improved sexual satisfaction for both the woman and her husband. In a later chapter, we will look at the problems of aging and intercourse.

# SECTION 5

## CONGRATULATIONS!
## YOU'RE GOING TO BE A MOTHER

# Chapter 16

# WHEN YOU'RE READY FOR A BABY

THERE IS NOTHING MORE EXCITING IN THE LIFE OF A COUPLE THAN THE thought of having a child. It is an act that forever unites two people. Their historical, spiritual, and even genetic legacy will continue to live on in their children long after the parents have passed on. In a sense, children are a testament that we have left something behind on this earth and a hope that whatever we started as a family will continue for generations to come.

But how do you know when you're ready to have a baby?

A generation ago it was not uncommon for women to have children in their late teens. Today, however, more women are postponing having children until their late thirties or early forties because of personal or professional goals. You may be one of these women. You may want to know what risks are involved with having a baby later in life. We hope to address these questions in this chapter.

## Exactly What Happens at Conception?

Aside from the obvious physical manner in which women get pregnant, it is actually a fairly complicated process. In order to get pregnant, several things must happen. First, the woman must release an egg from one of her ovaries. This is called *ovulation*. The egg is then captured by the fallopian tube and carried down the length of tube toward the uterus. This is accomplished by tiny hairs inside the tube called *cilia* that sweep the egg inward.

At the same time, there must be sperm that have made the difficult journey through the cervical opening, up the uterus, and into the tube. In an astonishing and biologically perplexing way, the tube sweeps the sperm in the opposite direction it is carrying the egg so that the two entities meet in the middle of the tube. One sperm, out of millions that began the journey, enters the egg in what is called *fertilization*. Once this occurs, the egg thickens its coating so no other sperm can enter.

This new creation of both the chromosomes of the egg and sperm begins to divide into many cells and is called an *embryo*. After a few days it is ready to make the journey to the uterus. No one knows how the tube coordinates the exact timing of entry, but it appears to be a critical element in the ability of the uterus to accept the developing embryo.

Once the embryo enters the womb, it floats for a few more days before attaching to the wall of the uterus. This is called *implantation* and results in the creation of chemicals that make the pregnancy test positive. The developing embryo becomes a fetus, and, if growth and development occur successfully, a baby is born.

## Take the Lifestyle Survey

When a couple is ready for children, many will do an inventory of their lives to see if they are in the best physical condition possible to conceive and nurture life. A survey of one's lifestyle before conception may reveal areas that need to be addressed before conception. What follows is a survey of things we discuss with our patients who are considering parenthood.

## Ditching Bad Habits Before and During Pregnancy

One of the first areas we explore with couples are their personal habits. These include smoking, alcohol consumption, drug abuse, dietary issues, and exercise routines. While normal children are born every day to parents with terrible personal habits, many couples want to optimize the fetal environment.

### Smoking

Cigarette smoke contains more than twenty-five hundred chemicals, of which nicotine and carbon monoxide are known to cause serious health problems. Because carbon monoxide directly impacts the ability of the fetus to use oxygen, smoking nearly doubles the risk of delivering a baby of low birth weight (less than five pounds). It also increases the chances of premature birth. Together, these two conditions increase the likelihood of cerebral palsy, mental retardation, learning disabilities, and even neonatal death.[1] Cigarette smoking also decreases fertility and increases the chances of miscarriage.

### DID YOU KNOW?

In the United States, 20 percent of women smoke cigarettes, and 11 percent do so during pregnancy.[2]

Smoking doubles the risk of placenta previa and placental abruption, as well as premature rupture of the membranes leading to preterm delivery. There is an increase in the stillbirth risk and a three-times higher incidence of sudden infant death syndrome (SIDS).[3]

The more a woman smokes, the greater the risks. For those who stop smoking, even in the third trimester, the risks are reduced. If all pregnant women stopped smoking, the stillbirth rate in this country would drop 11 percent and newborn deaths would decrease 5 percent.[4]

We try to encourage all women to stop smoking before becoming pregnant or as early as possible once they are pregnant.

Even if the woman does not smoke, secondhand smoke has also been implicated in increasing low-birth weight and SIDS risk. We strongly advise husbands who smoke during their wives' pregnancies to do so away from their wives' presence. Women who work in bars or other locations with significant exposure to secondhand smoke may want to consider a job change before becoming pregnant.

## Alcohol abuse

Alcohol use and its impact on fertility is a controversial subject. There is evidence that alcohol consumption in high levels causes an increase in estrogen for both men and women. Testosterone levels may be decreased for men, with a resultant drop in sperm count. Some studies suggest a decrease in the fertility rate of women who have five or more alcoholic drinks per week.[5] Others have shown mixed results, concluding a more negative impact on fertility from binge drinking.[6] The effects of alcohol exposure on the developing fetus have been thoroughly studied, and the results are conclusive. Warning labels are mandated by the surgeon general on all alcoholic beverage containers warning of the risks of alcohol to the developing fetus.

In the 1970s, fetal alcohol syndrome (FAS) was identified, linking the consumption of alcohol during pregnancy to birth defects. FAS is characterized by decreased fetal growth, abnormal facial features, and abnormalities of the central nervous system. The discovery of FAS prompted the surgeon general's office to do extensive public education and increase awareness among women to limit the amount of alcohol they consume while pregnant.

Those women who consume seven or more drinks per week, or had binge drinking of five or more drinks per episode, delivered babies who were significantly smaller and had behavioral problems. These children were more likely to exhibit problems with arithmetic, language, and memory; eye-hand coordination; attention deficits; and problems processing information.

Many school-aged children are not diagnosed with FAS but simply placed in the category of attention-deficit hyperactivity disorder (ADHD) or other behavioral disorders. FAS is the single most preventable birth defect in the United States. Because it is not known exactly how many drinks it takes to adversely affect a developing fetus, especially in the early stages of pregnancy, the surgeon general advises all pregnant women and those considering pregnancy to abstain from alcohol consumption.[7]

## Drug abuse

Marijuana is the most frequently used illicit drug in the United States. Many couples wonder if it impacts fertility and if they need to refrain from using it before attempting pregnancy. It appears that casual and occasional use may not affect fertility, but there is evidence that frequent use decreases fertility.

Men who smoke marijuana frequently have significantly less seminal fluid, the fluid that nourishes sperm, and a lower total sperm count. Their sperm also behave abnormally, swimming too fast and reaching the egg before it is ready to be fertilized. There appears to be impairment in the ability of the sperm to penetrate the egg as well.[8]

Women who smoke marijuana have the same chemicals secreted into their vaginal fluids that damage sperm in men. It is possible that when sperm are ejaculated into the vagina, these chemicals impair sperm as if the man had been the user.

Because the main ingredients of marijuana are stored in the fatty tissues, it can take months for them to clear the body. Those who desire pregnancy may need to abstain from marijuana use at least six months before fertility is returned to normal.

Marijuana does not seem to cause abnormal embryos or birth defects, but there is a trend toward smaller birth weights. Babies are often jittery as they withdraw from the drug. The difficulty in studying marijuana's effect in pregnancy is because most women who smoke it are also using tobacco and alcohol, making it hard to isolate the effect of marijuana alone. The supply of marijuana is often tainted with other chemicals such as pesticides, which may have their own effects on development.

## Prescription drug use

There are a variety of medical conditions for which women take medications. These drugs can cause fetal malformations and birth defects. The most common are those taken for high blood pressure and seizure disorders. Some are known teratogens, chemicals proven to cause birth defects.

Among the medications for high blood pressure, ACE inhibitors are the ones to avoid when trying to get pregnant. ACE inhibitors are not associated with malformations or adverse outcomes when used during the first trimester. But in the second and third trimester, ACE inhibitors have been associated with low amniotic fluid, stillbirth, kidney disease, and neonatal death. There have also been reports of abnormal fetal skull development, limited growth, and poorly developed lungs.[9]

Diuretics are commonly used hypertension medications. While they have not been implicated in birth defects, there are concerns regarding third trimester fetal neurologic development. Some studies have shown an increase in the incidence of schizophrenia in those patients exposed to diuretics during their third trimester.[10] There is also a concern regarding poor perfusion of the placenta with diuretic use.

There are alternative blood pressure medications with a long history of use during pregnancy. These include Aldomet (alpha-methyldopa) and some of the beta blockers such as labetalol.

The other class of drugs that are concerns for pregnant women are the antileptics, or antiseizure medications. In babies born to mothers with epilepsy receiving any anti-epileptic treatment, the overall rate of malformations has been demonstrated to be two to three times higher than the rate reported in the general population. This translates to a 10 percent chance of fetal abnormalities for women with seizure disorders. The malformations most commonly seen are cleft lip and cardiovascular abnormalities.

Neural tube defects, such as spina bifida, are also increased in women taking antiseizure medications. Folate supplementation prior to pregnancy has been demonstrated to reduce the incidence of such defects in women at high risk. They are advised to start taking folic acid supplementation (4 mg per day) as soon as contraception is discontinued.

Since taking multiple medications increases risk, it is best if seizures can be controlled with only one medication. There are also benefits to lowering the amount of drug as much as possible and splitting it into two doses per day instead of one.[11]

A woman may be tempted to stop taking her medications altogether, but that is a risky strategy that is best done in conjunction with a perinatologist. Having a seizure during pregnancy is also very detrimental to the developing fetus. Oxygen levels usually drop during a seizure, and this can impact the developing fetal brain. Women may also experience a seizure when driving or may otherwise injure themselves during a seizure.

## Managing Medical Conditions Before and During Pregnancy

Certain diseases can cause birth defects if not controlled before and during pregnancy. The two we most commonly see in our practice are diabetes and thyroid disease.

## Diabetes

Diabetes can be a difficult disorder to control. A woman who has type 1 or type 2 diabetes that is not tightly controlled has a higher chance of having a baby with a birth defect than does a woman without diabetes. The organs of the baby form during the first two months of pregnancy, often before a woman knows that she is pregnant. Out-of-control blood sugar levels can affect those organs while they are being formed and cause serious birth defects, such as those of the brain, spine, and heart. They may also lead to miscarriage of the developing baby.

There is a strong association between the degree of blood sugar control prior to pregnancy and the miscarriage rate. Poorly controlled blood sugars double the miscarriage rate. Your doctor can perform a test, hemoglobin A1C or glyco-hemoglobin, which measures the glucose control of the past three months. A normal range, and the goal of women planning pregnancy, is less than 6 percent. Moderate control is between 6 and 10 percent, and poor control is greater than 10 percent.

Patients with glycohemoglobin exceeding 11 percent have been shown to have miscarriage rates of up to 44 percent. Among the general population, major birth defects occur in 1 to 2 percent of the population. In women with diabetes and suboptimal glucose control prior to conception, the likelihood of malformation increased to 22 percent. If control was excellent, the risk was only 3 percent.[12]

An interesting fact is that no increase in birth defects occurs among women who develop diabetes after the first trimester. This suggests that glucose control in those first few weeks of pregnancy is critical in preventing birth defects. Since many women are not aware that they are pregnant in those first few weeks, preconception control is critical. This takes a team approach involving the patient, her endocrinologist, and her obstetrician.

## Thyroid disease

In the United States, about eight million women have either hyperthyroidism or hypothyroidism that is unrecognized and untreated.[13]

Untreated thyroid disease in pregnancy has been associated with offspring who have diminished intellect. It can also increase the risk of miscarriage and stillbirth. Ovulation is suppressed in thyroid disease, making conception difficult.

Because women are affected by thyroid disease seven times more than men, it is suggested that thyroid screening be done prior to conception. If a woman is diagnosed with a thyroid disorder, treatment and stabilization should be done prior to pregnancy. Even after conception, an endocrinologist will need to closely monitor the thyroid levels to ensure an optimum fetal environment.

# Proper Nutrition

While there is no specific diet that is best for preparing to become pregnant, it is always good to plan for the nutrition you would want to have if you were pregnant. Just as we advise women to quit drinking alcohol and stop smoking before conceiving, so do we advise certain dietary restrictions when considering pregnancy. The main reason is that many women are several weeks pregnant before they even realize it. It is common for patients to confess to eating or drinking something when they didn't know they were already pregnant. This leads to remorse and anxiety. It is always safest to assume before you do anything that you might be in early pregnancy.

We recommend women considering pregnancy begin to limit their caffeine intake to no more than two drinks per day. Excessive caffeine intake has been shown to increase the risk of miscarriage.[14] Since women may not know they are pregnant for the first few weeks, the damage by caffeine could already done.

While fish and shellfish are an excellent source of protein and omega-3 fatty acids, which are beneficial to the cardiovascular and nervous system, there has been some concern over the ingestion of seafood due to contamination of many of our waterways by lead and mercury. Lead and mercury are harmful to the developing fetus. Because these minerals are stored in the body and take many months to be removed, women who are considering pregnancy are advised to make the following dietary adjustments even before conceiving:[15]

- Do not eat shark, swordfish, king mackerel, or tilefish because they contain high levels of mercury.

- Eat up to 12 ounces (two average meals) a week of a variety of fish and shellfish that are lower in mercury. Five of the most commonly eaten fish that are low in mercury are shrimp, canned light tuna, salmon, pollock, and catfish. Another commonly eaten fish, albacore ("white") tuna, has more mercury than canned light tuna. So, when choosing your two meals of fish and shellfish, you may eat up to 6 ounces (one average meal) of albacore tuna per week.

- Check local advisories about the safety of fish caught by family and friends in your local lakes, rivers, and coastal areas. If no advice is available, eat up to 6 ounces (one average meal) per week of fish you catch from local waters, but don't consume any other fish during that week.

The one dietary supplement that has been found to be important preconception is the levels of folate or folic acid in the bloodstream that are available to the developing fetus during the first eight weeks of pregnancy. This is a critical time in the formation of the brain and spinal column. Deficiencies in folic acid have been shown to increase the risk of anencephaly, a condition where most of the brain is missing. There is also an increased risk of spina bifida, where the spinal column does not completely fuse and the spinal column is damaged. This can lead to lower body paralysis in the baby.

The recommended amounts of daily folic acid are 0.4 mg (or 400 mcg). Since it is important to achieve good blood levels by the time the second month of pregnancy occurs, it is difficult to "catch up" once you discover you are pregnant. It is far better to begin daily supplements at least three months before conception. Many breads, cereals, and pastas are fortified with folic acid, but most of our patients begin taking prenatal vitamins in advance. This gives them the recommended folic acid as well as essential vitamins and calcium to strengthen their own bodies in preparation for pregnancy.

## Preconception Exercise

There are really no restrictions on exercise in the preconception period. Many women will want to lose weight before becoming pregnant. This is a worthwhile goal, as pregnancies in women with a BMI over 30 (see chart on page 45) are more likely to be at risk for diabetes, large babies, preeclampsia, and cesarean section. Once a woman conceives, we do not recommend weight loss.

Those women who are underweight, meaning a BMI under 18, have more of a risk of delivering prematurely or having an underweight baby.[16] For both of these groups of women, a consultation with a registered dietitian may provide helpful nutritional guidance to optimize your pregnancy in advance.

Proper planning and good preconception health can optimize your chances of a healthy pregnancy and a healthy baby.

# Chapter 17

# INFERTILITY: CAUSES AND TREATMENTS

NFERTILITY, WHICH IS DEFINED BY THE MEDICAL COMMUNITY AS AN inability to create or sustain life in the womb, is a common problem. The general definition includes those couples who have regular sexual activity and have not achieved pregnancy in a year. This also includes couples who conceive but who repeatedly miscarry. The definition is often shortened to six months for those couples over age thirty-five due to the time constraints of their biologic clock.

The genetic health of a woman's eggs declines with age. The aging man makes significantly more abnormal sperm as well. These factors can lead to a higher rate of miscarriage because of the creation of abnormal embryos. Between one-fourth and one-third of all first trimester pregnancies end in miscarriage, a fact that is highly dependent on both the man and the woman's age. Other issues impacting fertility increase as one ages, including hypertension, diabetes, and thyroid disease.

About one-third of infertility is due to problems with the woman. This is contrary to what was traditionally thought for centuries. The woman was almost always felt to be at fault from ancient times until the recent twentieth century when medical science was able to discover many of the causes of infertility. One-third of infertility is from the man, and about 15 percent is a combination of both of them. There are 10 to 20 percent of couples for which medical science cannot determine the cause of their fertility problem.

*Trevor, a thirty-year-old, long-distance truck driver, and his wife, Susan, a thirty-two-year-old teacher, had been trying to have a baby for two years when they first came to see us. We reviewed both of their medical histories to see if anything was impacting their fertility. He had no unusual illnesses or previous trauma to the testicles. He noted no difficulties with achieving erection or ejaculation. Susan's periods were regular but came every twenty-three days and were very short. Her only previous medical problem was a ruptured appendix when she was eight. Trevor was often gone for one week at a time, but he still made time to be home during their fertile time each month.*

*We ordered a semen analysis from Trevor, which returned with a mildly decreased sperm count. Susan had a tubal X-ray, which revealed some scar tissue around her right fallopian tube, probably a result of a ruptured appendix, but her left tube looked good. A low progesterone level showed that Susan was not ovulating effectively, contributing to her short and frequent menstrual cycles.*

*Trevor saw a urologist who felt the sperm count was high enough for conception. The lower count came from his job as a trucker, sitting in the cab for prolonged periods of time. This causes increased scrotal temperature, which can lower sperm count. Susan underwent laparoscopy and had scar tissue removed from her right tube. A small dose of Clomid was prescribed to aid her ovulation.*

*Three months later, Susan became pregnant. She and Trevor were very excited and came to the office in the early stage of pregnancy. On ultrasound, there was no evidence of a pregnancy in the uterus. Because she was so early, we followed her pregnancy levels to determine the health of her pregnancy. When the levels reached a certain point, a repeat ultrasound failed to show an intrauterine pregnancy. A laparoscopy revealed a tubal pregnancy in the damaged right tube. This was removed, and Susan made a full recovery. Six months later, Susan became pregnant again; this time, she had a normal intrauterine pregnancy.*

## THE FACTS ABOUT INFERTILITY

About 12 percent of women (7.3 million) in the United States aged fifteen to forty-four have difficulty getting pregnant or carrying a baby, according to the National Center for Health Statistics of the Centers for Disease Control and Prevention. In the United States about 20 percent of women have their first child after age thirty-five. But one-third of couples in which the woman is over thirty-five have fertility problems.[1]

# Female Infertility

While aging is a primary factor of infertility, especially after age thirty-five, medical diseases can play a role as well. PCOS, which we have already discussed, is a common reason women do not ovulate. There is speculation that local insulin levels may be too high and suppress ovulation. Body fat stores estrogen and sends false messages to the brain that estrogen levels are sufficient, altering the signals sent by the brain to the ovaries to spur ovulation. Thyroid disease can send similar false signals from the brain, which disrupts ovulation. Certain medications for psychiatric or neurological conditions impact ovulation at the level of the brain. Even strenuous exercise and anorexia play a role in these brain chemistries.

Besides ovulation, the other factors causing female infertility involve reproductive organs such as the cervix, the uterus, and the tubes. The cervix is the entry point for sperm as it leaves the semen after ejaculation. Medical procedures for abnormal Pap smears such as cryotherapy and conization can cause scarring and tightening of the cervix. Medications that lower local estrogen content or raise progesterone levels shrink the cervical mucus that speed entry into the cervix.

Uterine abnormalities come into play when it is time for the embryo to implant. Fibroid tumors that grow into the uterine cavity may block implantation in ways similar to the IUD. Even deeper fibroids divert blood supply as they grow and can lessen the likelihood that an implanted embryo will survive. Embryonic abnormalities may even have occurred while a woman was forming in her own mother's womb. These abnormalities can cause the shape of the intrauterine cavity to be irregular and hamper the development of the fetus.

Finally, the fallopian tubes are crucial to the successful fertilization of the egg. They must be unobstructed to allow the egg to enter and the sperm to unite with it. If they are blocked or scarred, it is as if the woman has had her tubes tied. Partially damaged tubes may allow fertilization, but impairment of the cilia may cause the enlarging embryo to implant in the tube before it can reach the uterus. This is the cause of ectopic pregnancies.

A final factor in female infertility is endometriosis. This is a poorly understood phenomenon where it appears that cells belonging to the uterine lining have implanted themselves along the lining of the pelvic cavity. Some theorize that during menstruation, blood containing viable cells is back-washed out the tubes and collects in the pelvis. There, cells can attach to other organs such as the lining of the ovaries, intestines, or other pelvic structures. When the woman has her menstrual cycle, these cells "menstruate" as well, causing a reaction by the body. The body's response to this is scar tissue formation, which can damage the tubes. Chemicals are secreted by the endometriosis lesions that seem to poison the eggs and may hamper fertilization. Endometriosis is usually suspected if a woman has severe premenstrual and menstrual pain that resolves after menses. This is not always the case as endometriosis can also be silent.

## Fertility Evaluation for Women

The basic infertility evaluation of a woman is based on the factors mentioned above. The first thing that is evaluated is ovulation. If an egg is not released, there can be no pregnancy. There have been charts made of basal body temperature measurements to predict when ovulation will occur and to document that it did indeed occur. We've included an example of a basal body chart here. This chart required the woman to awaken each morning and immediately take her temperature. This was graphed as a menstrual calendar. The theory was that as progesterone rises, so does the morning body temperature of a woman. Rising progesterone signals ovulation. This method is also used for natural family planning.

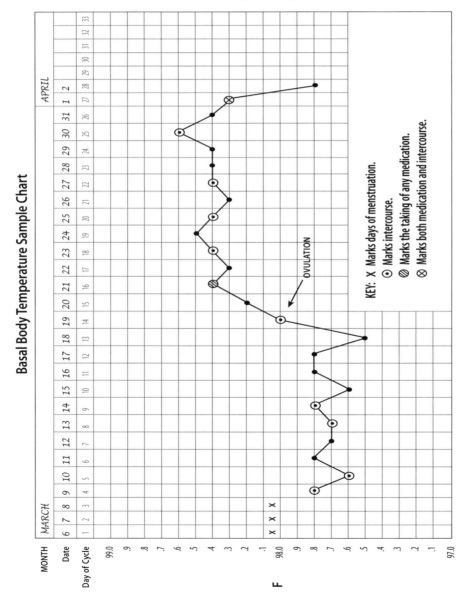

Basal Body Temperature Sample Chart

The problem with this technique is that any activity by the woman raises her basal temperature, so the measurement has to be done before she even leaves the bed. If she has had a viral or bacterial infection that month, the entire calendar becomes invalid. The stress this puts on the woman to accurately chart her daily temperature is quite significant. The graph is also more of an historical document in that it records ovulation occurring but tells nothing of the quality of that event.

Since the advent of accurate and rapid blood tests to measure progesterone levels, the basal body temperature chart has been widely abandoned in favor of blood tests. We ask women to have a progesterone level tested on Day 21 of their cycle (Day 1 being the first day of their period). This level determines not only if they ovulated that cycle but also the quality or strength of that ovulation. This is useful in determining if medication is needed to help ovulation.

Some older women will have an FSH drawn on Day 3 of the cycle. This is a hormone that "talks" to the ovary to recruit an egg to ovulate each cycle. The "louder" it has to shout (i.e., the higher the FSH), the less likely a woman can conceive, even with medical help.

Secondly, we evaluate the female organs themselves. Transvaginal ultrasonography may be used to assess if the egg was ovulated, to look for ovarian cysts or tumors, and to evaluate uterine abnormalities such as fibroids. Another test is a hysterosalpingogram, or HSG. This is an X-ray of the uterus and tubes done by injecting radioactive material through the opening of the cervix into the uterus. The dye is then spilled out of the tubes if they are open. Abnormalities of the lining of the uterus, such as polyps, fibroids, or embryonic defects, can also be identified. If tubes are scarred closed or if the dye collects at the end of the tube, this signifies reduced fertility.

The drawbacks of this test are that it is uncomfortable to experience and the data from the tubes is not always correct. Some women experience uterine cramping from the material injected that can temporarily cause tubal spasm. The tubes will appear closed on X-ray when in fact they may be perfectly fine in their natural state. For this reason, if there is an abnormal HSG, confirmation is needed.

This brings us to the third area, which is surgical tests. An abnormal HSG of the uterus requires hysteroscopy. This involves placing a scope attached to a camera through the cervix to visualize the uterine cavity. The patient is generally asleep. Any abnormalities are directly seen and often treated in the same operative setting to enhance the ability of the embryo to implant. Laparoscopy is a surgical procedure where the same camera is placed through a scope in the navel to evaluate the internal pelvic organs. This is useful in verifying any tubal disease, adhesions, fibroids, or endometriosis. Often treatment can also be done in the same operative encounter.

## Treatment for Female Infertility

Sometimes lifestyle changes are not enough to address female infertility. A variety of fertility medicines are used to treat women who do not ovulate or who do so poorly. The most common is clomiphene citrate (or Clomid). This medicine causes ovulation by acting on the pituitary gland. It temporarily decreases the level of estrogen in the body and causes the pituitary to "yell louder" at the ovaries, enhancing ovulation. It is often used in women who have PCOS or other problems with ovulation.

Clomid is taken by mouth for five days in the beginning of the menstrual cycle, while the woman is still on her period. Since estrogen is temporarily decreased, most women experience hot flashes and some mood changes while on this drug. Ovulation can also be painful, and ovarian cysts occasionally are large enough to require treatment.

Another oral medication is metformin (or Glucophage). It is an oral diabetes medication that is helpful for women who have insulin resistance and PCOS. This drug seems to normalize elevated insulin levels surrounding the ovaries in women with PCOS without decreasing blood sugar in nondiabetics. It is taken daily and will be about three months before its effects are seen. Sometimes clomiphene citrate is combined with metformin to improve ovulation. If ovulation is not achieved through oral medication, injectable drugs are the next step.

Human menopausal gonadotropin (Repronex, Pergonal) is often used for women who do not ovulate on oral medication. Human menopausal gonadotropin (hMG) acts directly on the ovaries to stimulate ovulation and is an injected medicine. A similar injectable medication is follicle-stimulating hormone, or FSH (Gonal-f, Follistim). It works much like hMG by directly causing the ovaries to ovulation. These medicines are usually injected by the patient's husband.

Negatives for these drugs include pain from daily injections, significantly higher cost, and a sharp increase in the possibility of multiple fetuses: twins, triplets, or greater. Women who are pregnant with multiple fetuses have more problems during pregnancy, and their fetuses have a high risk of being born prematurely with all of the health and developmental problems that go with it.

When women are taking medications to enhance ovulation, fertility specialists often try to enhance the chances of conceiving by adding intrauterine insemination (IUI), even if there are no abnormalities with the husband's sperm. Those on clomiphene can suffer decreased cervical mucus production from the decrease in estrogen inherent in the medication. This can impede passage of the sperm into the uterus. Those who have been diligently timing ovulation with injectable medications do not want to risk missing the small window of opportunity for fertilization after spending hundreds of dollars on drugs. IUI insures that the sperm will be deposited close to the egg at the optimum time.

Those women with endometriosis or uterine abnormalities may require surgical treatments, as has been previously mentioned. Until the 1980s, if the tubes were blocked, surgical correction was often offered but was not always successful and had the potential of increasing a woman's chances for an ectopic pregnancy. Since then, the science of assisted reproductive technology (ART) has been developed. This is a term that describes several different methods used to help infertile couples.

ART refers to any method that assists the union of egg and sperm through scientific means. Common methods of ART include in vitro fertilization, or IVF, which is the most effective ART.[2]

With IVF, fertilization occurs outside of the body. It is often used when a woman's fallopian tubes are blocked or when a man produces too few sperm. Many couples seek IVF when the cause of their infertility is unknown. Specialists called *reproductive endocrinologists* treat the woman with a drug that causes the ovaries to produce multiple eggs. Once mature, the eggs are removed by a needle under ultrasound guidance in the specialist's office. They are put in a dish in the lab along with the man's sperm for fertilization. After three to five days, healthy embryos are implanted in the woman's uterus.

Because the success rate of IVF is directly related to the number of embryos that are implanted, multiple pregnancy is a high likelihood. Due to the extreme high risks to high-order multiples (greater than triplets), only three to four embryos are placed at a time. Others can be frozen for later use. Even then, only a small percentage will attach to the uterus and survive, if any at all.

A variation of IVF is zygote intrafallopian transfer (ZIFT), where the very young embryo is transferred to the fallopian tube instead of the uterus. It is hoped that more natural implantation will occur and increase the pregnancy success rate. This can only be done in the presence of normal fallopian tubes and thus represents a smaller subset of ART.

Success rates of ART vary and depend on many factors. Some of these include the age of the partners, the reason for their infertility, and the quality of the fertility clinic.

The CDC collects success rates on ART for most of the fertility clinics in the United States. One can ask the specialist for the specific success rates of the clinic you are considering.

> **ASSISTED REPRODUCTIVE TECHNOLOGY STATISTICS**
> According to the 2003 CDC report on ART, the average percentage of ART cycles that led to a healthy baby were as follows:[3]
> - 37.3 percent in women under the age of thirty-five
> - 30.2 percent in women aged thirty-five to thirty-seven
> - 20.2 percent in women aged thirty-seven to forty
> - 11.0 percent in women aged forty-one to forty-two

ART can be expensive and time-consuming. The average cost of an IVF cycle in the United States is $12,400.[4] But it has allowed many couples to have children that otherwise would not have been conceived.

An infertility group whom we work with, RMA for Texas, has created a chart (on facing page) that they use for their patients as they decide what, if any, fertility treatment they might want to pursue. It gives success rates and costs so patients can make informed decisions. They have graciously allowed us to reproduce it here.

# Male Infertility

Male infertility comprises one-third of cases and focuses on sperm. Certain conditions may be associated with male infertility. These conditions include infection of the prostate or testicles from STDs or other bacterial causes. The prostate gland is the main organ responsible for making semen, the vehicle that carries sperm out of the man with ejaculation. Infection alters the semen quality. It also brings white blood cells that mistakenly attack swimming sperm in their attempt to destroy harmful bacteria.

Other conditions include varicocele. These are varicose veins of the scrotum. It is thought that the pooling of blood from these veins causes an increase in the local temperature of the testes, impacting sperm survival.

Abnormal male chromosomes impact sperm formation. One such condition is known as Klinefelter's syndrome. Instead of the usual XY chromosomes that most men have, these men have an extra X chromosome, making them XXY. This may be from a faulty egg or fertilization by two sperm instead of one. While not every man with extra chromosomes has infertility issues, some do.[5]

There are other sources of male infertility. Some men have undergone radiation treatment for cancer therapy and have sustained damage to the testes as a result. Others have had diseases such as mumps that can cause shrinking of the testicles, or they have experienced traumatic injury to the testicles. Even previous surgical procedures from childhood such as hernia repair can impair blood flow to the testes.

| RMA *for Texas* | | NORMAL FERTILE COUPLE | INFERTILE TIMED INTERCOURSE | CLOMIPHENE + INSEMINATIONS | INJECTABLES + INSEMINATION | IVF < 35 YEARS |
|---|---|---|---|---|---|---|
| DIMENSION | Pregnancy rate | 20%/month | 1–2%/month | 8%/month | 17%/month | 48%/month |
| Time | 1 month | 20% | 2% | 8% | 17% | 48% |
| Time | 2 month | 36% | 4% | 15% | 31% | 73% |
| Time | 3 month | 49% | 6% | 22% | 43% | 86% |
| Time | 6 month | 74% | 11% | 39% | 67% | 93% |
| Time | 12 month | 93% | 22% | | | |
| Time | 18 month | 98% | 30% | | | |
| Time | 24 month | 99% | 38% | | | |
| Social/Logistics | | N/A | learn an ovulation predictor method | some office visits, monitoring | learning self injection, blood tests, monitoring, several office visits | learning self injection, daily injections, frequent blood tests, monitoring, several office visits |
| Medical Risks | Singleton | 99 out of 100 | 99 out of 100 | 13 out of 14 | 12 out of 15 | 2 out of 3 |
| Medical Risks | Twin | 1 out of 100 | 1 out of 100 | 1 out of 14 | 1 out of 5 | 1 out of 3 |
| Medical Risks | Triplets | 1 out of 8000 | 1 out of 8000 | 1 out of 250 | 1 out of 20 | 1 out of 25 |
| Medical Risks | Quadruplets | extremely rare | extremely rare | 1 out of 350 | 1 out of 33 | 1 out of 110 |
| Medical Risks | Hyperstimulation requiring hospitalization | N/A | N/A | very rare | 1 out of 100 | 1 out of 100 |
| Financial | cost $ | - | - | $600–900.00 | $1,500.00 | $8500 + meds |
| Emotional | Emotional credit card | assess individually | assess individually | assess individually | assess individually | assess individually |

## Fertility Evaluation for Men

An analysis of the man's semen is a key part of the basic workup. He is asked to abstain from intercourse for at least three days. The sample is obtained by masturbation into a sterile cup that is then analyzed in a lab about one hour later. There are several characteristics that are evaluated from the sample.[6] The first is volume of semen produced in the ejaculation. The normal is 1–6.5 ml. Next, the time it takes for the semen to go from a clumpy state to a liquid one is measured. This is called *liquefaction*. A liquid state is crucial if the sperm are to leave the semen and enter the cervix, as only the sperm migrate up the cervix. The normal time to liquefaction is around twenty minutes. Anything over sixty minutes is considered abnormal.

The sperm count is of critical importance. This is measured in sperm per milliliter of semen ejaculated. The normal count is between 20 and 150 million sperm per milliliter. This may seem like an excessively large amount when only one is necessary for fertilization. But the environment of the vagina is so harsh and the journey so difficult that of the millions ejaculated, only a few dozen make it to the egg. A man is less fertile if his count is below 20 million, and significantly so if below one million. But there have been successful pregnancies for even those men with very low sperm counts, so this is not an absolute.

The next characteristic evaluated from the semen analysis is sperm mobility (or motility). It is of no use to have sperm that cannot swim and make the journey needed to fertilize the egg. Mobility measures the percentage of sperm that move in a forward direction. A least 60 percent of the sperm should be moving in the correct direction for optimum fertility. Morphology is another characteristic identified with fertility. This is measured as a percentage of sperm with normal shape. Abnormal shapes include two-headed sperm, sperm with missing tails, and rounded sperm heads. These characteristics make it more difficult to fertilize the egg. Normal forms should make up at least 70 percent of the specimen for it to be optimal. Other values measured in the semen analysis include the pH and any signs of infection.

If a low sperm count or a high percentage of sperm abnormalities are found, blood tests may be done to measure testosterone or a biopsy of the testes may be ordered. It is standard practice in our office to send the husband to the laboratory for the semen analysis and to interpret the results for him and his wife. The husband is usually referred to a urologist for evaluation of any abnormalities. This is a specialist in male reproductive disorders. Often the semen analysis is repeated to ensure that the first result was truly representative of his condition.

# Fertility Treatment for Men

One of first things that a urologist will recommend to men who are trying to conceive a child is to minimize those factors that impair sperm production. Scientists have measured a steady decline in the sperm count of men in Western countries over the past few decades.[7] This is likely due to many factors in our society. Reducing alcohol, marijuana, cigarettes, and obesity improves both quality and quantity of sperm. Those who work in fields where exposure to radiation, pesticides, or lead is involved may need to take precautions to guard themselves.[8]

There is some debate about the role of temperature in sperm production. Some feel that the higher the temperature of the scrotum, the lower the sperm count will be. Those who do vigorous exercise in tight clothing (such as cyclists) or who sit for long periods of time (such as long-distance truck drivers) may be decreasing their sperm counts. Men are often advised to avoid hot tubs and tight underwear due to several studies that show even small increases in scrotal temperature can make a big difference in sperm count.[9] There are even studies expressing concerns over men placing laptop computers in their laps for prolonged periods of time.[10] Whether or not these temperature changes are enough to take a man from fertile to infertile, those with already low counts could benefit from these lifestyle changes.

Some urologists and fertility specialists advocate intrauterine insemination (IUI) as another type of treatment for male infertility. IUI is known by most people as artificial insemination. In this procedure, the woman is injected through the cervix with specially prepared sperm from her husband to concentrate and place those sperm as close to the opening of the fallopian tube as possible. This reduces the tremendous loss in numbers that occurs in the normal journey from the vagina to the tubes and shortens the "swim" necessary to the waiting egg. Because the timing of this procedure is critical to its success, the woman must also be ovulating on the same day.

Finally, for those with very low counts, poor motility, or high numbers of abnormal shapes, a technique called intracytoplasmic sperm injection (ICSI) can be offered. In this technique, a single sperm is extracted and inserted into an egg to achieve fertilization. This embryo is then placed into the uterus. This technique is sometimes used in those couples where the man has had a previous vasectomy and there is no other way to extract sperm from him.

## (i) RESOURCES

You can find out more about infertility by contacting the National Women's Health Information Center (NWHIC) at (800) 994-9662 or any of these organizations:

- American College of Obstetricians and Gynecologists (ACOG) Resource Center; (800) 762-2264; http://www.acog.org
- American Society for Reproductive Medicine; (205) 978-5000; http://www.asrm.org/
- Resolve: The National Infertility Association; (888) 623-0744; http://www.resolve.org
- International Council on Infertility Information Dissemination, Inc.; (703) 379-9178; http://www.inciid.org/

## IT'S IN THE WORD

If you and your spouse are struggling with infertility, remember that God placed examples in His Word to guide you. One foundational truth is that it is God's will for you to have children. If it is His will, then you can cling to it. Fertility was considered a blessing from God bestowed upon the righteous. (See Psalm 127; 128.) Even the creation of life within the womb is beautifully told by David in Psalm 139:13–16.

There are many scriptures that deal with God as the opener and the closer of the womb. (Read Genesis 21:1–2; 25:21–26; 29:31–35; 30:22–24; Exodus 23:25–26; Deuteronomy 7:12–14.) In biblical times, there was no medical knowledge of fertility and everything was thought to be the woman's fault. Nevertheless, God heard their prayers and made them pregnant. His promise to those who trust Him is that He will be faithful. As medical professionals, we are an extension of that promise, His hands at work in the lives of our patients.

# Chapter 18

# THE FIRST TRIMESTER

*Janelle came to our office when she was seven weeks pregnant. It was her second pregnancy. During her first pregnancy, she miscarried around eight or nine weeks. She was getting nervous because, although she was nauseated and was experiencing breast tenderness, she had all of those symptoms in her first pregnancy until about nine weeks. At that time in her first pregnancy, she went in for her first prenatal visit. The doctor performed an ultrasound but was unable to detect a heartbeat in the fetus. She did not have any other signs of a miscarriage, no bleeding or cramping. She underwent a D&C. Now, four months later, she was pregnant again. She was worried that the same thing would happen this time.*

*We performed an ultrasound, which showed a strong heartbeat, and repeated the ultrasound two weeks later to reassure her. Janelle had an uncomplicated pregnancy and went on to deliver a healthy baby boy.*

## Morning Sickness

Bringing a new life into the world is exciting, though it may not feel that way at first. For many women, one of the first signs that they are pregnant is feeling nauseated. It is not known what causes this, but it may be related to the rapidly rising levels of a hormone known as human chorionic gonadotropin (hCG). This is the same hormone detected in your urine by a pregnancy test and is responsible for maintaining the pregnancy once the corpus luteum regresses. In a normal pregnancy it doubles every forty-eight hours, and in twin pregnancies it can rise quicker and reach higher levels.

Morning sickness is, like its name, more pronounced in the morning, though it can occur at any time during the day. People who experience it often get some relief once they eat, and they do not have problems unless they have an empty stomach. Some women find it helpful to keep crackers next to their bed to eat before getting up in the morning. Eating several small meals throughout the day to keep your stomach from being empty can help. Many women who find it difficult to take their prenatal vitamin in the morning can take it at night or may substitute a children's chewable vitamin and folic acid for their prenatal vitamin. Most people who suffer from morning sickness will vomit on occasion. There are several medications that can help relieve these symptoms, including some over-the counter preparations that your doctor can recommend. Usually nausea and vomiting do not cause any serious problems and will subside as the first trimester ends.

Occasionally, what initially began as morning sickness can progress into a more serious condition known as *hyperemesis gravidarum*. This is severe nausea and vomiting where patients are unable to tolerate any food or liquids. This can lead to extreme dehydration and weight loss and requires hospitalization with intravenous (IV) fluid administration.

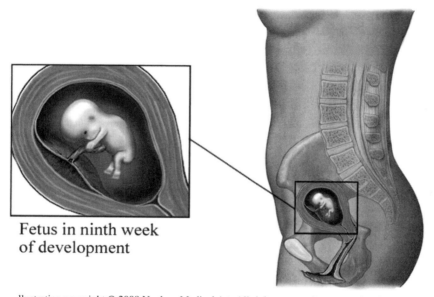

Fetus in ninth week of development

llustration copyright © 2008 Nucleus Medical Art. All rights reserved. www.nucleusinc.com.

## Body Changes

One other prominent symptom early in pregnancy is breast tenderness, which is caused by hormonal stimulation of breast tissue. The ducts in the breast are stimulated to grow in both quantity and size in preparation for milk production. The amount of fat in the breasts also builds up. By six weeks of pregnancy, your breasts may grow one whole cup size and may keep growing in size and weight during the first three months.[1] If you plan on nursing, it is a good idea to buy nursing bras when you are pregnant. Your breasts will usually stay larger throughout your pregnancy and while you are breast-feeding.

In addition to the increase in the amount of milk glands, there are other changes that occur in the breasts. Blood flow to the breasts increases, causing prominent bluish veins under the skin. The nipples become more pointed, and the areola (darkened skin around the nipple) darkens and gets larger in size. You may notice small, raised bumps on the areola region. These glands produce an oily substance responsible for keeping the nipple and areola soft.

Toward the end of the first trimester, your breasts may begin to leak fluid. This fluid is called *colostrum* and varies in color from clear to yellow. This is not an indication of whether or not you will be able to breast-feed, so do not worry if your breasts do not leak.

Another common symptom in the beginning of pregnancy is feeling bloated. As the uterus grows, there is less room in the abdominal cavity for the bowel, and pressure is exerted on the bladder. This leads to the need to urinate frequently. Some of the hormones produced during pregnancy slow the bowels down, leading to constipation and problems with gas. Drinking plenty of water, eating high-fiber foods, or taking a stool softener can all help relieve this discomfort.

Despite these changes, it is often hard to judge your pregnancy. At this point, you cannot feel the baby moving, and you may not be showing. Near the end of the first trimester, you will be able to hear your baby's heartbeat at your doctor's office, which will provide you with reassurance that everything is going well.

## Emotional Changes

In addition to undergoing physical changes, your emotions will fluctuate too. You may be happy that you are pregnant, yet still experience sadness or moodiness. Getting plenty of rest will help, as will reaching out to family and friends for support. It is very common, especially for first-time parents, to worry about their baby and whether or not they will be good parents.

Many parents expecting a child worry that something may be wrong with their baby. While there are some tests that help detect abnormalities, such as blood work or ultrasound, no test is perfectly reliable or accurate. Most newborns do not have any problems. You can do your best by eating well, taking a prenatal vitamin, exercising moderately, and avoiding things that could harm your baby, such as alcohol, drugs, or cigarette smoke.

Many women faced with childbirth fear the birthing process itself. Attending classes that prepare you for childbirth and discussing the birthing process with your doctor may help allay those fears. There are different options for pain control when you are in labor. There are also techniques that help you go through labor without medication, which will be discussed in detail in the chapter on labor.

Many couples worry about whether or not they will be good parents. Especially if you have never been around infants, it may help to take a class on baby care. You will learn how to feed, bathe, and dress your baby and change his or her diaper. If you have a friend with a baby, spend time with her or consider volunteering in your church nursery. The nurses and lactation consultants in the hospital are a wonderful resource for you to take advantage of before heading home with your baby. Your doctor or the baby's doctor may be able to recommend books for you to read to help prepare yourself for your new role as a parent.

It is a life-changing event to bring a child into the world. It is normal to feel that your life will never be the same, and that doesn't have to be a bad thing. You will experience a whole new world and a new perspective on life. It truly is a gift from God, and you will experience countless blessings.

## The Abnormal Pregnancy

Sometimes your fears may be justified, and there is a problem with your pregnancy. We sometimes have patients tell us they "don't feel pregnant" or they are having pain and bleeding. We take these concerns very seriously as they may be a sign of an abnormal pregnancy.

### Miscarriage

It is estimated that between 12 and 15 percent of all pregnancies end in miscarriage;[2] however, it is difficult to estimate because some will occur before a woman even knows she is pregnant. Most miscarriages occur during the first trimester and are caused by chromosome abnormalities. These are usually due to chance and not because of an underlying genetic disorder of the parents. Because the rate of chromosome abnormalities increases with a woman's age, the chance of having a miscarriage increases as you get older.

There are certain conditions that can predispose a woman to having a miscarriage. For example, women with uncontrolled diabetes are more likely to miscarry. Infections can lead to miscarriage if they involve the uterus. Structural abnormalities of the cervix or uterus can lead to pregnancy loss, usually in the second trimester. Sometimes problems with hormones can lead to miscarriage, in which case your doctor will usually provide a hormone supplement in future pregnancies.

The most common sign of a miscarriage is vaginal bleeding. Most women who experience vaginal bleeding or spotting during the first trimester of pregnancy go on to deliver healthy infants. However, anytime a woman experiences bleeding early in pregnancy, it is referred to as a threatened miscarriage. Other signs that you may be having a miscarriage are low backache and cramping along with bleeding. Occasionally, a woman will not have any symptoms of miscarriage, and it will be discovered at a routine doctor's visit that there is no heartbeat in the fetus.

If you think you may be having a miscarriage, it is important to contact your doctor. He or she will perform a pelvic exam and usually an ultrasound. If there is any tissue left in the uterus, or if you are experiencing heavy bleeding, your doctor may recommend a procedure called a *D&C*, which stands for "dilation and curettage." This is when your cervix is gently opened and the contents of the uterus removed. Sometimes medications are prescribed to aid in the process as well.

You should not worry that you did something to cause a miscarriage. There is no proof that engaging in everyday activities such as exercise, working, or sex causes miscarriage. Birth control pills do not cause a woman to miscarry. You should be able to get pregnant again and carry the baby without any problems following a miscarriage. In fact, you can ovulate as soon as two weeks following a miscarriage, so if you do not want to become pregnant, you should ask your doctor about birth control options.

Some women who have a miscarriage will have another the next time they become pregnant. If a woman has had two or more miscarriages, her doctor may do further testing. This usually includes a complete physical exam and blood work to detect chemical or hormonal abnormalities. The woman's and her husband's chromosomes may be checked to see if there are any abnormalities that could affect the development of a fetus. Diagnostic procedures such as hysterosalpingography (an X-ray of the uterus and tubes after dye is injected), hysteroscopy (viewing inside the uterus with a camera), laparoscopy (viewing inside the abdominal and pelvic cavity with a camera), ultrasound, or sonohysterogram (instilling saline into the uterus, then viewing with an ultrasound) may be performed to aid in evaluation. You may be referred to a specialist for further evaluation.

## Ectopic pregnancy

Sometimes the embryo can be trapped in the fallopian tube or float out into the abdominal cavity. When the developing pregnancy grows outside the uterus, it is known as an ectopic pregnancy. This occurs in about one of every fifty pregnancies and is almost always in the fallopian tube.[3]

As the fetus begins to grow, it can cause the fallopian tube to expand and can lead to rupture of the tube. This is a surgical emergency and can lead to hemorrhage and death if not treated. If the fetus is still small and the tube is not ruptured when an ectopic pregnancy is found, medication can be used to treat you by dissolving the pregnancy. There is no way to transplant the developing embryo from the tube into the uterus.

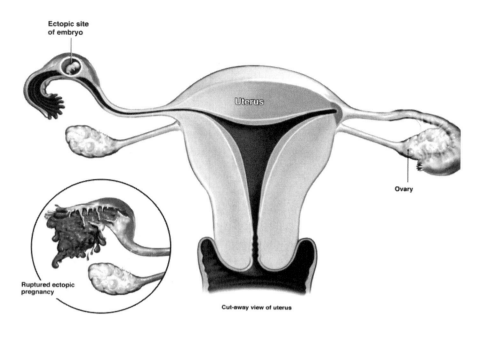

There are risk factors that can predispose a woman to higher chances of ectopic pregnancy. Prior ectopic pregnancy, previous tubal surgery such as tubal ligation, other abdominal or pelvic surgery (which can lead to scar tissue formation), pelvic inflammatory disease, sexually transmitted diseases, infertility, and endometriosis can all increase the chance of a woman developing an ectopic pregnancy. Symptoms of an ectopic pregnancy include vaginal bleeding, lower abdominal discomfort (often more pronounced on one side), weakness or dizziness (due to blood loss), and shoulder pain (due to the buildup of blood underneath the diaphragm).

If you think that you may have an ectopic pregnancy, you should contact your doctor immediately. Testing may take time and need to be repeated to establish a definitive diagnosis. If detected early, you may be able to undergo treatment with a medication called *methotrexate*. This is given as an injection and works on growing cells. During treatment, your doctor will monitor your pregnancy hormone levels. If they do not fall in response to the medication, a repeat dose or surgery may be indicated. Surgery may be needed if tubal rupture occurs.

If you do need surgery, it may be done as a laparoscopic procedure placing small incisions on the abdomen to place a camera and instruments through, or you may have an incision on your lower abdomen from exploratory surgery. Sometimes your tube can be opened and the pregnancy removed; however, if it is ruptured, the tube may be damaged and need to be removed.

If you have had an ectopic pregnancy, you are at increased risk in subsequent pregnancies. Let your doctor know as soon as you become pregnant so that he or she can make sure you do not have another ectopic pregnancy.

# Genetic Testing

Many couples worry that their child may be born with a problem, or birth defect. Birth defects are rare, occurring in only three to four per one hundred births.[5] Some birth defects are caused by environmental factors (exposure to a harmful agent), others are passed from the parents to the affected child, and some are a combination of the environment and inheritance.

Genetic disorders can be passed from parent to child in several different ways. Each parent gives their child twenty-three chromosomes, and each chromosome carries several genes. These chromosomes pair up in the child for a total of forty-six chromosomes, with one copy from the mother and one from the father. Some genes are dominant; some are recessive. If a gene is dominant, only one copy from one parent is needed for the disorder to manifest itself. If a gene is recessive, both copies (one from each parent) are needed for the problem to occur in the child. Some disorders are sex-linked and are carried on the X chromosome (one of the chromosomes responsible for sex determination). Female babies have two copies of the X chromosome (one from each parent), so if a disorder is recessive and carried on the X chromosome, the female is not usually affected if they have a normal X chromosome from the other parent. However, males have one X chromosome and one Y chromosome; therefore, if the X chromosome carries the disorder, there is not another normal X chromosome and the child will be affected.

Chromosome disorders can be caused by a damaged, missing, or extra chromosome and occur when the egg and sperm are joining together. One of the most common chromosome disorders is Down syndrome, which is caused by an extra copy of chromosome 21. These disorders occur more commonly as a woman ages. You may be at increased risk for having a child with a birth defect if you are thirty-five or older when your baby is due.

Other factors that increase your chance of having a baby with a birth defect are having a family or personal history of birth defects, having a previous child with a birth defect, taking certain medications during your pregnancy, and having diabetes that is not well controlled.

There are tests that can be performed to assess your risk for certain birth defects. Carrier testing is offered if either parent carries a genetic defect or if you are at an increased risk of carrying the genetic defect based on your history. Cystic fibrosis is a common genetic disorder that all women should be offered testing for. If a woman is found to be a carrier for a recessive disorder, her partner can be tested to see if the baby is at risk of being affected.

There are some screening tests offered to all women, regardless of risk factors. These tests indicate if a woman is at an increased risk of having a baby affected with a chromosome problem such as Down syndrome (trisomy 21) or trisomy 18, or with a structural abnormality such as a neural tube defect or an abdominal wall defect. Commonly referred to as triple screens or quad screens, these tests look at three or four substances in a woman's blood and, depending on which substance is elevated or decreased, can help estimate a woman's risk of having a baby affected with one of the disorders listed above. There are other things that can cause abnormal values. For example, a screen can only be done between fifteen and twenty weeks of pregnancy, and if a woman is further along than she thinks, the test may be falsely abnormal. Carrying more than one baby can also affect the results. Just because the test is abnormal does not mean there is something wrong with the baby.

There is a different screening test that is offered during the first trimester that can screen for Down syndrome (trisomy 21) or trisomy 18. It combines a blood test with an ultrasound to estimate a woman's risk of having a baby affected with one of those disorders. The blood test measures two markers in a woman's blood, and the ultrasound is used to measure the thickness on the back of the baby's neck (nuchal translucency). Other tests can then be done to confirm the diagnosis.

One diagnostic test that can be performed in the first trimester is chorionic villus sampling. This is usually done between ten and twelve weeks and is similar to an amniocentesis. A small tube or needle is passed through the vagina and cervix or the abdomen to obtain tissue from the placenta for culture. This tissue can be tested for chromosomal disorders or other defects. There is less than 1 percent chance of miscarriage following this procedure.[6]

As a Christian, you may struggle with the thoughts of pursuing these tests. A child is truly a gift from God, and you may feel that you should accept whatever gift is given to you. While that may be true, some people find that it is easier to prepare for how their life will be changed if they are caring for a child with special needs. As a Christian, you can still accept God's gift if deciding to undergo one of the tests mentioned above.

The first trimester of pregnancy can be both exciting and intimidating. You may be overjoyed with the thought of bringing a child into your world, but overwhelmed with nausea and sickness. You may also be excited about having a baby, but worried that something may be wrong with him or her. Rest assured that God will give you the strength you need to make it through this time, and He has prepared a special life for you to care for.

# Chapter 19

# THE SECOND TRIMESTER

THE SECOND TRIMESTER IS USUALLY THE MOST ENJOYABLE TIME DURING A pregnancy. By the start of the second trimester, most of the time morning sickness resolves. This is also when you will begin to look pregnant, or to "show." And best of all, you now can feel your baby move. If this is your first pregnancy, you may make it almost halfway through your pregnancy before you feel your baby move. Usually you will feel the first little flutters around eighteen weeks. At first, the movements you feel may seem like trapped gas, or butterflies in your stomach. If you have been pregnant before, you may feel movement a little earlier, around sixteen weeks. However, do not worry if you do not feel movement until twenty weeks.

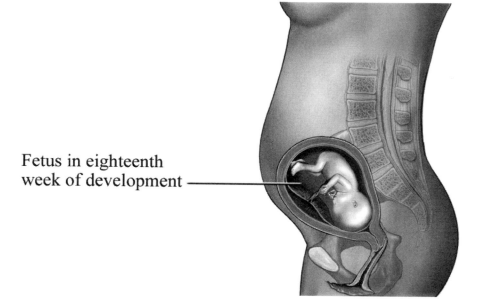

Fetus in eighteenth week of development

As your baby grows, the movements will become more distinct. By the time you reach your third trimester, you may be able to identify specific body parts protruding under your skin.

# Genetic Testing

As discussed in the previous chapter, maternal serum screening is offered in the second trimester. This is a blood test that is done between fifteen and twenty weeks to screen for neural tube defects, abdominal wall defects, trisomy 18, and Down syndrome (trisomy 21). It is commonly referred to as the quad screen because it looks at the following four substances in a woman's blood to help estimate her risk of carrying a fetus with one of the above disorders:

1. Estriol—a hormone similar to estrogen, found in the mom, baby, and placenta
2. Human chorionic gonadotropin (hCG)—a hormone made by the placenta responsible for maintaining the pregnancy
3. Alpha-fetoprotein (AFP)—made by the fetus but passed into the maternal bloodstream in small amounts
4. Inhibin A—a hormone produced by the placenta

| Birth Defect | Estriol | hCG | Inhibin A | AFP |
|---|---|---|---|---|
| Neural tube defect or abdominal wall defect | Normal | Normal | Normal | High |
| Down syndrome | Low | High | High | Low |
| Trisomy 18 | Low | Low | Normal | Low |

If the screening test is positive, indicating an increased risk of having a baby affected with one of the above disorders, a diagnostic test can be performed.[1]

# Ultrasound

A detailed ultrasound exam may also be performed if genetic screening indicates that there may be an abnormality. This is usually performed after eighteen weeks and may be done by a specialist. Other indications for a detailed ultrasound include a family history of birth defects, or an abnormality on a basic ultrasound.

Most doctors will perform a basic ultrasound between eighteen and twenty weeks to evaluate the fetal position, size and number, placental location, amniotic fluid volume, heart rate, and anatomy. This is when you can learn the sex of your baby, if you desire. Most of the time a transabdominal ultrasound is performed, with the probe of the ultrasound placed on the abdomen. However, in special situations such as evaluating the cervix or placenta, and during the first trimester, a transvaginal ultrasound may be performed.

There are now centers offering keepsake ultrasound videos and pictures using the new 3-D and 4-D technology. This offers a "lifelike" look at your baby inside the womb. These can be performed in the second trimester but are normally done in the third. Usually these are not performed at your doctor's office and require that your doctor give permission for this to be done. Some concerns exist about repeated exposure to ultrasound, though it seems to be safe. Also, the technicians performing these exams are not trained to interpret the images and may not detect abnormalities with the fetus. It is best to check with your doctor before having this done.

# Medical Problems That Complicate Pregnancy

Some women will bring into their pregnancies various health issues that can make their pregnancy "high risk." By knowing about these conditions ahead of time, your obstetrician can take special care to evaluate you and your fetus throughout the pregnancy. Sometimes we will get assistance from a pregnancy expert called a maternal-fetal medicine specialist. These men and women have done extra training to evaluate and manage those pregnancies that are high risk. They typically do not deliver babies but act as consultants during the second half of pregnancy. Some of the medical conditions that are considered high risk are listed below.

### High blood pressure

High blood pressure can be present before pregnancy and, if not controlled, can lead to heart failure or strokes. It can also affect the growth of the baby. Some of the medications prescribed for blood pressure control are contra-indicated during pregnancy, so it is important to consult your doctor so your medication can be switched if necessary. Your doctor will monitor you closely during your pregnancy because your blood pressure can fluctuate. Your blood pressure will be checked at each visit and your abdomen will be measured to ensure that your baby is growing appropriately. Nutrients and oxygen flow from the mother into the placenta and pass through the umbilical cord to the baby. Having uncontrolled high blood pressure can increase resistance to blood flow through the placenta and can deprive the growing baby of nutrients and oxygen. If your doctor suspects your baby is not growing adequately, he or she may perform an ultrasound to evaluate for possible growth restriction.

### Diabetes

Diabetes can be present before pregnancy or can develop as a result of it (gestational diabetes). If you have diabetes before you get pregnant, it is best to have it well controlled. Having diabetes can increase your risk of miscarriage and of having a baby with a birth defect. The most common birth defects among diabetics are heart defects, kidney defects, and spinal abnormalities. They are more likely to occur when the blood sugar is too high and the disease is not under good control. Other problems that are more common in pregnancies complicated by diabetes are macrosomia (an abnormally large baby), stillbirth, and respiratory distress syndrome (due to delayed lung maturity).

Risk factors for developing gestational diabetes include the following: age (twenty-five years or older), being overweight, having a family history of diabetes or personal history of gestational diabetes, or being an ethnicity that has a high rate of diabetes (Hispanic, Native American, or Asian). You may be screened for diabetes if you have one of the above risk factors, or your doctor may screen all of his/her patients (universal screening).

The screening test that is used is a one-hour glucose challenge test. It is performed at the end of the second trimester, between twenty-four and twenty-eight weeks. It consists of drinking a sugary liquid and then having your blood sugar drawn exactly one hour afterward. If the screening test comes back abnormally high, your doctor will then order a three-hour glucose tolerance test. You will need to be fasting for this test and will have four blood samples drawn—before drinking the liquid, after the first hour, after the second hour, and after the third hour following drinking it. The three-hour test will tell your doctor if in fact you do have gestational diabetes.

Having gestational diabetes or diabetes present prior to pregnancy puts you at risk for complications during pregnancy and delivery. Women with diabetes have to follow a special diet that may need adjustments during pregnancy. It is also important to exercise, as that will help keep blood glucose levels down. Medications such as insulin shots may be prescribed to help regulate blood sugar levels and may need to be adjusted from time to time. Blood glucose levels need to be monitored closely and kept within a desired range. The risk of complications is decreased with good blood sugar control.

## Asthma

Asthma is another common medical condition that can be affected during pregnancy. There are many changes to the lungs during pregnancy, and some people experience worsening of their asthma. Most medications are safe to take during pregnancy, but you should discuss your treatment regimen with your doctor. You may need additional medication if you notice that you are using your inhaler more frequently. If asthma is not controlled, it can deprive the baby of oxygen. It is important to get regular prenatal care so that your health and the baby's health can be monitored.

## Heart disease

Heart disease is less common, but it can affect 1 to 4 percent of pregnant women.[2] Heart problems such as congenital heart disease (problem that you were born with), rheumatic heart disease (such as mitral valve prolapse), previous heart surgery, or heart attack all require special care during pregnancy. Specific risks during pregnancy and delivery depend on the severity of the problem. It is important to discuss these risks with your doctor before you get pregnant, if possible. Usually your doctor will refer you to a high-risk specialist (maternal-fetal medicine doctor) and will also want you to see a cardiologist.

Blood volume increases 40 to 50 percent during pregnancy; therefore, your heart has to work harder. There is also an increased risk of developing blood clots during pregnancy. If you have a condition that predisposes you to developing a blood clot or having a stroke, you may need to be placed on a blood thinner. During labor there is additional stress on the heart, so your doctor may recommend shortening the amount of time you push by using a vacuum device or forceps to help deliver the baby.

## Seizure disorders

Some women have epilepsy or seizures prior to pregnancy. Most of these women will have healthy babies, but they are at risk for having a baby affected with a birth defect. Cleft lip and palate, heart defects, and neural tube defects are all more common in women with a seizure disorder. These may be caused by some of the medications used to prevent seizures. Some medicines lower the amount of folic acid, which can lead to neural tube defects. If you plan on getting pregnant, it is important to take folic acid supplements. Do not stop your anticonvulsant medication if you get pregnant without talking to your doctor, because having a seizure can harm your baby.

## Thyroid disorders

Thyroid disorders are common among women of reproductive age. If the thyroid is overactive (hyperthyroidism) or underactive (hypothyroidism), it can lead to problems during pregnancy. Some of the problems in babies born to women with uncontrolled hypothyroidism are growth restriction (smaller than normal baby), preterm delivery, and cretinism (a form of mental retardation). These women are more likely to develop preeclampsia and have placental abruptions. Babies born to women with uncontrolled hyperthyroidism also are more likely to have growth restriction and preterm births. Women with uncontrolled hyperthyroidism may suffer from a condition known as *thyroid storm*, which is a medical emergency that can lead to heart failure or coma if not treated.

Thyroid disorders can usually be controlled with medication. Thyroid hormone levels will be monitored by your doctor and your medication will be adjusted, if necessary. The only medication that is contraindicated during pregnancy is radioactive iodine because it can affect the baby's thyroid also, causing hypothyroidism.

# Chapter 20

# THE THIRD TRIMESTER

*Karen's first pregnancy was uncomplicated, and she delivered a full-term, healthy baby girl. When she came into our office during the twenty-eighth week of her second pregnancy, it had been uncomplicated up to this point. She stated she was experiencing some vaginal discharge and lower abdominal cramping. Upon examining her, we discovered her cervix was dilated. We sent Karen to labor and delivery for treatment of premature labor. But despite aggressive efforts to stop her labor, she delivered her son later that evening. Immediately, he was admitted to the intensive care nursery and placed on a breathing machine. Over the next month, he was weaned from the machine and then discharged the following month. Today he is a healthy toddler and does not have any problems despite these complications during her pregnancy.*

## What's Happening?

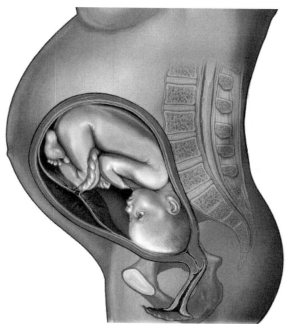

The third trimester is an exciting time as the fetal movement is a lot stronger and you can see the movements through your skin. Your husband can also begin to feel the baby, which makes him more a part of this process. Up until now, he has had to take your word for things and watch your body change from a distance. But now he can experience some of the things you do when he feels the baby kick through your skin.

This trimester is also the time of rapid fetal growth. From about the seventh to ninth months, the baby doubles in size. Just when you think you can't possibly hold any more or stretch any further, he/she sprints up the growth chart to prove you wrong.

The rapid growth may bring some unpleasant side effects to your skin, such as stretch marks. These are actually tears in your skin that resemble scars and are bright pink. Over time, these fade to a more natural skin tone and shrink in length and width.

Some people recommend cocoa butter or other creams to prevent stretch marks. The truth is, there is no way to prevent them. You inherit the condition from your mother. Since they come from the inside out, putting creams on the surface doesn't do much good except make your skin feel better. Certain races and nationalities get stretch marks more than others. Some of the over-the-counter scar therapy treatments are helpful after the birth to lessen the appearance of stretch marks.

Most women will also notice a brown line begin to form in the middle of their abdomen that starts at the bottom and progressively rises higher as the pregnancy goes along. This is called the *linea nigra* and is a normal sign of pregnancy.

Hands and feet may begin to swell in the late third trimester. Some of this is from the weight of the baby pressing on your lower pelvic blood vessels. The blood pumps down the legs, but it gets harder to get it back up. This causes the blood vessel to "leak" fluid into the surrounding tissues. Salt can also leak out, causing water to follow it. This is one reason women swell. It may be from obvious things like eating Chinese food or from more subtle things like drinking too many sodas. If you work outside the home or are on your feet a lot, swelling will almost surely happen. We only get concerned about it if it is accompanied by high blood pressure. If you have sudden swelling, you may be asked to come to the office to check your blood pressure. We will discuss this later in this chapter.

As the third trimester comes to an end, you will notice more contractions occurring, especially in the evening. Some may be mild tightening only, and some may be stronger, the so-called Braxton-Hicks contractions.

# Braxton-Hicks Contractions

These contractions are named after an English doctor, John Braxton Hicks, who first described them in 1872. They are usually felt during the third trimester, but many women who have already had a baby can feel them in the second trimester. Typically, they are relatively painless and are usually felt as a tightening or hardness in the abdomen. However, sometimes they are painful, making it difficult to tell them apart from true labor contractions.

Braxton-Hicks contractions are also known as false labor pains, because they do not usually cause the cervix to dilate much. They do get your body ready for labor and can soften and open your cervix a little. They usually become more frequent the closer you get to your due date and are more common following sexual intercourse, physical activity, and in the evening. They can also occur when a woman is dehydrated, so it is important to drink plenty of fluids. If you are having Braxton-Hicks contractions prior to thirty-seven weeks, it is important to monitor them. If you have more than four or five in an hour, you should call your doctor.

## WHEN TO STOP WORKING

If you are one of the many women who work outside of the home, you may wonder when would be a good time to stop working during your pregnancy. At your initial visit, you should discuss the type of work you do, so that your doctor can recommend any restrictions that may be necessary during your pregnancy. If you develop any complications during your pregnancy, such as preterm labor or high blood pressure, your doctor may put you on bed rest. Most women with uncomplicated pregnancies continue working until they are too uncomfortable to continue. For some, this is right up to the time they go into labor. It is important to communicate with your doctor any concerns you have about working and decide together when would be a good time to stop.

# Fetal Monitoring

There are special circumstances during pregnancy that require close monitoring of the fetus during the third trimester. Monitoring is done to evaluate the conditions inside the uterus to make sure the baby is getting the oxygen and nutrients he or she needs. The simplest test to perform is to note your baby's movements throughout the day. This is called *fetal kick counts*, and your doctor may suggest that you begin doing this in the third trimester. Normally, your baby should move about ten times in two hours; however, your baby may move more than that. If you feel like there is a decrease in normal movements for your baby, you should notify your doctor.

There are other ways to monitor the fetus. One is called a *nonstress test*. During this test, two straps are wrapped around your abdomen to hold monitors in place. One monitor tracks the fetal heart rate and the other monitors the contraction pattern. A nonstress test is performed for up to forty-five minutes, until there are two increases in the fetal heart rate of at least fifteen beats per minute for fifteen seconds (an acceleration). These two increases need to occur within a twenty-minute time period for the test to be deemed reactive. Sometimes it is more helpful to see what happens when the fetus is stressed, so your doctor may order a contraction stress test. During this test, contractions are stimulated until three occur in a ten-minute window. The fetal heart rate is observed for accelerations and decelerations (a drop in the heart rate below the baseline).

Another way to evaluate fetal well-being is with ultrasound. Your doctor may perform an ultrasound to assess the baby's growth and movements. The amount of amniotic fluid is also measured, as it can help determine if the placenta is working properly. The placenta is also examined during some ultrasound exams to see if it appears healthy. A biophysical profile is a test performed with ultrasound that looks at the volume of amniotic fluid, the baby's gross body movements, as well as fine movements, and the baby's breathing. Often, a nonstress test is also performed, which provides reassurance that the intrauterine environment is healthy for the fetus.

These tests are sometimes performed routinely in high-risk pregnancies complicated by high blood pressure, diabetes, twins, or other problems. They can also be performed if there is a concern something could be wrong; for example, if you do not feel your baby moving. Monitoring is also performed during labor, which we will discuss in the next chapter.

## Gestational Diabetes

When diabetes occurs only during pregnancy, it is called gestational diabetes. Usually, it will resolve after delivery, but it does put you at risk for developing diabetes later in life. If you are diagnosed with gestational diabetes, you will be instructed on how and when to check your blood sugar. You will be placed on a special diet. Many times, gestational diabetes can be controlled with diet and exercise. If your blood sugar measurements are still high, your doctor may prescribe either a medication or insulin shots to control it.

You will need to be seen more often during the third trimester if you have diabetes. Your doctor will perform nonstress tests, which monitor the baby's heart rate to determine fetal well-being. He or she may also perform ultrasound exams to monitor the baby's growth. If your blood sugars are not well controlled, your baby can grow very large (a condition known as *macrosomia*). Babies with macrosomia often have problems at birth with their blood sugar and may have jaundice and difficulty breathing. Babies born to mothers with diabetes often have shoulders and trunks that are larger than their head. This increases the risk of shoulder dystocia during delivery. Shoulder dystocia is when, after delivery of the head, the shoulder gets stuck in the birth canal. This can be relieved by special maneuvers, or your doctor may perform a cesarean if he or she feels the baby is at risk for this.

If your baby needs to be delivered early due to diabetes, you may need to undergo an amniocentesis. The fluid can be tested for a substance that indicates if the baby's lungs are mature. A couple of months after delivery, you should be retested for diabetes because having gestational diabetes increases the chance that you will develop diabetes later in life.

## Pregnancy Hypertension/Toxemia

When hypertension, or high blood pressure, develops only during the second half of pregnancy, it is termed gestational hypertension, or pregnancy-induced hypertension. This condition usually resolves after the baby is born. If you develop gestational hypertension, you may need to be seen more often to have your blood pressure checked and to be monitored for signs of preeclampsia.

Preeclampsia, also known as toxemia, occurs when high blood pressure leads to stress on the kidneys, causing protein to leak into the urine. It can affect all organs of the body and, in its most severe form, lead to seizures (eclampsia). Symptoms of preeclampsia include headaches, visual changes such as blurry vision or seeing spots, abdominal pain, and edema (swelling of the hands and face). It is not clear why some women develop preeclampsia, but there are factors that can increase your risk. If this is your first pregnancy, or if you have had preeclampsia in a previous pregnancy, you are at risk. Women who are very young (in their teens) or older (over age thirty-five) are at risk. Other factors that predispose you to developing preeclampsia are having gestational or chronic hypertension, having other medical problems such as diabetes, being overweight or obese, and having multiple babies (such as twins).

If you develop preeclampsia, your doctor will monitor your blood pressure closely. Your baby will be monitored for signs of distress and poor growth. If you have lab work or symptoms indicating that your organs or your baby are affected, you may undergo induction of labor. Delivery is the only cure for preeclampsia and may be done before you are full term. Medications are sometimes given to lower blood pressure and to prevent seizures.

# Premature Labor and Delivery

Babies born before the thirty-seventh week of gestation are premature, or preterm. Twelve percent of all babies born each year are preterm.[1] Premature babies can suffer a variety of complications, which are more severe the earlier they are born. They may suffer problems requiring prolonged hospitalization following birth and may have problems later in life with development, hearing, and vision.

Sometimes delivery is a result of premature labor or preterm rupture of membranes; other times it is necessary to deliver a baby early due to a problem in the mother or fetus. Most of the time, preterm labor occurs without warning. There are some risk factors that have been associated with it:

- History of preterm labor in a previous pregnancy
- Multiple gestation (twins, triplets, etc.)
- Infection
- High blood pressure
- Vaginal bleeding during pregnancy
- Very young (younger than seventeen) or older (over age thirty-five)

Symptoms of preterm labor include pressure in the lower abdomen or low back pain, vaginal bleeding, increased discharge or leaking amniotic fluid, and contractions. If you think you may be having contractions, it is important to monitor how frequent they occur. If you feel your abdomen tighten for about forty-five seconds and then relax, and that happens more than four or five times in an hour, call your doctor. He or she will want you to come in so that your cervix can be checked to see if it has dilated (started to open) or effaced (thinned out). Your doctor may also perform other tests, including monitoring the baby's heart rate and the uterine contractions. An ultrasound exam may be performed to evaluate the baby's weight and to see if the cervix has shortened. A test called *fetal fibronectin* can help predict whether or not delivery may occur. If delivery is likely but not imminent, your doctor may recommend a steroid shot to help mature the baby's lungs. Steroids help reduce the likelihood of developing respiratory distress syndrome when given between twenty-four and thirty-four weeks.

If you go into labor and there are no signs that the baby is in distress, your doctor may prescribe medication to stop your labor. These can be given in a pill form, as an injection, or as an intravenous infusion. Some side effects include shortness of breath, dizziness, and racing pulse. You may also be hospitalized or placed on bed rest. Progesterone injections are sometimes given to help prevent preterm birth.

Sometimes it is necessary for your baby to be delivered prematurely. If there is a complication to your pregnancy such as high blood pressure or infection, your doctor may recommend delivery. The risk of delivering is carefully weighed against the risk of continuing the pregnancy. Sometimes tests are done to see if the baby is ready to be delivered. An amniocentesis can be performed to evaluate the baby's lung maturity. After delivery, your baby may have to stay in the hospital after you are discharged. The length of the baby's stay depends on how premature he or she is. Babies born after thirty-two weeks usually do not have long-term complications, whereas babies under twenty-four weeks rarely survive.

If your water breaks before thirty-seven weeks, it is termed preterm premature rupture of membranes. If there is no sign of infection or compromise of the baby, attempts are made to prolong the pregnancy. Most of the time, you will be hospitalized, placed on bed rest, and given antibiotics to help decrease the chance of infection. As mentioned earlier, steroid shots are also given before thirty-four weeks to help mature the baby's lungs.

## Breech Babies

Most of the time, babies assume the head-down position midway through the third trimester if they haven't already. If not, the baby is said to be in the breech position, either with the buttocks or feet positioned to come first through the birth canal. About 3 percent of full-term births will be complicated by breech presentation.[2] Some of the risk factors for breech presentation include having a previous pregnancy that was breech, being pregnant with more than one baby, preterm birth, having an abnormal amount of amniotic fluid (either too much or too little), and placenta previa. Sometimes babies are breech because of a birth defect that prevents them from going to the head-down position. Some are breech because the shape of the woman's uterus will not allow them to turn.

If your baby is still breech around thirty-six weeks, your doctor may offer to perform a procedure called *external cephalic version*. This is where your doctor turns the baby by placing his or her hands on your abdomen and, with gentle pressure, guides the buttocks up while pushing the head down. Usually this is not painful, though you may feel some discomfort during the procedure. This is successful about 50 percent of the time and will often allow a vaginal delivery to occur. Occasionally, a complication can arise during a version. Sometimes the baby does not tolerate it very well, and there is a drop in the fetal heart rate. The placenta could separate from the uterus, causing a placental abruption. It could also cause you to go into labor or cause your water to break.

If you elect not to have a version, or if it is unsuccessful, your doctor will likely recommend a cesarean delivery. This is because it is not safe to deliver a breech baby vaginally. The head, or vertex, is usually the largest part of the infant and could potentially get trapped in the birth canal after delivery of the body. Sometimes the umbilical cord comes out before the baby, and compression of it cuts off the blood supply to the baby. However, there are some special circumstances where a vaginal delivery is an option. If a woman is pregnant with twins and the first twin presents with its head down, the second twin can usually be delivered from the breech position if it is not significantly larger than the first twin.

## Twins

Twins occur when a woman is pregnant with two babies. Approximately one out of every thirty-two births in the United States are twins.[3] Twins can result from a single egg dividing and becoming two fetuses (identical twins) or, more commonly, as a result of two separate eggs being fertilized by two sperm (fraternal twins). There is an increased rate of twinning as well as other multiple pregnancies (triplets, quadruplets) because more and more women are undergoing fertility treatments, which cause multiple eggs to be produced at one time. Other risk factors for having a multiple pregnancy are family history of twins and being over the age of thirty-five.

Most of the time, twins are detected on an ultrasound exam. There are some signs that may indicate you are pregnant with twins, such as extreme nausea and vomiting during the first trimester or feeling more fetal movement in the second trimester. Your doctor may notice that your uterus is larger than expected or may hear more than one heartbeat.

A twin pregnancy is considered high risk because of the special needs of the mom and developing babies, and the increased risk for complications. Instead of needing an additional three hundred calories per day to support a single pregnancy, a woman carrying twins needs an additional five hundred calories. She should gain fifty to sixty pounds, which is double what someone carrying one baby should gain. Twin pregnancies are at an increased risk for preterm labor and delivery, high blood pressure, anemia, preterm rupture of membranes, and problems with growth. Your doctor will monitor you closely if you are pregnant with twins. An ultrasound will be done each month to evaluate growth, and your doctor visits will be more frequent, usually weekly beginning in the third trimester.

There are special considerations with delivery of twins. Depending on the position of the babies, a cesarean delivery may be necessary. Twin vaginal deliveries are performed in the operating room in the event an emergent cesarean is necessary. Two obstetricians are present; one performs the delivery, and the other monitors the other baby's heart rate and position with the ultrasound. There are usually two teams from the intensive care nursery, one for each baby. Most twins are born by thirty-seven weeks, and many have problems with prematurity.

# Chapter 21

# CHILDBIRTH

YOU MAY WONDER IF YOU WILL KNOW WHEN YOU ARE IN LABOR. SOMETIMES women think they are in labor, but they are not. We often tell our patients not to worry—when you are in labor you will know. Very few women who are in labor don't know it. You may wonder when it will happen and how.

I (EAK) spent the last few weeks of my pregnancy wondering when it would happen to me—and I am an obstetrician! Would my water break in the middle of my office, or would I start contracting? Would I be able to handle the pain, or would I go to the hospital before it was time?

Your doctor can provide you with the reassurance that together you can determine when labor has begun and when you should go to the hospital.

As you get closer to your due date, it is a good idea to prepare for your delivery. Install the baby's car seat and make sure you know how to use it. You should know how to get to the hospital and have an alternate route in case there are any delays. Keep your car's gas tank full. Arrange for child care or pet care, if needed. Try to preregister at the hospital to avoid filling out paperwork when you arrive in labor. You will also want to talk with your doctor about who can be with you in the delivery room and if cameras or videotapes are allowed.

Pack your bag a few weeks before your due date. Include items in your bag such as:

- Bathrobe
- Two to three nightgowns
- Nursing bras and panties
- Slippers
- Socks
- Toiletries, including a toothbrush, toothpaste, and comb/brush
- Glasses if you wear them or contacts (you may not be able to wear your contacts)
- Blankets for the baby and an outfit for the baby to wear home
- Comfortable clothes for you to wear home

Your husband may want to bring:
- Camera, film, and batteries
- Cell phone and phone numbers of friends and family
- Books or magazines

# Is This the Real Thing?

You may have experienced what you thought were contractions during your pregnancy, but they were not true labor contractions. These are Braxton-Hicks contractions, which we discussed in the previous chapter. Unlike real labor contractions, Braxton-Hicks contractions stop when you walk, rest, or change positions.

Real labor contractions are usually painful and occur in a regular pattern. Your abdomen will tighten all over for about thirty to forty-five seconds during the contraction. The pain may begin in your back or may radiate into your pelvis. Usually the contractions will become closer together and stronger as labor progresses. When you begin to have contractions, you will want to monitor the time from the start of one contraction to the start of the next. If they keep coming no matter what you do and increase in intensity, it is likely that you are in labor. Discuss with your doctor when you should call or go to the hospital if you think you may be in labor. You should also call if your baby is not moving as well as it normally does.

Sometimes you may think you are in labor, but it turns out to be a false alarm. Your doctor may monitor you for a couple of hours before determining if you are truly in labor or not. Early labor is the time period that it takes your cervix to dilate up to 4 centimeters. This can take a few hours or even a day or more. During this time you may want to walk around, take a shower, try to relax, or even sleep, if you can. Once you are in active labor (when your cervix goes from 4 to 10 centimeters), your contractions will get stronger and your water may even break. You may experience vaginal bleeding as your cervix dilates. Your doctor will admit you to the hospital once you are in active labor.

# Lamaze and Bradley Methods

One of the biggest fears most pregnant women have is experiencing the pain of labor and how they will deal with it. There are many techniques as well as options for pain control during labor. You may want to develop a birth plan that describes your wishes for what is done when you are in labor. This will help you communicate your wishes with your doctor and the labor and delivery nurses. During the 1940s, on opposite sides of the Atlantic, two obstetricians developed labor methods—the Lamaze method and the Bradley method—that would be used for decades to come.

Developed by French obstetrician Ferdinand Lamaze, the Lamaze method uses alternatives to medication to help control the pain of labor. These techniques initially focused on breathing, but now this method is an expanded philosophy of increasing a woman's confidence in her ability to give birth. Lamaze classes teach women "how to respond to pain in ways that both facilitate labor and increase comfort." You do not have to go through labor without pain medication if you participate in Lamaze. In fact, the classes describe your options and leave you with the ability to make an informed decision regarding pain medication and other interventions.

Typically, Lamaze classes have at least twelve hours of instruction and include the following information:

- Using videos of live births to review normal labor and the delivery process
- How to be active and informed during the childbirth process and how to communicate with your health-care team so that your needs are met
- Breathing techniques
- Other techniques to relax and manage pain such as walking, different positions, and massage
- Tips for partners to be supportive and encouraging
- The value of one-on-one professional support during labor
- Complications that can occur during labor and delivery and how they may be managed by your doctor
- Options for pain management, including epidural anesthesia
- Your first interactions with your baby
- Breast-feeding[1]

(i) Most hospitals offer classes or you can find one close to you by contacting Lamaze International at www.lamaze.org.

The Bradley Method, developed by American obstetrician Dr. Robert Bradley, focuses on childbirth as a natural process for women to embrace. With proper preparation, 90 percent of women who deliver vaginally are able to do so without medication. It is a twelve-week program that focuses on mental, physical, and emotional preparation for pregnancy, childbirth, and the post-partum period. The classes also educate partners to be supportive coaches.

The classes address the following topics:

- Nutrition and its impact on a growing fetus
- Exercise and its importance during pregnancy
- Dealing with common pregnancy symptoms
- Relaxation techniques during labor and birth, helping you to focus on and manage your pain
- Helping your partner gain skills to be an active participant and effective coach during the labor process
- The stages of labor and how to cope with each one
- Avoiding unnecessary medical interventions
- Reducing your risk for cesarean delivery, and what to do if it is medically necessary
- Making your birth plan and communicating with your medical team
- Breast-feeding[2]

(i) To find classes in your area, call the American Academy of Husband-Coached Childbirth at (818) 788-6662 or (800) 4-A-BIRTH.

You may also want a trained attendant to assist during your childbirth. Some people will hire a doula for this purpose, while others choose to have a nurse-midwife provide them with care and coaching. A doula is a nonmedical assistant who provides emotional support during labor and delivery. They can offer suggestions on providing comfort during labor, but they do not have any medical knowledge of the process and are not there to deliver the baby. A nurse-midwife can provide prenatal care as well as care during labor and delivery of the baby. This is sometimes done under supervision of a physician in a hospital setting or birthing center, but it may also be done in your home.

Having a child at home or in a birthing center may provide you with a more natural feel to the birthing process. Most women will do just fine under these circumstances. However, when an emergency arises or a problem surfaces requiring the training of a physician, it is comforting to be in a hospital setting. Many hospitals are catering to women in this important phase in their life and are providing them with the most comfortable and natural experience possible.

# Fetal Monitoring During Labor

Since most women will choose to deliver in a hospital setting, and since that is the setting in which we practice, we will talk about what will happen when you get to the hospital. When you are admitted to labor and delivery, one of the first things your nurse will do is monitor your baby. This can be done by auscultation, using a handheld Doppler ultrasound to measure the fetal heart rate intermittently. It can also be done continuously by hooking your baby up to an electronic fetal monitor. This monitor is placed around your abdomen, and the fetal heart rate traces on paper or a computer screen.

A normal fetal heart rate ranges anywhere from 120 to 160 beats per minute. It is also normal for the rate to change from beat to beat. This is called variability and provides reassurance that the baby is doing well. The average heart rate is termed the baseline. Increases from the baseline are called accelerations and are normal and reassuring. Decelerations are decreases from the baseline and can be concerning if they occur repeatedly during labor.

It is important to know what is happening to the fetal heart rate during and following your contractions. For that reason, your nurse either will palpate your abdomen to determine when contractions occur, or another monitor will be placed around your abdomen to trace the contraction pattern. If your nurse or doctor has any concerns about the baby's heartbeat, he or she may take steps to help it improve. Things that can sometimes help include changing your position, giving you oxygen to breathe through a mask, giving you IV fluids, stopping medication that is making you contract or giving you a medication to stop contractions, or putting extra fluid up around the baby.

Sometimes it is difficult to trace the fetal heart rate due to the baby's position or movement. In these cases, your doctor may want to place an internal monitor. This can only be done if the bag of water is broken, as the monitor is attached to the baby's scalp. It is unlikely that this will hurt your baby, and it can provide a more accurate tracing of the fetal heart rate. An internal monitor can also be used to monitor contractions. Unlike an external monitor, this intrauterine pressure catheter can measure the strength of your contractions, providing more information to your doctor.

# Pain Relief: Drugs and Epidurals

The amount of pain a woman feels during labor varies, because each person perceives pain differently. Pain can be stronger if the baby is large or is in a certain position. Pain is also usually greater if your water is broken or if your contractions are strong. Some women are able to manage their pain with the breathing and relaxation techniques they learned in classes. Sometimes the pain is difficult to manage through breathing techniques alone. There are other options for pain management, including medications and epidural anesthesia.

Pain medications are usually given through an IV (intravenous line) during labor. The medications vary based on your doctor's preference but commonly consist of a narcotic, and sometimes an antiemetic (antinausea) medication is given along with it. The concern with these medications is that they can pass through your bloodstream into the baby's, so you can only receive limited doses. They cannot be given too close to the time the baby is delivered because they can suppress the newborn's reflexes and drive to breathe.

Local anesthetics are numbing medications that can be given before or after delivery. Local anesthesia can be injected next to a nerve that supplies the pelvic area with sensation in order to take away pain when the baby passes through the birth canal. An episiotomy is a cut made to widen the birth canal to assist with delivery. Local anesthesia can be used if an episiotomy needs to be performed or if a laceration needs to be repaired with stitches.

An epidural is a popular form of pain management during labor and delivery. This consists of a catheter placed by an anesthesiologist through the bones of your spine into a space next to the spinal cord. Medication can then be injected into, or continuously infused through, the catheter while you are in labor. The low doses of medication used do not usually cause problems for the baby. There are some complications that can occur with epidurals, however. An epidural can cause your blood pressure to decrease. To help counteract this, you will be given IV fluids prior to the placement of your epidural. Sometimes you can get what is called a *spinal headache* if the covering of the spinal cord is pierced with the needle. This headache may last several days and is usually relieved by lying down. Let your doctor know if you experience this because a procedure called a blood patch can help this headache go away.

Many people worry that getting an epidural will slow their labor down. This has been studied thoroughly, and it does not seem to cause this problem. Your doctor may recommend that you wait until you are in active labor or are dilated at least 4 centimeters because latent, or early, labor can take awhile. The degree of numbness depends on the individual and the amount and type of medication used. Some women will still be able to feel their contractions and vaginal examinations, while others will be so numb it is difficult for them to push. A catheter will be placed in your bladder since you will be numb and unable to sense the urge to void. Your anesthesiologist can adjust the degree of numbness in order to make you as comfortable as possible.

You should not worry that by using pain medication or getting an epidural your experience will be unnatural. It takes strength to go through labor, regardless of the pain relief method chosen. You will not be judged as weak if you choose medication to assist with pain control. We tell our patients you do not get any extra points for suffering. Together with your doctor, you can decide what is best for you when the time comes.

## The Things No One Ever Tells You About

At a Christmas party a couple of years ago, I (EAK) got involved in a conversation with people I had just met who asked what kind of work I do. Upon finding out I am an obstetrician, one girl began talking about episiotomy. Another girl had no idea what she was talking about and asked me to explain what it is. I told her it wasn't something she probably wanted to discuss at a Christmas party and left it at that. However, it made me realize there is a lot about the process of childbirth a woman about to experience it may not know.

First of all, labor and delivery is a process that makes it hard to maintain your dignity. You will feel exposed and vulnerable. Your husband and any other family or friends you choose to involve in the process will see you in a light you may feel is less than desirable. Many people get nauseous during labor, and you may throw up. During the process of pushing the baby out, you use some of the same muscles used to have a bowel movement, and you may in fact do so while pushing. In the past, enemas were used in the early stages of labor to help evacuate any stool prior to the birth of the baby. Now, most obstetricians have abandoned that process, as it served no benefit to either mom or baby.

As for episiotomy, it is sometimes necessary to assist in delivery of the baby. This is where your doctor may need to cut to widen the vagina so the baby will fit. Sometimes this is done in an attempt to keep the vagina from tearing badly. We used to think it was preferable to perform this procedure rather than letting the woman tear; however, current studies have shown women are more likely to suffer complications of incontinence following episiotomy because it can create a weak point, making further tearing more likely.[3] Most obstetricians now try to avoid episiotomy for these reasons. If you do tear or need an episiotomy, stitches will be placed to repair the area. These sutures will dissolve on their own but will require some care and avoiding intercourse for a time while they heal.

After delivery, your body will be overcome with a rush of adrenaline, causing extreme shaking. This normal and natural response worries some moms. After the baby is born, the delivery is not yet complete. The placenta, or afterbirth, needs to be delivered. This often does not require any work or pushing from the mom, but it can be felt and, when completed, provides a sense of relief.

# Induced Labor

During your prenatal course, your doctor is constantly evaluating the health of your baby in the intrauterine environment. There may come a point when he or she decides it may be more risky to continue the pregnancy than to deliver your baby. If that is the case, he or she will recommend an induction of labor. Some reasons for inducing your labor include the following: your water bag has broken and labor has not started on its own, you have passed your due date by one or two weeks, there is an infection in the amniotic fluid (amnionitis), your baby is not growing properly (growth restriction), or you have a condition such as diabetes or high blood pressure that can affect you or your baby if the pregnancy is continued.

Sometimes your doctor may allow induction of labor for elective purposes, for example, if you live a long distance from the hospital or if you have a history of rapid deliveries and are worried you may not make it to the hospital on time.

Induction of labor is not without risks, however. Being induced can put you at an increased risk of needing a cesarean section. This is especially the case if your cervix is not "ripe." Your cervix will be examined by your doctor to evaluate both dilation and effacement (thinning). If your cervix has not dilated or effaced much, he or she may use a cervical ripening agent the evening before to begin the induction process. This is usually placed into the vagina and helps to soften the cervix.

If your cervix has already started to dilate, your doctor may strip your membranes to get you to go into labor. This is done by sweeping the examining finger over the membranes that connect the bag of water to the lower part of the uterus. This causes your body to release chemicals that ripen the cervix and may cause contractions. Other ways to induce labor include breaking your water and giving a medication called *pitocin* through the IV. To break your water, your doctor will perform a vaginal exam and then make a hole in the amniotic sac. This is usually not any more uncomfortable than a standard vaginal exam. However, once your water is broken, your contractions will usually get stronger and become more painful. Sometimes labor is started or augmented with pitocin, which is given through your IV. This medication is a hormone that is found naturally in the body (oxytocin) and is responsible for causing contractions.

# Assisted Deliveries: Vacuum and Forceps

Most of the time, deliveries occur without any problems. However, there are some cases where your doctor may need to intervene for your health or the health of your baby. As discussed in chapter 19, there are certain medical conditions affecting the mother that can make pushing hard on her body. Sometimes the mom just becomes exhausted after hours of pushing and is too tired. The baby's position may make it difficult for the mom to push, and sometimes the heart rate will drop down, necessitating a quick delivery.

One way your doctor can assist in the delivery of your baby is by placing forceps around its head. These look like big spoons and work by guiding the head under the pubic bone through the birth canal. Another device that is sometimes used is a vacuum extractor. This is a suction cup that attaches to the baby's head with an attached handle that allows your doctor to pull as you push. Most of the time when these devices are used, there are no problems.

# Cesarean Section

About one out of every four babies is born by cesarean section in this country, making it a very common procedure these days. Sometimes it is planned, while in other cases it is performed because of a problem or emergency that arises during labor. Some reasons for performing a cesarean delivery include the following circumstances:

- Previous cesarean delivery: You or your doctor may choose to perform a repeat cesarean section rather than allow you to go into labor and deliver vaginally. This depends on several factors and should be discussed with your doctor in detail.

- Breech presentation: If your baby is breech (buttocks or feet presenting first into the vagina) and you are in labor, your doctor will likely recommend a cesarean delivery. Cesarean delivery will also be recommended if your baby is lying sideways in your uterus (transverse).

- Placenta previa: This is a condition where the placenta covers all or part of the cervix, blocking the baby from coming through the birth canal.

- Infections: Certain infections, such as genital herpes or HIV, may increase the chance of the baby becoming infected if delivered vaginally. It is important to talk with your doctor if you have these infections.

- Multiple pregnancy: Twins or higher order multiples (triplets or quadruplets) are often delivered by cesarean. However, many women can safely undergo vaginal delivery of twins.

- Failure to progress: About one out of every three cesarean deliveries is performed because the cervix does not dilate fully or the baby's head does not descend into the pelvis to allow for a vaginal delivery.

- Fetal distress: If labor or contractions become stressful on the baby, it may be safer to deliver your baby by cesarean.

If you undergo a planned cesarean delivery, a spinal block is usually used for anesthesia. This is similar to an epidural in that medication is put next to the spinal cord; however, a catheter is not placed, so it is a single dose. In the case where a cesarean is performed for a problem arising during labor, an epidural can usually be used if already in place. The anesthesiologist simply injects additional medication into the catheter to numb the lower abdomen and pelvis. If an emergency cesarean needs to be performed, you may have to undergo general anesthesia (get put to sleep).

**Incisions for Cesarean Section**

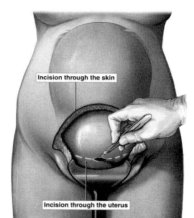

Illustration copyright © 2008 Nucleus Medical Art. All rights reserved. www.nucleusinc.com.

## Removal of Baby

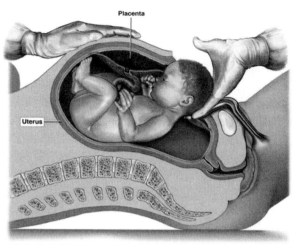

Illustration copyright © 2008 Nucleus Medical Art. All rights reserved. www.nucleusinc.com.

Most of the time, a cesarean section is performed through a small horizontal incision on the lower abdomen just above the pubic bone. This is commonly referred to as a "bikini cut." A similar, small horizontal incision is usually then made on the uterus, through which the baby is delivered. The placenta is then removed, and the uterus is then sewn back up. The procedure takes about thirty minutes to do. If you are awake, you may feel some pressure or tugging as your baby is pushed out of you by the assistant or doctor performing the surgery, which is normal. Most of the time, you are able to see your baby immediately and may even be able to hold him or her in the delivery room.

# Chapter 22

# THE POSTPARTUM MOTHER

*You would think that OB/GYNs are taught a lot about breast-feeding. Our basic education taught us that it was best for the baby, as it provides important antibodies, especially during the first six months. As a new mom, I (EAK) always planned to breast-feed, but I really had no idea what I was doing or what to expect.*

*Breast-feeding takes a lot of time and commitment. It is not easy to get up every two to three hours around the clock to feed for thirty minutes to an hour for several months. I was exhausted, and although I had a supportive husband, he couldn't breast-feed for me. Even if I wasn't breast-feeding that often, I needed to pump. Incorporating breast-feeding into my work routine was also challenging. Sometimes work was so busy, it was hard to find time to eat, much less pump. I had to make sure I was eating and drinking enough not just for me but also for my baby. I also had to fit several pumping sessions into my day.*

*It can also be painful, especially at first. There were times tears came to my eyes and I literally cried when my son latched on. When I decided to wean, after six months of breast-feeding, the pain of engorgement was worse than anything else I experienced following delivery.*

*Breast-feeding does provide both you and your baby with so many bene-fits and a unique bond. I am happy that I persevered despite the rough spots, as I believe it was the best for both of us and is what God intends for us as mothers to do, if possible. I also think my experience has given me knowledge to support my patients that I would not otherwise have if I hadn't personally experienced it.*

## Physical Changes

It took nine months for your body to change into something that was capable of carrying both a full-term baby and all the extra fluid needed to support it. Your breasts have grown, and extra fat has been deposited on your body to provide reserve. Do not expect these changes to reverse overnight, or even by your six-week checkup. Some will never quite go back to the way they were.

One of the first things you will likely notice following delivery is how sore you are. Your body just had an incredible workout. You will be exhausted.

Obviously, you will be the most sore in your pelvis following a vaginal delivery, and your abdomen following a cesarean. You will be swollen from all of the extra fluid, which will pool in your feet and lower legs but will also be noticeable in your hands and possibly your face.

It takes six weeks for your uterus to return to its normal pre-pregnancy size, but it will shrink to half of its full-term size in the first twenty-four to forty-eight hours following delivery. Still, most women are surprised to see that they still "look pregnant" after delivery and have to wear maternity clothes. As your uterus contracts back down to its normal size, you will feel cramps and experience bleeding. Your bleeding will be heaviest in the first one to two days after delivery and will lighten up after that.

If you are breast-feeding, you will notice that when you nurse, your uterus will contract strongly. This is due to the release of oxytocin, which helps with milk letdown and is the same hormone that triggers uterine contractions. Therefore, you may experience heavier bleeding when this occurs, and that is normal. Generally you can expect your bleeding to subside in two to six weeks following delivery. If you continue to bleed beyond six weeks, you should contact your doctor. You should also call your doctor if you ever bleed so much that you saturate a pad in an hour or if you have a fever or foul-smelling discharge.

Your doctor will usually see you back in the office four to six weeks following delivery, and possibly sooner if you had a cesarean. At this visit, he or she will examine you to make sure your uterus has returned to its normal size and your vagina is healed from any stitches that were placed. Until then, it is recommended that you use pads, not tampons, and avoid intercourse. After assuring you that everything is healed, you will be able to have sex again.

The first few times you have sex following the birth of your baby, you will likely experience some discomfort. If you had stitches, the area where the stitches were will be tender. If you are breast-feeding, low estrogen levels may cause vaginal dryness. Using a lubricant during intercourse can help.

If you are exclusively breast-feeding, your period may not return for the time you are feeding, but that does not mean you cannot get pregnant. If you are not breast-feeding, your period will usually return six to eight weeks following delivery, but fertility can return before that. You may ovulate before your first cycle. It is best if you can give your body some rest between pregnancies. Eighteen months is recommended to avoid an increased risk of preterm labor and low birth weight.[1]

# Breast-Feeding

Breast-feeding provides the best nutrition for your newborn baby. It also helps establish a bond between mother and child. God designed it so that you have everything you need to provide for your infant as soon as he or she is born. Still, breast-feeding can be challenging as some infants do not take to it as well as others. It takes a lot of work to teach your body and your baby how to tackle breast-feeding.

If you plan to breast-feed, it helps if you attend a breast-feeding class while you are still pregnant. These classes are usually taught by certified lactation consultants who will review in detail how to get started, common problems you may run into and how to deal with them, and pumping if you plan to go back to work. You can also talk to your doctor and your pediatrician if you have questions or concerns. If you have friends or family members who have breast-fed, they may be able to offer advice and support.

When you are in labor, let your nurse know that you are planning on breast-feeding. She can help you get your baby to latch on soon after the birth, when your baby is naturally alert and awake. This helps to establish the bond between mother and child and teaches your baby how to suck. Babies are born with a reflex called the rooting reflex that will help them nurse.

Initially, your breasts will secrete a thin, yellow substance called *colostrum*. This contains all the nutrients your baby needs to grow during its first few days of life and antibodies to help fight off disease. After three to four days, your milk will come in. Some women wonder if they will know when this happens. Like labor, you will know when it happens. Your breasts will become engorged, or full, and may be tender. If you experience redness or have a fever greater than 101 degrees, contact your doctor immediately, as these are signs that you could be developing an infection (mastitis).

The best way to relieve engorgement is to feed your baby. Sometimes, if your breasts are very full, it can be hard for your baby to latch on. If you can express some milk manually first, that will help. You may also try getting in a warm shower or applying a warm compress to help your milk flow. If feeding does not relieve your discomfort, you might try using ice packs afterward to reduce some of the swelling. If you do not want to breast-feed, using ice packs and wearing a tight bra will help to relieve engorgement. If the breasts are not stimulated to produce milk, they will quickly dry up.

You should feed your baby every two to three hours. This amounts to eight to twelve breast-feeding sessions in a twenty-four-hour period. As you might imagine, this can become exhausting. It is important to help your baby establish good technique so that he or she can be efficient at nursing. Bring your baby close to your nipple when you see signs of hunger (rooting at your breast, making sucking motions, or putting hands to mouth). Try not to wait until your baby is crying, as that is a late sign of hunger. As you bring your baby close, touch your nipple to the baby's lower lip to trigger the mouth to open. When your baby opens his or her mouth, place the entire nipple and areola (the dark area around the nipple), squeezing your breast, into the baby's mouth. You will know that your baby has latched on properly if he or she begins to suck and you can hear or see him or her swallow. If your baby is latched on correctly, breast-feeding should not hurt you.

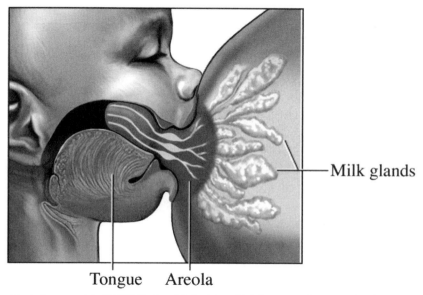

Milk glands

Tongue    Areola

Illustration copyright © 2008 Nucleus Medical Art. All rights reserved. www.nucleusinc.com.

There are several different positions to use while breast-feeding. Experiment to find what is most comfortable for you and your baby. Whatever you choose, it should feel comfortable and natural; you should not feel like you are having to force your baby to stay in a certain position.

A common and very natural position is the cradle hold. In this position, you have your baby cradled in your arms. With your left arm supporting his head, he will feed from your left breast while your right arm supports his legs and feet, and vice versa. In this position, use your right hand to squeeze your nipple and place it into his mouth before using this arm to support his legs and feet.

With the cross-cradle hold, you will support his body with your left arm and, cupping his head into your hand, will feed him from your right breast, and vice versa. This position frees up your other arm and hand, which can help you to ensure you get your nipple into his mouth correctly.

Another position you may want to try is the football hold. Similarly to the cross-cradle position, you will cup your baby's head into your hand while supporting his body with your arm, but instead of laying your baby across your chest to feed on the opposite breast, he will feed on the side you are holding him and will be therefore tucked under your arm. (See illustration below.)

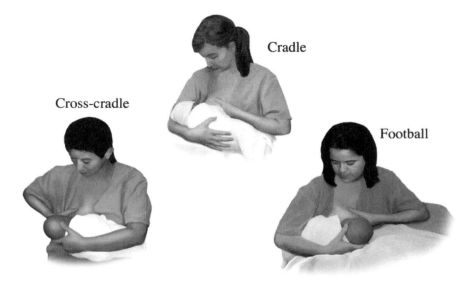

You may find that one of these positions is right for you or that they all work under different circumstances. If your baby is having trouble getting a good latch, make sure to experiment with all of the positions as you may find one that works better for you. There are several products on the market to help you and your baby get comfortable while nursing. You may find that a good comfortable chair is all you need, but you may also want to experiment with a footstool and breast-feeding pillows, though usually any type of pillow can help provide the support you need.

There are several ways to tell that your baby is getting the nourishment he or she needs. You will know if your baby is getting enough milk if he or she seems content after nursing. Your breasts will be full and firm to the touch before nursing and should feel softer afterward. Your baby should have at least six wet diapers and three bowel movements per day. Your baby's stool will be soft and yellow and may occur after each feeding. Initially, your baby will probably lose a little weight, but should be back up to his or her birth weight after two weeks and should continue to gain weight.

You do not need any special clothes for nursing other than a few good nursing bras. It is best if you purchase these during your pregnancy when you shop for new bras due to your increased breast size. Even though your breasts will be larger when your milk initially comes in, they will go back down to the size they were during pregnancy after the first couple of weeks. Some nursing bras have cups that are adjustable so that you can make the bra bigger or smaller as your breasts fill with milk and empty as you feed your baby. The most important feature is having clasps that are easy to open with one hand, as you will probably be holding your baby with the other hand. You will also want to make sure your bra is comfortable. It is helpful to have someone fit you so that you make sure to buy the correct size. You will also want to wear a bra at night to give you a little support. In addition to good nursing bras, you will need nursing pads to help absorb any milk that may leak in between feedings.

You will need to follow a balanced, healthy diet while breast-feeding; you actually need more calories than you did when you were pregnant. You will need an additional five hundred calories a day over what you needed before you were pregnant. You also need more calcium (1,000 mg) and an extra serving of protein (four instead of three). Your doctor may recommend continuing your prenatal vitamin while breast-feeding. Make sure you drink plenty of fluids, at least eight glasses of water daily. Dehydration can decrease your milk supply. You may notice that your baby is sensitive to some foods you eat; if so, try eliminating them from your diet for a few days to see if your baby gets better.

If you breast-feed, you really shouldn't diet. Because of all the extra calories used to breast-feed, you will likely notice that you are back to your normal weight within a few months. You should start an exercise routine once your doctor says it is OK.

You may notice that your sex drive is low while you are breast-feeding. Sore or leaking breasts can be uncomfortable to touch. Breast-feeding causes your estrogen levels to remain low, which delays ovulation but can also lead to undesirable side effects such as vaginal dryness. You may want to use a lubricant during intercourse, or talk with your doctor if that does not help. Because your estrogen levels are low, you probably won't have a period while you breast-feed. However, you can ovulate before your period returns, so relying on breast-feeding as birth control will not always be effective. There are forms of birth control that are safe to use while breast-feeding.

# Birth Control for Breast-Feeders

Of the many birth control methods discussed in an earlier chapter in more detail, one method many Christians feel comfortable practicing is natural family planning, also known as the rhythm method. However, if you are breast-feeding, it can be difficult to practice this method because you will most likely not have a period to track your cycle. You will have to check your cervical mucus every day for possible evidence of ovulation. Taking your temperature can usually help increase the accuracy of this method; however, your basal body temperature can be affected by lack of sleep or irregular sleep patterns that are common when you have a new baby. Another drawback to this method is limiting your opportunities for sexual activity. After having a baby you may not feel like having sex regularly due to changes in your body, discomfort, or sheer exhaustion. Placing restrictions on when you can safely engage in intercourse may be difficult.

Another type of natural family planning is using the lactational amenorrhea method. This method relies on the low levels of estrogen during breast-feeding to inhibit ovulation. As mentioned previously, breast-feeding will not completely protect you from getting pregnant. However, according to the Bellagio Consensus (www.fhi.org), you have less than a 2 percent chance of getting pregnant if the following three criteria are met:

1. You must be in the first six months postpartum.

2. You must be nearly exclusively or exclusively breast-feeding.

3. You must be amenorrheic (not have had a period).[2]

It is possible that the lactational amenorrhea method can be used beyond the first six months; however, that is when most children are receiving supplementation from solid foods and their breast-feeding requirements decrease. It is not known what level of breast-feeding is necessary to maintain these low pregnancy chances, or how often ovulation occurs before your menses returns; therefore, it can only be recommended under the guidelines stated above.

If you choose to breast-feed, either exclusively or partially, and would like additional protection, there is a birth control pill that will not affect your milk supply. The "minipill" consists of progestin only, whereas a regular birth control pill contains both estrogen and progestin. You will not have a period on the minipill, and it is important that you take it every day because the dose is lower than that in a regular pill; missing a pill may put you at risk for pregnancy.

An alternative to the minipill is an injection, Depo-Provera, that we discussed earlier. It contains progestin and will not affect your milk supply.

Most women may experience side effects such as weight gain, depression, and a decrease in bone density. It is important to take calcium to help counteract the bone loss that can occur while on the shot.

Barrier methods can be used with breast-feeding and offer a hormone-free alternative to other forms of contraception. Another option that is convenient for new moms to consider is an intrauterine device (IUD).

If you know you do not want any more children, you or your husband may choose to undergo a sterilization procedure. Both tubal ligation and vasectomy are permanent and over 99 percent effective. Your doctor may be able to perform a tubal ligation immediately following delivery using the same anesthesia you had while in labor.

Whatever method you choose, consideration must be given to your choice to breast-feed or not, and your desire for future children. It is important to discuss all of your options with your partner and doctor before you deliver your baby so that you are prepared when you are able to engage in intercourse again.

## Postpartum Changes

It is true that your life will never be what it was before. It is normal to miss time you used to enjoy by yourself. Now getting to take a shower or leaving the house may seem like monumental tasks. After the birth of our son, I (EAK) experienced a time when I had been cooped up inside the house with our baby for days. Once when my husband came home from work, I decided to go out for a walk to the mailbox. Even though our son had just eaten and was sleeping when I left, as soon as I shut the door, he awoke and screamed the whole time I was gone. This time can be trying on fathers too. They miss the wife and life they had before the baby, and often feel like they can't help as much as they would like to.

To make matters worse, you will be incredibly sleep deprived, which will only enhance these emotions. It is important to try to sleep when your baby sleeps. Leave the laundry, cooking, and cleaning for your family. More than likely you will have people who want to help, so let them. You will be consumed with feeding your baby and diaper changes every two to three hours initially. If you are breast-feeding, once your milk is established, you should pump a bottle for your husband to feed to your baby.

You may be mourning the changes that have taken place in your body. Many women enjoyed being pregnant, and they miss the feeling of having their baby moving inside of them. There isn't much that is enjoyable about the postpartum body. You may still look pregnant and will probably have to wear your maternity clothes for a while. Your perineum will be sore following a vaginal delivery, and your abdomen will be sore following a cesarean. Once your milk comes in, your breasts will be tender and uncomfortable. Your body just doesn't feel like your own anymore, and you may wonder when it will return to "normal."

Usually after the first week or two, your body is less sore and feelings of sadness are overcome by the joy of having a child in your life. Your body is not yet back to normal, your routine changes, and even though you are still sleep deprived, the baby blues usually fade away. If your sadness intensifies, however, you may be suffering from postpartum depression.

## Postpartum blues and depression

Because of the extreme fluctuations in your hormones following delivery, you may experience feelings of sadness two or three days after the birth of your baby. Usually these feelings are mild and will subside within a week or two. If they become more intense or last longer, you may be suffering from postpartum depression.

It seems strange that at such a happy time in your life you might feel sad. Many women are surprised that they feel alone and drained following their baby's birth. It does not mean that you are a bad mother. And you are not alone; about 10 percent of new mothers will suffer from postpartum depression.[3] It can occur after any birth, not just the first, and does not always happen immediately following delivery. Depression within the first six months after delivery may be postpartum depression. It can affect anyone but is more common in women who suffered from depression or anxiety prior to pregnancy. If you have had postpartum depression in a previous pregnancy, you are more likely to have problems with it again. Other stressors, such as moving, losing a loved one, or work-related stress, can precipitate postpartum depression. It is also more common in women who have marital problems or those who lack a social network and have few family members or friends to support them.

 Some of the symptoms of postpartum depression include:
- Loss of interest in things you normally enjoy
- Strong sense of depression or anger
- Loss of appetite or overeating
- Less energy and motivation to do things
- Trouble sleeping (insomnia, sleeping too much)
- Increased crying or tearfulness

- Feeling worthless, hopeless, or overly guilty
- Feeling restless, irritable, or anxious
- Intense concern or worry about the baby
- Unexplained weight loss or gain
- Feeling like life isn't worth living
- Having thoughts about hurting yourself
- Worrying about hurting your baby or being afraid to be left alone with your baby

If you feel like you have some of these symptoms, you should contact your doctor. He or she can talk with you about options for treatment, including counseling and medications. Let your doctor know if you are breast-feeding, so that he or she can decide which medication may be best for you to use.

You can also help yourself by letting others help you. Just because you are your baby's mom does not mean that you have to do everything. Get help with child care, errands, and housework. Do something for yourself each day, even if it is just taking a shower and putting on makeup. Try to exercise by walking each day, or take some time to yourself to read or write in a journal. Remember that it is still normal to feel overwhelmed from time to time. Having a baby is not easy, and it does not come with instructions. Becoming a mother takes patience and time.

If the stress becomes too much, get some help. Your doctor can provide you with resources in your community. Whatever you do, do not take out your frustrations or anger on your baby. If you ever feel like you might, put your baby in a safe place such as the crib, or ask someone else to hold him or her. Walk away, get in the shower, or go somewhere where you can't hear your baby's cries until the feelings pass. Try to figure out what might help you avoid that from happening again.

Getting help does not make you a bad mom or an unsuccessful one. Share your feelings with your spouse, and listen to his concerns as well. Remember that you are not alone; you are now a family.

# Chapter 23

# THE LIFE OF A
# PERIMENOPAUSAL SOCCER MOM

*Sheila has been our patient for many years. She first came to see us for the care of her initial pregnancy and continued with us through the birth of her twins. Sheila always prided herself on staying in great shape and exercising consistently. She was always at her goal weight within a few months of giving birth.*

*When the twins were three years old, Sheila and her husband decided that the desire for more children was no longer there. The twins were very time-consuming, and they had always thought they would only have three children. They never expected to reach that goal in only two pregnancies! But as the twins got older and the older child entered elementary school, Sheila wanted more permanent birth control.*

*Both she and Ted had discussed, and debated, who would be the one to get "fixed." Sheila felt she had done enough work delivering three babies and that Ted should have a vasectomy. Ted was willing, but as a high school football coach, it was difficult to find time in his schedule to have a surgery and recovery period.*

*One of things that bothered Sheila most about her body was the stretch marks and excess skin she retained after the twins. No matter how many aerobics classes and abdominal crunches she did, there was always a "pooch" that never flattened. We explained to Sheila that the skin and abdominal wall had stretched beyond its ability to shrink back. While her muscle tone was excellent, the wall of the abdomen had been permanently pulled apart. No amount of exercise would be able to reverse the changes that had taken place because of the twins.*

*We suggested a consultation with a plastic surgeon so she could know the options available to her. This extremely motivated and body-conscious woman wanted to know everything that could be done to restore her once flat stomach.*

*After her consultation, Sheila informed us that she had decided to have an abdominoplasty, or "tummy tuck." Was there any way we could tie her tubes at the same time as her other surgery? She would already have child care arranged and be recovering anyway. This seemed a perfect time to do both things.*

*We agreed and have participated in this similar surgical combination many times before. Often, the insurance will pay for the hospital and anesthesia charges if cosmetic surgery is done at the same time as a covered surgery in the patient's health plan. This can save the patient money and let her leave with the added benefit of permanent birth control. Most plastic surgeons will not recommend abdominoplasty if future childbearing is desired.*

*Sheila had a "tummy tuck" and laparoscopic tubal ligation over spring break. By the summer, she was able to wear a bikini again, something she never dreamed she would do again. Her self-confidence has increased, and she is facing a new stage in her life with boldness and determination. The hard work she has done in the gym is finally fully evident with the removal of excess skin and stretch marks. Her muscles are back together, and she is able to demonstrate the "flat" stomach that was hiding underneath the entire time.*

## Changes Due to Pregnancy

Even if women can avoid the temptation to compare themselves with the Hollywood ideal, there are changes that occur in life that can dramatically alter their appearance. Perhaps the most that we see are those caused from pregnancy.

The recommended weight gain in pregnancy is between twenty-five and thirty pounds. Whatever a woman gains over that amount will usually still be with her after her six-week checkup. But even if women return to their weight goal, there are stretch marks, weakened abdominal muscles, and sagging breasts. No amount of exercise or diet will lift a breast or remove a single stretch mark. And even the skeletal shape of a woman changes after pregnancy. My (SAF) wife was dismayed that certain dresses did not zip up the back the way they used to before children. It was not excess weight but changes to her skeleton.

During pregnancy, the rib cage spreads itself horizontally to make room for the lungs, which must now compete for room with the expanding abdomen. Breathing changes from an up-and-down movement of the diaphragm to a more horizontal stretching of the chest. After childbirth, it is not uncommon for the rib cage to stay stretched in its horizontal position.

Similarly, during pregnancy there are hormones released that allow the pelvic bones to widen in an attempt to give the baby more room for vaginal delivery. This widening does not completely reverse. The combination of the wider rib cage and hips changes a woman from a straighter silhouette to that of the classic, hourglass figure.

# Cosmetic Surgery

Christian women often struggle with whether it is proper to alter the body God gave them or fix changes that occur with childbirth or aging. I (SAF) remind them that they have been born into a fallen world and the body we have now is subject to decay and change.

Cosmetic or "plastic" surgery is typically divided into three types: enhancement, repair of damage done by childbirth or aging, and reconstruction.

Common surgeries to enhance one's appearance are rhinoplasty ("nose jobs") and breast augmentation. Almost 12 million cosmetic procedures were done in 2007, with breast augmentation and rhinoplasty as the number one and two procedures, respectively.[1] These are often done on younger women to alter their appearance. But some women will find their breasts have shrunken after pregnancy and breast-feeding. They may be dissatisfied with the appearance of their breasts and seek to have them filled in with breast implants. Similarly, a breast lift can reverse the effects of gravity and pregnancy stretching on already full breasts. These women do not seek larger breasts but simply wish for them to be put back in their original position on the chest wall.

Other common procedures to reverse the effects of childbearing are abdominoplasty (or tummy tuck) and liposuction. Women who gained a lot of weight during pregnancy and then lost it will be left with extra skin that hangs down over their pubic bone. Others who had larger babies or are smaller framed may have had their abdominal muscles pulled apart and are unable to get them back together. This leaves them with a "pooch" that no amount of exercise can remove.

Abdominoplasty seeks to restore the abdominal wall to its previous state of tone and firmness by removing excess skin and fat, then sewing the muscles back together in the midline. This creates a flatter appearance to the stomach. The scar is quite large but low in the bikini area. The plastic surgeons also use liposuction to remove "love handles" on the sides, back, and upper thighs. These areas are often resistant to weight loss alone.

Procedures that reverse the signs of aging include face-lifts, brow lifts, and eye lifts. The face-lift is generally the complete package. Some need only the eyes or brows done. Plastic surgeons often recommend doing several smaller procedures over time instead of one large makeover to make the changes appear less dramatic and more "natural" in appearance. These facial procedures can make a person appear ten years younger.

All the above surgical enhancements are expensive, estimated at $5,000–$15,000 per procedure. That has led many to explore other options. People travel to Mexico, the Dominican Republic, or the Orient for cosmetic surgery that is half the cost, but they have experienced severe complications at the hands of poorly trained surgeons, according to a *Dateline NBC* investigation.[2] Our strong recommendation is to use a board-certified plastic surgeon in the United States for all cosmetic surgery. As with any surgical procedure, there are risks of complications, including death.[3] The quality of the surgeon—and ultimately your life—is far more valuable than the price of the procedure.

A nonsurgical procedure that is extremely common is Botox injections, followed by Restylane. Botox is made from botulism toxin, a nerve agent that paralyzes the muscles of the face to decrease wrinkles, especially in the forehead and eyes. Restylane is a filler that plumps up the lower facial area to remove deep creases. A competitor is Juvéderm. All of these are temporary, lasting four to six months on average, and must be repeated to maintain the cosmetic effects.

Reconstructive surgeries are those used to correct defects from birth (such as cleft palate), to reconstruct breasts in breast cancer patients, and to correct traumatic injury to the body from accident or burns. They can be some of the more fulfilling surgeries that a plastic surgeon ever does. Some might also include breast reduction in this category as it is more than cosmetic for most of our patients. Many women whose cup size is DD and larger experience back and shoulder pain, and the bra straps can dig into the shoulder blades, causing grooves. These women are limited in their ability to do breast self-exams, and even mammography is more difficult. Reducing the size of the breasts to a C or D cup is more than cosmetic for these women; it is therapeutic.

When patients ask us what we think about plastic surgery, and more importantly what does God think, we ask them a series of questions.

- What are they trying to achieve with this surgery?
- Can they afford the surgery?
- Are their husbands in agreement with the surgery?

The answers to these questions are crucial in determining what God thinks about it. In this society that places so much importance on appearance, it is easy to become trapped in the race to always look young. It is tempting to try to become what one sees on the magazine covers or on television. Remember that most of the women paraded for your viewing pleasure have all had plastic surgery and continue to have procedures to keep their careers viable. If you want to enhance or change something that has always bothered you, or you are aging prematurely, or childbirth has made significant changes to your body that you cannot overcome, plastic surgery may be an answer. But remember that we all age and change, no matter how many procedures we have. We need to be authentic about who we are, not caricatures of our former selves.

## IT'S IN THE WORD

Too often we fall victim to the "standards" set by this world, measures of beauty that change with the seasons. These vary by country and culture; the "lucky" ones are born in the right place and at the right time in history to take advantage of their genetic predispositions. The rest of us are left with the temptation to compare ourselves with others. But Paul cautions against that very thing when he writes to the church in Corinth: "We do not dare to classify or compare ourselves with some who commend themselves. When they measure themselves by themselves and compare themselves with themselves, they are not wise" (2 Cor. 10:12). If we can see the beauty in all of us as unique expressions of God's creative genius, we can break free from the worldview of this current age and embrace who we really are in Christ.

# Make Time for Yourself

If there is ever a time in the life of a woman where she is likely to neglect her own personal health care, it is the phase between motherhood and menopause, when most of her time is spent raising her children. As the children grow older, the number of extracurricular activities they participate in increases. She typically drives all over town taking the kids to lessons, sports activities, parties, and dance lessons, only to drive them back home to begin helping with homework, preparing dinner, getting them bathed and off to bed, and finally collapsing into bed herself at the end of the day, having spent little time on herself. Just reading about it is exhausting!

As we have mentioned in an earlier chapter, when childbearing is complete, many couples choose permanent birth control. It is not uncommon in our office to have women miss their annual exams in the years right after a tubal ligation or vasectomy has been completed. It is often only when a medical problem brings them back to us that we realize how long they have gone without personal health care.

When we question them about this, it is often the same story of spending time in the pediatrician's office instead of ours. With no need for birth control, one must choose to be examined. We cannot force it.

Additionally, we see women who are now spending a large amount of time caring for their aging parents. They may be taking them to doctor's appointments or caring for them at home, neglecting their own health maintenance. Often we hear stories of years spent nursing a loved one with cancer or a stroke, finally returning to care for their personal needs upon the death of that parent.

The dilemma is that the period between age thirty and fifty lays the foundation for personal health later on. Without regular contact with a health-care provider, preventative measures are delayed and the damage to your body may have already been done.

As this stage of your life blends with the next stage, remember that there are people dependent upon you as a wife, a mother, a sister, and a daughter of your family. While you take care of them, you do them no favors if your own health suffers. Your children may be forced to care for you years before your time.

# SECTION 6
## LIVING LIFE AT MIDLIFE AND BEYOND

# Chapter 24

# EVERYTHING MENOPAUSE

The menopause phase is a challenging time in a woman's life. It can be a difficult part of growing older for a woman, both physically and emotionally. Anything that affects the body and the emotions also impacts sexually and spiritually.

*Frieda was a fifty-two-year-old woman who had always been healthy, rarely visiting a doctor's office except for her yearly examinations. This year, however, she was early for her annual exam. Frieda had not come to be examined but to talk. During the past year, she had begun to feel night sweats that disrupted her sleep. This resulted in memory loss, fatigue, and irritability. Recently, she was embarrassed by daytime hot flashes that caused her face and chest to flush. Everyone around her knew she was suffering from menopausal symptoms.*

*Being health-conscious, Frieda had tried herbal remedies such as soy and black cohosh, but she found them only minimally effective in curbing her symptoms. In addition to the hot flashes and night sweats, Frieda began to notice that intercourse was becoming more uncomfortable. Lubrication was lacking, and, even with store-bought remedies, she felt her vaginal skin tearing during sex.*

*At her visit, we discussed her symptoms and the remedies she had already tried. We drew blood to check the level of estrogen she still had and to exclude thyroid disease as a cause of symptoms. A later visit gave us the opportunity to explain that Frieda had, in fact, entered menopause.*

*While Frieda was initially reluctant to begin hormone replacement therapy, she found the symptoms so disruptive to her life that she reconsidered. We discussed oral, vaginal, and transdermal remedies. Because Frieda was already adept at taking her daily vitamin supplements, she elected to begin an oral therapy that combined estrogen and progesterone. A plant-based preparation suited her desire for natural ingredients.*

*In a follow-up visit three months later, Frieda was pleased with her decision to begin HRT (hormone replacement therapy). Most of her hot flashes and night sweats were gone, although she still had one or two each day if she became excited or angry. Intercourse was more comfortable, and her job performance improved with a better night's sleep.*

*Our plan is to reevaluate her HRT regimen at each annual exam. We will factor in any changes in her health or medications that might increase her risks of taking HRT. Over time, our plan is to gradually decrease her dose of hormones so that she eventually weans off medication without having a relapse in symptoms.*

# What Is Menopause?

In the Western world, the average age of menopause is fifty-one, with the ages from forty to fifty-eight encompassing the natural statistical curve. Menopause before age forty is considered "premature," whether it happened spontaneously (i.e., naturally) or through surgery, chemotherapy, or radiation. Every woman who lives long enough will proceed through this phase of life called menopause.

Menopause is defined as the period of time when the available eggs in the ovary have dwindled and the estrogen levels have dropped dramatically. Menopause has fully arrived when a year has passed since a woman's last period and certain blood levels signify the end of ovarian function.[1] Medically, it is a set moment in time. But for most women, the process leading up to it can last several years. All of life after menopause is termed "postmenopausal."

## Menstrual changes

Perimenopause is the time period of transition from normal menstrual cycles to the complete absence of cycles. It generally lasts for four to seven years and is often the time period women refer to when they complain of "going through menopause." There is an early phase where menstrual cycles begin to become irregular, usually in the early forties. The later phase begins in the late forties and is signified by missed cycles and menopausal symptoms. The quality of the eggs not "chosen" earlier in life is poorer and results in lower estrogen levels. This in turns prevents consistent ovulation of the egg and causes weak progesterone levels. The lower progesterone levels lead to irregular or missed menstrual cycles.

Changes in menstruation can be the first symptom that brings a woman to our offices. It is very rare to abruptly stop having periods and never have them again. For most women, the transition from fertility to menopause is an inconsistent and unpredictable one. Cycles can be closer together or farther apart. They can be shorter than usual or longer and heavier. We prefer to be contacted if periods become extremely heavy, last longer than seven days, are closer than twenty-one days from the start of one to the start of another, or if there is b eeding after intercourse. Sometimes bleeding can occur between periods and may need evaluation as well. Any bleeding in the postmenopausal period, after twelve months or more of no menses, requires investigation for the possibili y of uterine or cervical cancer.[2]

Some of the tools that can be used to evaluate abnormal bleeding are ultrasonogra phy or sonohysterography to look for polyps or fibroids. Endometrial biop sy can sample the lining of the uterus to exclude precancerous or cancerou changes. Hysteroscopy is a surgical tool to look directly into the uterus for abnormalities. Other conditions can cause irregular menstrual bleeding or missed periods, such as thyroid disease that may need evaluation.

With the completion of menopause comes amenorrhea or loss of menstruation. While the cessation of menstrual periods is a blessing for most, it also signals the end of fertility. While it is rare to find a woman who still wants to have a child in her fifties, the very fact that she can never have one again can bring a time of mourning. Even women who have had a tubal ligation find that they become sad when the last egg is gone. Their hormonal and physiological pro cesses have been geared toward fertility and childbearing. They must face the realization that new life will no longer come from their wombs. For some, this calls for a radical reshaping of their self-image. For others, this means that they are getting "old."

On the positive side, the lack of menstruation frees a woman to be sexually active whene ver she wants. She will not be a victim of some ill-timed blood flow or painful n enstrual cramps. There is a freedom that exists after menopause. Birth contro is not an issue or a burden. Sex can be for fun instead of carrying the fear of u nwanted pregnancy. Even the sexual drive will be restored as the body becom s accustomed to its new hormonal reality. The ovaries continue to produce a sr iall amount of weak estrogen, and the production of testosterone still continu s. With the balance of hormone shifted to the male side, some women even have an increase in libido after menopause is completed.

## Hot flashes

As women enter menopause, there will be about 15 percent who experience no symptoms at all except a loss of menstruation. They will not complain of hot flashes o : mood swings or anything their fellow sisters in menopause are going throu h. In fact, they may have a difficult time understanding what the other 85 percent are experiencing. But the majority of women will have varying degr es of difficulty as they transition through this phase of life. How much it both ers them will determine what remedies they seek.

At the beginning of menopause, nightly hot flashes are the most bothersome, waking women in the middle of the night, often covered in sweat, only to then become cold again. This repeated interruption in sleep patterns deprives women of the restorative deep sleep that one needs to feel rested and refreshed the following day. As a consequence, many women entering menopause also suffer fatigue and poor concentration due to sleep deprivation.

As menopause progresses, the hot flashes begin to intrude upon the daytime hours and can be socially embarrassing, with facial flushing, sweating, and feeling hot when no one else in the room does. Women can become more irritable as well, and many seek relief from this uncontrollable furnace within. The core body temperature does not actually increase, but the skin temperature can raise four to seven degrees in a matter of seconds, only to plummet again a few moments later.

No one knows what causes hot flashes, but some speculate that hot flashes come from an area in the brain called the hypothalamus, which is the temperature regulation center. Signals may be sent from this center that dilate blood vessels on the skin in a attempt to cool the body, leading to the "flushed" sensation that often begins in the torso and spreads upward. This can occur several times an hour or only a few times a day. It generally stops occurring a few years postmenopausal, but we have personally had patients who continue to experience hot flashes into their seventies.

### Other symptoms of menopause

Decreasing estrogen levels have been linked to increasing irritability, depression, sleep deprivation, and loss of memory. No definitive studies have established estrogen loss as the cause, although women who have surgically lost their ovaries seem to experience these symptoms at a greater level than those who enter menopause gradually.

The presence of hot flashes and night sweats can disrupt the normal sleep patterns. Poor sleep in turn leads to irritability, depression, and poor concentration. Relieving hot flashes or promoting better sleep may resolve some of these issues. We will look at the role of estrogen for the relief of hot flashes later in this chapter. Sleep aids can range from herbal (valerian root), to antihistamine (Simply Sleep, Unisom, Tylenol PM), to prescription (Ambien, Lunesta, Rozerem). The latter can be troublesome in long-term use and require the supervision of a physician.

The lack of estrogen to the vagina leads to thinning of the vaginal lining and dryness. This in turn causes painful intercourse. Estrogen loss changes vaginal pH and its microorganisms, making it more difficult to defend against yeast or bacterial infections. The ligaments that hold the female organs in place can weaken, letting the bladder, uterus, or rectum prolapse into the vagina, bringing discomfort with standing or intercourse.

Bladder control can be partially lost, leading to wetness or urinary tract infections. An overactive bladder may develop that leads to the sensation of always needing to urinate. While these changes may not be specifically tied to hormone loss, they are frequent menopausal complaints.

# The Estrogen Controversy

Whether or not the symptoms we have just described are severe or troubling to you will determine how you seek treatment. Everything we have described about menopause is a natural transition. But some women experience this transition more acutely and severely than others. It is not a question of being "tough" enough. Your experience is your own and cannot be compared to others.

### The dangers

The main question that comes with menopause is whether or not to take hormone supplements. Of all the remedies known to mankind, nothing relieves hot flashes and night sweats like estrogen. It is the hormone that the body is crying out for, and every other remedy is a pale substitute. Estrogen used to be prescribed to almost every menopausal woman in the United States at some point in her life. It was thought for decades that estrogen would prevent heart disease, strokes, osteoporosis, and certain cancers, while improving the quality of life for those suffering from hot flashes and mood swings.

This prescribing pattern came to an abrupt end in 2002. That was when the Women's Health Initiative (WHI), a large national study of thousands of women, stopped its study of hormone replacement therapy (HRT) early because it was finding that the women who were taking hormones were doing worse than the women who were taking placebo (or fake) pills.[3]

For many years, there was a body of evidence that showed HRT, specifically estrogen, was beneficial in raising "good" cholesterol and lowering "bad" cholesterol. Because it was assumed that this would be an improvement for the heart, HRT was recommended as a way to prevent heart attacks and strokes. Since most women did not have a rise in cardiac events until after menopause, it was thought that female hormones protected women and that replacing them could continue this "fountain of youth."

Many of us spent the 1980s and 1990s vigorously advocating HRT for everyone. The problem with the early studies was that the number of patients studied was small and the data was based on questionnaires that asked about past use and present disease. There had not been a large trial of HRT versus placebo to see what would actually happen in the future. This type of study is much more powerful in reaching conclusions, but it takes a lot longer to complete and requires thousands of participants.

Over the past several years, a few of these large studies began releasing their findings. The first study to question the value of HRT was the Heart and Estrogen/Progesterone Replacement Study (HERS). Women with previous heart disease were recruited in the hope that adding hormones to their system would reverse the effects of hardened arteries and improve their lives. In the first year of the study, those who took the hormones began dying of heart attacks and strokes at a faster rate than those taking the placebo or "sugar" pills.[4] We immediately stopped advocating hormones as a treatment for heart disease but still clung to the hope that healthy women might find prevention for future heart attacks if they could keep their cholesterols levels balanced with the hormones.

The WHI study released early findings in July of 2002 showing no benefit for healthy women who took hormones to prevent heart attacks. In fact, a small number of women actually did worse than expected. For every ten thousand women who took combined estrogen-progesterone (in this case, the drug Prempro), there were seven more cardiac events, eight more strokes, eight more pulmonary embolism, and eight more invasive breast cancers than women taking the placebo. On the positive, or prevention, side, there were six fewer colorectal cancers and five fewer hip fractures.[5] While these numbers represent a very small change (five to eight women out of every ten thousand), taken together the statistics showed definite negative effect for women taking the combined hormones compared with those who didn't. This revealed a flaw in our thinking about hormones. Just because it seemed to do one thing in the laboratory did not mean it translated to better health in real people. It took enough women studied to be able to figure this out. The four main studies published to date have over twenty thousand women in them. Overnight, the sale of Premarin, which had been the most prescribed drug in the United States, dropped precipitously.

Other research on HRT confirmed the possibility of a cancer risk. There seems to be a small but definite rise in the risk of breast and ovarian cancer with continued use of estrogen and progesterone. Those who took the hormone more than four or five years began to see an increase, and it continued for those taking hormones ten or more years.[6]

It was once hoped that estrogen could prevent the development of dementia, or Alzheimer's disease. But the WHI also showed that estrogen used over many years can actually increase the risk of dementia, probably through a series of undiagnosed strokes.

## The benefits

To make things a bit more confusing, a second arm of the WHI study enrolled ten thousand women taking estrogen alone who had already had a hysterectomy. Overall, there was no cardiovascular harm from using estrogen alone for up to seven years of the study. When broken down by age, those who began estrogen early in menopause and concluded use by age sixty may have had a small cardiac benefit.[7] In a second study, those women who took combined estrogen and progesterone and started it within four years of menopause had less heart disease than those who never took hormones at all.[8] While this benefit has not been definitively established, two further studies are currently ongoing to determine if beginning estrogen early, before heart disease has already occurred, might be of some benefit. These are expected to be completed in 2009–2010.

Reanalysis of the data from concluded studies also shows that combined hormones do not increase breast cancer in the first four years and that estrogen alone for up to seven years seems to reduce breast cancer![9] These are certainly controversial times for hormone therapy.

More proven benefits of both estrogen and progesterone include relief of hot flashes, night sweats, vaginal dryness, and pain with intercourse. In fact, no other drugs come close to providing the kind of relief that HRT and ERT can provide for these symptoms. Hormone replacement therapy is also a strong prevention of osteoporosis in the hip and spine.

From an FDA standpoint, estrogen and progesterone are approved for short-term use (ideally, less than five years) in the treatment of moderate to severe hot flashes, night sweats, and osteoporosis prevention. Women with a uterus should have progesterone added to their estrogen to prevent uterine cancer. Women who do not have a uterus should be on estrogen alone, as the addition of progesterone offers no benefits and the potential for more complications.

# What Do We Recommend?

Our advice to women now is different than it was a decade ago. Some of the promise of estrogen is in its prevention of osteoporosis and fractures. Millions of women suffer from osteoporosis and have sustained vertebral fractures, causing their spines to hunch over, or a hip fracture that has left them bound to a walker or wheelchair. A visit to any nursing home in America will reveal hallways lined with old women who are immobile and dependent on others to even take them to the bathroom. Much of this could have been prevented by better bone health as they aged.

Estrogen is a powerful preventative of spine and hip fractures. For the longest time, it was the only preventative we had that could take calcium and bind it back into the bones. But over the last few years, new drugs have been developed that not only prevent osteoporosis but also can reverse some of the bone loss that has already taken place. Some of these agents even appear to prevent breast cancer and may decrease the risk of heart disease. These new "designer" drugs called SERMs are targeting the areas that need help without the side effects of HRT. With the advent of such therapy, the need for HRT is greatly diminishing. We will discuss these drugs further in the next chapter.

But the new drugs also cause hot flashes! For those women who are suffering from these unexpected swells of heat and perspiration, awakening them in the night and embarrassing them in the daytime, hot flashes may be the worst part of menopause. If you have had a sudden loss of estrogen through hysterectomy, the hot flashes will be even more severe. For those with severe hot flashes or mood swings, there is nothing like estrogen to make them feel "normal" again. If the current data holds true, there is no harm in taking HRT for a few years to aid in the transition of menopause until the hot flashes subside, generally by age fifty-five. This is, of course, provided you have not had breast cancer or heart disease before. Only your doctor can review your individual history and advise you on your options.

## What About Bioidentical Hormones?

Since the very public advocacy of Suzanne Somers, there has been a surge of interest in "natural" or "bioidentical" hormone therapy. The thought is that much of the research cited earlier focused on drugs that were manufactured from animal sources (Premarin) and synthetics (MPA progesterone). Some believe that plant-based drugs (phytoestrogens) might be more "natural" and thus free of the health concerns such as those from the WHI.

Tailoring the dose of drug to the individual patient was also a strong desire as many women found themselves unsatisfied with traditional dosing regimens for prescription hormones and wanted the ability to have the compounds adjusted to fit their specific needs. Compounding pharmacists combine several hormones into a gel, tablet, or suppository. These hormones include estrogen, progesterone, testosterone, and DHEA.[10]

To determine the correct combination and dosage for each woman, a saliva test is done to ascertain the woman's current hormone concentrations. While this seems logical and scientific, there are potential problems that should be understood by anyone wanting bioidentical hormone therapy.

First, the "normal" range for salivary hormone concentrations is broad, and all practitioners are adjusting doses not based on final levels achieved but on subjective symptom relief. Second, the salivary samples are often shipped to reference labs with no guarantee that the hormone concentrations remain stable during shipping. Unlike blood, saliva is not a stable fluid.

Finally, these compounded drugs have never been tested for serious long-term side effects. Because they are compounded by the pharmacist, the FDA does not require the same warning labels as it does for products made by pharmaceutical companies. This is an oversight, not an endorsement of the safety of the product. Because each "batch" is individualized, the FDA has no way of knowing what a patient is receiving. The government continues to caution that until large studies are done on every potential hormone product, which will never happen, results from WHI apply to all HRT preparations.[11]

## Other Options

There are natural, herbal preparations that can help with hot flashes, such as ginseng, black cohosh, red clover, and soy. Soy is a main dietary ingredient in the Orient, and many of those cultures lack a word for "hot flashes." Because the typical American diet is not rich in soy, many supplements are available to boost soy intake with the hope that hot flashes will be reduced. This dietary supplement is safe but fairly weak in its ability to reduce hot flashes.[12]

Black cohosh is widely used in Europe and is approved by their regulatory board for the use in treating vasomotor symptoms (hot flashes and night sweats). In the United States, the most popular brand is actually made by a large pharmaceutical company under the name Remifemin. Doses of 40–80 mg per day have been shown to be effective in reducing hot flashes.[13] There do not appear to be any long-term side effects to black cohosh except the very rare case of liver disease. In our experience, women who have been the most satisfied with herbal remedies have been those with milder vasomotor symptoms.

Some serotonin agents previously used for depression have been found to improve hot flashes and are often prescribed to women who have had breast cancer and cannot take estrogen. In one study, the drug Paxil produced a drop in hot flashes by 67 percent.[14]

## What If I Still Want Estrogen?

As we have mentioned earlier, there is nothing quite like estrogen to restore the feelings of well-being and prevent vasomotor symptoms. It is the standard by which every other treatment is compared. If a woman is at low risk (does not have a history of breast or uterine cancer, heart disease, stroke, blood clots, or diabetes) then a short course of estrogen for moderate to severe symptoms is safe and beneficial. If she has a uterus, progesterone must be added to protect against uterine cancer.

We cannot take the place of a face-to-face consultation with your gynecologist, but here are some general guidelines. First, take the lowest dose for the shortest time needed. Try to finish using estrogen within five years if you can. Some people cannot wean off, and that is understandable. But the majority of people can be gently weaned down in dose and get off hormones within five years.

The most popular hormone replacements before 2002 were Premarin and Prempro. Prempro is for women with a uterus, and Premarin is for those without one. These are still very good products, but because of the WHI, they have fallen out of favor somewhat. We have patients who are doing very well with them, and we do not automatically switch to something else.

While there is no evidence to prove this, some feel that a more natural estrogen and progesterone regimen might avoid some of the issues that came from the animal-based hormones of the WHI study. Plant-based hormones are available that do not have to be compounded. These are on every insurance formulary in America and are less expensive than paying for the compounding products out of pocket. They come in a variety of forms, depending on what is desired. These include oral pills, creams, patches, vaginal rings, and injectables.

Examples of oral estrogen products are estradiol (generic), estriol (generic), Enjuvia (a brand substitution that is close to Premarin but made from plants), Gynediol (brand-name estradiol), and Femtrace (brand-name estradiol). For those who need the addition of progesterone to the estrogen tablets, there is Activella, Femhrt, and Angeliq. These are really lower doses of previously manufactured birth control pills on the market for many years. It is thought that since there have been no cardiac or breast issues with low-dose birth control pills, using even lower doses for menopause might be safer. Again, this is an unproven theory that may have more to do with the age of the woman taking the products than the product itself.

Some women do not want to take an oral medication or may feel that they are not getting good intestinal absorption from the pills. They may desire a more direct route in the hopes of maximizing symptom relief. Medically, by absorbing the drugs directly into the bloodstream, one avoids the liver and may decrease the risk of blood clots.

Examples of estrogen creams are Premarin, EstroGel, and Estrasorb. Premarin is usually inserted vaginally, while the last two are spread on the arms or legs like a body lotion. A vaginal ring that is available is called Femring. Patches include Climara and Vivelle. For those who need progesterone added to the estrogen, patches include Climara Pro and Combipatch.

Some women only need relief of vaginal dryness or painful intercourse and do not want estrogen circulating throughout the bloodstream. Local estrogen can be applied that will not enter the bloodstream and can be safely used even with health conditions that would otherwise prevent estrogen use. These include Premarin cream, Vagifem (a vaginal tablet), and Estring (a vaginal ring). Your gynecologist can help you decide which of the available products may be right for you, at what dose, and for how long.

# Chapter 25

# SURGERY 101

*After speaking to a women's group at church, I (SAF) was approached by Ruth, a woman in her early sixties. She asked to speak to me about a personal problem, and we found a quiet spot away from the others. Ruth explained to me that she and her husband, Roger, had not been able to be sexually active for some time due to erectile dysfunction. But recently, he had been given a prescription by his urologist and was experiencing strong erections again. Now she was having problems of her own.*

*Ruth had noticed for some time that her vagina was falling out. She had had a hysterectomy ten years earlier, and over the past two years, the vaginal tissues would protrude past the opening if she was on her feet for any length of time. This was not too troublesome for her as she could easily push it back in whenever she wanted.*

*But now that Roger wanted to be sexually intimate again, she found intercourse very uncomfortable. The vaginal tissues were becoming irritated from exposure to the air and contact with her underwear. Roger had to push the vaginal tissues in before he could enter the vagina, something she found very distasteful and embarrassing. It certainly did not put her in the mood for sex!*

*I invited Ruth to make an appointment with one of my partners who specializes in vaginal repairs of this nature. He confirmed that her entire vagina was now protruding through the opening and would need a mesh graft to keep it in place. He also recommended a bladder lift to control urinary loss once the vagina was back in its proper position.*

*Since Ruth was in good health, she elected to undergo the procedures. Both the vaginal repair and bladder lift were accomplished as an outpatient surgery, and Ruth was home later that day. After a six-week recovery period, Ruth was cleared to become sexually active again. Roger was thrilled with the "new" Ruth. They had recaptured a part of their marriage they thought was over. Even though this involved medication for Roger and surgery for Ruth, both feel it was worth the trouble and have encouraged their friends to not abandon sex as they age. Intimacy is worth the price.*

# Gynecologic and Urologic Surgery

As you have already noticed, your body goes through many changes in the perimenopausal and menopausal period. There is generally a slowing of metabolism and some associated weight gain. Bone loss can occur, and a woman may notice a loss in height. These issues are discussed in other chapters. For this chapter, we would like to focus on gynecologic and urologic surgery. These are the procedures that are commonly done by OB/GYNs across the United States. This chapter will give you some insight into the conditions that can be treated with surgery, the various options for surgery, and what to expect from these procedures. Think of this as a "pre-op" visit.

Some of the most common surgeries in the United States are gynecologic. Many times they are done to relieve a disease process in the uterus itself that is causing troublesome menstrual cycles. Often, other means have failed to alleviate the situation, and this is the next option.

Some of the transitional issues in this period of life include changes in the menstrual cycle. Menstrual periods can become longer, heavier, and closer together, with more cramping and clotting. This can be the result of irregular ovulations and poor progesterone levels that do not effectively eliminate the monthly lining of the uterus. Supplementing progesterone through either very low dose birth control pills or progesterone-only formulations may be all that is needed to regulate the periods. But often, there are physical changes in the uterus itself that need surgical correction.

Gynecologic surgery is also used to treat the effects of childbirth and gravity on the female organs. A falling bladder, uterus, or rectum is an example of pelvic prolapse. One or all three of these areas may be involved at the same time. Urinary leakage, back pain, or difficulty in passing stool can be symptoms of this condition.

## Uterine surgery

We will begin with the most common surgeries, those that treat abnormal uterine bleeding. As mentioned in the previous chapter, unusual uterine bleeding may require evaluation to determine if physical abnormalities of the uterus need correcting or if the lining of the uterus is abnormal. The original surgery for this was the dilation and curettage, commonly called the D&C. This is an outpatient procedure that involved dilating the cervix to admit a sharp instrument or suction catheter that scrapes the lining of the uterus to remove polyps or obtain a sample to exclude cancer.

Because a D&C is done "blindly" without the benefit of visualizing the exact location of the scrapings, it has been enhanced with a device called a hysteroscope. This is a camera that is inserted into the dilated cervix to visualize the birth canal and the inside of the uterus. This is most helpful in diagnosing polyps, fibroids, or abnormal growth of the lining. Often, instruments can be advanced under direct visualization to remove the abnormality more precisely.

An additional outpatient technique that is used to help women who suffer from excess blood loss is endometrial ablation. After hysteroscopy has excluded or removed any abnormalities, a device can be inserted that attempts to destroy the uterine lining and cause the surfaces of the uterus to scar closed. This reduces the available lining that is shed each month and can significantly improve the menstrual cycle. Common techniques use heat from water or electricity to destroy this layer of tissue. Because the lining will be damaged, the desire to bear children must be complete; permanent birth control is ideal. At least 75 percent of women who have endometrial ablation require no further treatment.[1] This outpatient procedure often requires only one or two days of recovery.

Often the source of abnormal bleeding or pelvic pressure can be uterine fibroids. These are muscle tumors that are rarely malignant. They can grow into the lining of the uterus, causing heavy bleeding, or they can enlarge the wall of the uterus, pressing on pelvic structures such as the bladder, rectum, or abdominal wall. We commonly see fibroids that can make a woman appear four months pregnant and rise up to the level of the navel when standing or lying down. The treatments are based on location and the desire to preserve the uterus for future childbearing.

If the fibroids are protruding into the lining of the uterus, hysteroscopy can be used and the tumors can be removed vaginally. If the location is in the wall of the uterus, an abdominal approach is necessary. Small fibroids can be removed through a laparoscope that is inserted into the umbilicus and assisted by two or more small puncture sites on the abdominal wall. Instruments are inserted into these additional sites, and a camera is attached to the umbilical port to visualize the surgery on a television monitor. The pieces of the tumor are then removed by electrical cautery. This outpatient surgery requires one to two weeks of recovery.

Larger fibroids may require opening the abdomen by laparotomy. This allows the entire uterus to be elevated through the abdomen and the tumor removed by hand. For those women desiring children, efforts are made to protect the fallopian tubes and prevent scar tissue formation. Recovery from this inpatient procedure is four to six weeks.

Some conditions require the complete removal of the uterus. These conditions include precancerous changes of the cervix, uterine prolapse, uterine fibroids, endometriosis, and severe pelvic pain. Whether the surgery is done vaginally or abdominally depends upon the nature of the disease and the training of your surgeon. Each case is individual and often requires a second opinion to help in decision making.

Whether the ovaries are removed with the uterus is also an individual decision based on the disease, the age of the patient, and any family history of female cancer. As mentioned in the previous chapter, the sudden loss of ovarian function by hysterectomy is a leading cause of severe hot flashes. The likelihood of requiring hormone replacement is increased by removing the ovaries. This decision is one that should be made with as much knowledge as possible.

A laparoscopic hysterectomy is sometimes an option, whether done completely or aiding a vaginal approach. The recovery time is usually shorter due to the smaller incisions and may be from two to three weeks. A simple vaginal hysterectomy is also a two to three week recovery with a one-night hospital stay a common expectation.

Abdominal hysterectomy is a hospital stay of two to three nights, with four to six weeks recovery. This is the least appealing approach for most patients, but it may be a necessity based on your particular medical condition.

## Ovarian surgery

Sometime during the reproductive years, most women will experience some problem with their ovaries. Common abnormalities include ovarian cysts. These are usually what are termed "functional," meaning that in the course of the normal function of ovulation cysts can form. This may be from failure of the egg to actually "pop out" and rupture the lining of the ovary. The following cycle, hormones that would target another egg for ovulation begin to swell the previous cyst to greater size. Often these will spontaneously resolve within one to two menstrual cycles. They can occasionally rupture, causing pain severe enough to bring women to the emergency room.

If unruptured, the heavier ovary can twist during physical activity and cause pelvic pain. A large unruptured cyst may require surgery to relieve the patient's pain. Those cysts larger than 6 centimeters are at higher risk of twisting on their attachments in a condition called *ovarian torsion*. This strangulation of the blood vessels leading to the ovary will lead to the death of that tube and ovary. This is a more emergent surgery if the ovary is to be saved.

Other causes of ovarian cysts are endometriomas, a form of endometriosis where the lining of the uterus attaches to the ovary and "bleeds" with each menstrual cycle. Over time, this leads to a "chocolate" cyst, where old blood accumulates in the ovary. These can be very painful and may inhibit fertility.

Tumors can grow in the ovary and can be either benign or malignant. The most common tumor in the reproductive years is a cystic teratoma or dermoid. This is made from cells that can grow into a variety of tissues. We tell our patients that it is similar to an egg trying to develop into a baby without the sperm. Hair, teeth, bone, fat, and even thyroid tissue can grow in these cysts. Because of the weight of these tissues, the ovary can easily twist. It is often when that happens that the diagnosis is made. On X-ray or ultrasound, the teeth or bones will show brightly and are a key to diagnosis.

These tumors, while very bizarre, are almost always noncancerous or benign. There is a variety that is cancerous, however, so these are almost always removed as a precaution. The opposite ovary has about a 10 percent chance of developing a similar tumor over time.[2]

Other ovarian tumors include cystadenomas. These are the tumors one reads about in magazines or hears about on television that can weigh up to one hundred pounds. Cystadenomas are usually benign but continue to grow until they are removed. Many patients mistake their enlarging abdomen for obesity and are shocked to discover they have a tumor. Cystadenomas can also be cancerous and are the type that can be screened with a blood test called a CA-125. This is used to help physicians determine before surgery if the tumor is likely to be malignant. It is a poor "cancer" screen for the general population who have no symptoms and no ovarian tumors.

Because ovarian cancer is difficult to diagnose and often has spread before being discovered, physicians often want a tissue diagnosis of ovarian cysts and tumors they discover. This is not the case for a simple cyst in a young woman, but a complex cyst in an older woman must be evaluated. While ultrasound, CT scans, and MRIs are helpful to determine certain characteristics of the ovary, there is no substitute for actually looking at the tissue under a microscope to exclude cancer.

Most health professionals do not recommend needle biopsy for fear of rupturing the tumor and spreading cancer inside the abdomen. Many can be diagnosed and treated through laparoscopy, a technique where a camera is inserted in the navel and small ports are placed in the abdomen to guide instruments into the patient. These small incisions lead to a shorter recovery time and less pain. The camera guides the surgeon and allows for a better view at times than if the abdomen was actually opened up. Most benign tumors can be removed laparoscopically. Simple functional cysts or endometriomas can also be treated this way, preserving the rest of the ovary and leading to improved fertility for younger women seeking to avoid scar tissue.

If the ovary appears to have cancer or the tumor is too large or is adhered to other structures, an abdominal incision called a laparotomy is necessary.

This is the same incision used for abdominal hysterectomy or cesarean sections and requires a longer hospital stay and postoperative recovery. But for certain circumstances, it may be the safest route for the patient. In these situations, the ovary is almost always completely removed.

## Endometriosis and tubal surgery

As mentioned earlier, a condition exists called endometriosis, which is when the lining of the uterus grows outside the uterus in other areas of the pelvis. There are many theories as to its origin, but one is that menstrual fluid is back-washed out the fallopian tube and cells attach to other structures and live off of their blood supply. Since they are the same cells as those found inside the uterus, they "menstruate" each month along with the other cells of the uterus. Because internal bleeding is very irritating to the pelvic organs, scar tissue can form around endometriosis, leading to tubal blockage. Endometriosis itself secretes a chemical that is thought to poison the egg during ovulation and reduce fertility, as we have discussed in an earlier chapter. Both laparoscopy and laparotomy are used to treat endometriosis.

The tubes can also be scarred from past STDs, such as gonorrhea and chlamydia, and from pelvic infections, such as a ruptured appendix. Laparoscopic surgery can be improved with the aid of microscopes to guide the removal of damaged tissue and reattach the ends of the tubes together. This same technique is used to reverse the effects of a prior tubal ligation. For those women desiring permanent sterilization, tubal ligation is also done through the laparoscope as described in a previous chapter.

## Bladder surgery

The result of childbirth, especially large babies or many lifetime deliveries, is that the pelvic muscles are weakened and stretched in a large percentage of women. As women age, the muscle strength also diminishes and pelvic hernias can occur that allow organs to fall into the vaginal space. The bladder is an organ that when standing lies above the vagina. With pelvic prolapse, the base of the bladder can fall into the vagina, causing feelings of pressure. The path of the urethra can be kinked, leading to difficult and incomplete emptying of urine. This leads to more frequent urination and nocturnal urination.

The urethra itself can be dislodged from its connections and fall into the vagina. Abdominal pressure from coughing, sneezing, heavy lifting, or exercise can cause pressure to be transmitted to the urethra that overcomes its ability to stay closed and leads to leakage of urine. Nearly 40 percent of women over age forty have bladder leakage.[3]

For women who have "overactive bladder" with the sensation of needing to empty their bladders frequently, medications that relax the bladder muscles are very helpful. Common drugs used include Detrol, Ditropan, Sanctura, Enablex, Oxytrol, and VESIcare. Common side effects result from the relaxation of related muscle groups and include dry mouth, constipation, and dizziness. But for bladders that have "fallen," surgery often brings the most patient satisfaction. To determine which approach is right for any particular patient, a series of tests called *urodynamics* is often recommended. This gauges the ability of your bladder to hold urine and its tendency to have muscle spasms. The pressure point where leakage occurs is also measured. This allows the gynecologist or urologist to customize a treatment plan that fits the needs of the patient.

Should bladder surgery be needed, it is an outpatient procedure with only a few days of recovery. If other abdominal surgery is required, a bladder lift can be done through that incision. This attaches the tissues around the urethra to the pubic bone for support. This same approach can be done laparoscopically through small incisions, whether or not other laparoscopic procedures were planned.

More commonly now, bladder surgery is done vaginally with minimal incisions used. The most popular approach is the "sling." This is based on the concept of a hammock that supports the urethra and keeps it from falling when abdominal pressure is exerted. It is not so much "lifting" the bladder as it is providing support should it try to fall. Several approaches are popular and are usually chosen based on the experience and expertise of your surgeon. The results are very similar.

One approach that we use is the Gynecare TVT-OT system. (See illustration on page 236.) A mesh is placed vaginally under the urethra and threaded through the pelvic wall on each side to exit the under surface of the thigh near the buttock. Discomfort is minimal and patient satisfaction is high. Ninety-eight percent of patients were still satisfied after seven years.[4]

For more information, you can visit the Gynecare Web site at www.gynecare.com.

### Vaginal prolapse

Whether due to a previous hysterectomy or damage done during childbirth, vaginal prolapse is a common occurrence. Like a hernia, the walls of the vagina can fall, letting the organs on the other side of that wall push into the vagina. The bladder, which acts as the "ceiling" for the vagina, can drop downward into the vagina in what is called a *cystocele*. Many women experience a pressure sensation when standing for any length of time. They may have difficulty completely emptying their bladder. I liken this to a teapot where the spout is higher than the bottom of the pot. To fully empty, it must be tilted forward. This can happen to the bladder as well.

When a woman has had a hysterectomy, the space that the uterus previously occupied is now vacant. The ligaments that held the bladder to the uterus have been severed, and the bladder may come loose over time, especially with activities that tense the abdominal muscles. These activities include straining for bowel movements, lifting heavy objects, or pushing heavy things. Those who have chronic coughs, such as smokers, often are repeatedly pushing down on the bladder with each cough. Over time, these types of activities loosen the attachments of the bladder, even in women who still have their uterus.

Others give a history of delivering large babies, a greater number of babies, or rapidly delivering their children. These events can also cause an internal injury to the vagina that never heals properly.

The "floor" of the vagina is the rectum. Childbirth injury is the most common reason for weakness in this region of the vagina. A hernia of the floor of the vagina is called a *rectocele*. Women with this condition complain of difficulty passing stool. Constipation is an issue for them, and they may feel the vagina bulge forward when they try to push the stool out. Often, women find that pressure with their hand pushing the vagina back into place aids in defecation. Occasionally, women will insert their fingers into the rectum to pry out the stool that is "stuck" in this pouch of vaginal tissue.

If the uterus is present, it can drop into the vagina and pull the other walls of the vagina with it. This is often corrected by vaginal hysterectomy. If the uterus has already been removed, the top of the vagina where the cervix was attached can itself become dislodged and protrude out of the opening of the vagina in what is called *vaginal vault prolapse*.

## KEGEL EXERCISES

For many decades, minor degrees of prolapse were aided by Kegel exercises. These exercises are designed to strengthen the muscles around the openings of the urethra, vagina, and rectum. Like any other exercise, they will only improve vaginal muscle tone if done consistently and with the right muscles in use. To do a proper Kegel, a woman squeezes the muscles that she would use to stop the flow of urine. One can initially try to locate these muscles while urinating, but the exercise is not designed to be done during actual urination. Once those muscles are identified, the woman attempts to hold them tightly closed for ten seconds. They are then released. This pattern is repeated approximately ten to twenty times in a row for a minimum of three times a day.

It is easy to "cheat" and try to use the stronger muscles of the leg, buttock, or abdomen. But those are not the muscles you are trying to strengthen when you have vaginal weakness. If these exercises are done on a regular basis, a woman will see results in about two to three months. Her ability to hold urine without leakage or to have a better bowel movement will improve. Many women use these exercises to tighten the opening of the vagina to improve sexual satisfaction, both for their partner and themselves.[5]

For more severe prolapse of the vaginal walls, surgery is often done. Traditionally, the walls of the vagina are opened in the area of the weakness, and the muscles that have been spread apart to allow the hernia are located and sewn back together. This can be done over the bladder or rectal areas. Vaginal vault prolapse requires a different approach as this is a problem of disconnected internal ligaments. The top of the vagina can be sewn vaginally to a ligament in the hip called the sacrospinous ligament. This requires a measure of skill as the ligament is difficult to locate and is near some large blood vessels that are difficult to repair if injured during the procedure. An abdominal approach ties the top of the vagina to the pelvic bones where they connect to the spine. This is called a sacrocolpopexy and has its own "scary" blood vessels to avoid.

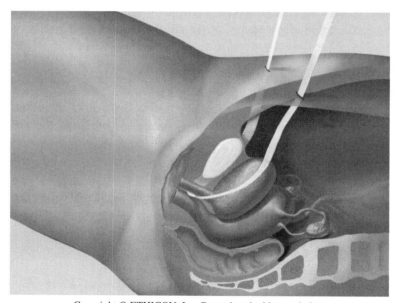

Copyright © ETHICON, Inc. Reproduced with permission.

Taking a cue from the general surgeons in their approach to groin or abdominal hernias, a new technique has been developed to use mesh to cover over the defects in the vagina. Instead of trying to pull together weak tissues and hope they stay closed, synthetic mesh has been developed to lay over the defects, whether under the bladder or over the rectum. They can even support a falling vaginal vault. Only a few gynecologists have been trained in these techniques, but it is worth investigating if you are faced with surgical decisions of this nature.

## Vaginal rejuvenation

Childbirth often leads to stretching of the opening of the vagina. This can be a blessing for the young wife who has previously found intercourse uncomfortable. Many women relate that intercourse is much better after childbirth. But some find with time that the vagina is not as tight as they would like. Many liken it to having a clapper in a bell, with the penis moving around inside but little pleasurable contact being made with the vaginal walls. The looseness of the labia can prevent contact with the clitoris during intercourse, and orgasm can be more difficult as a result. Both husbands and wives have sought our expertise in repairing the changes that childbirth or a failed episiotomy repair has wrought in their sex life.

Beside the previously mentioned Kegel exercises, surgery can be performed to tighten the vaginal muscles and ligaments. This is similar to the approach one takes in doing an episiotomy, except that attention is paid to reuniting tissues that have been spread apart. The extra skin is then removed.

On the opposite end of the spectrum, there are women who have been sewn too tightly during their episiotomy repair. This can leave them with the inability to have intercourse because of the pain experienced with stretching this scar tissue. A procedure called *perineoplasty* is used to release the scar tissue and relax the vaginal opening.

Some secular press has been given to labial reduction surgery, which makes the labia smaller. Some women have had the labia stretched due to childbirth injury and find the tissues get "caught" by the penis with intercourse, pulling the labia into the vagina. This can be uncomfortable, and we are able to trim them back to their original state for more satisfying sex. The argument for trimming them for a better cosmetic appearance is in the eye of the beholder, and we do not have many requests for surgery due to appearance only.

One final thought on gynecologic surgery is in the area of vaginal rejuvenation. Much has been made in the media and women's magazines about "tightening" the vagina to increase sexual pleasure. Physician are now advertising this service in newspapers, magazines, and on billboards in our city, as I am sure they are in many major cities in the country. This has not been endorsed by any reputable medical organization in America and, in our view, is a chance to con women out of thousands of dollars.

The American College of Obstetricians and Gynecologists, the governing body for OB/GYNs in the United States, has recently issued the following statement regarding vaginal rejuvenation procedures: "These procedures are not medically indicated, and the safety and effectiveness of these procedures have not been documented.... Women should be informed about the lack of data supporting the efficacy of these procedures and their potential complications, including infection, altered sensation, dyspareunia [painful intercourse], adhesions, and scarring."[6]

These are by no means the only surgeries that may be offered to patients to treat gynecologic or urologic conditions. We hope the information presented here will be a good starting point for a conversation with your own personal physician.

# Chapter 26

# LIFE BEYOND FORTY: MAINTAINING YOUR HEALTH

*My (SAF) wife, Sandy, has always been faithful to have regular Pap smears and mammograms. I suppose she doesn't have much of a choice if she wants to avoid being hounded by me! But when her reminder card comes to the house, she makes her appointment and keeps it.*

*On her last visit, she mentioned that she wanted a mammogram. Being in her forties, she had the choice to have them every year or every other year. While many of my patients choose the every-two-year option in their forties, Sandy has always liked the reassurance of a negative exam. She lost a sister to bone cancer when Sandy was in middle school.*

*I had suggested a new mammogram facility that had opened near our office. I knew that the radiologist there was excellent. When Sandy went for her mammogram, she noticed that they took longer than usual and did more X-rays than usual. After her visit, the report came back with a suspicious spot, which they recommended should be biopsied.*

*I reassured Sandy that this was part of the process, that most of these mammogram findings end up to be nothing at all, and that the radiologist was just being thorough. But deep down, she felt that something was wrong.*

*After the biopsy was taken, we received the unexpected news that she had breast cancer. Fortunately, it was a very small tumor that the Lord led them to find. Her lymph nodes were all negative, and she needed no chemotherapy or radiation.*

*We believe the Lord used this screening test to alert us. It could have easily been three years before the tumor would have grown to the size where she or I could feel it. By then, the lymph nodes likely would have been positive for cancer, and she would have had to undergo chemotherapy and radiation. Sandy is a strong advocate for mammography to all the women she meets. She is a living illustration of the value of screening for disease.*

## The Annual Well-Woman Exam at Forty and Older

Once a woman reaches age forty, there are certain areas of the body that we need to monitor more closely. She is either perimenopausal or menopausal, and her body will undergo dramatic changes again. A thorough OB/GYN will perform the following tests and screenings: mammography, colonoscopy, osteoporosis screening, cholesterol, heart disease, and diabetes.

## Mammography

One out of every eight women will get breast cancer during her life.[1] In 2008, about 182,460 women will be diagnosed with breast cancer, and 40,480 will die from the disease.[2] When detected early, the five-year survival exceeds 95 percent. Mammograms are one of the best methods for early detection, yet 13 million women in the United States age forty or older have never had a mammogram.[3]

There are many reasons for this, such as cost, access to health care, ignorance about risk, and fear of discomfort or radiation exposure. The American Cancer Society recommends yearly mammograms beginning at age forty to help detect breast cancer. If you have a family history of breast cancer in a first-degree relative, you may need to start sooner. If you are a woman, you are at risk for breast cancer. You do not need to have a family history of cancer or an abnormal breast exam to undergo mammography.

A mammogram is an X-ray of the breast tissue used to detect abnormalities in both symptomatic and asymptomatic women. Mammography was initially developed in 1969, though X-rays have been used to examine the breasts for over ninety years. Since then, there have been great technological advances, even in the last twenty years. One change is the amount of radiation delivered during the exam. The machine used to image the breasts produces lower energy X-rays with less tissue penetration than a normal X-ray.

A screening mammogram takes two views of your breasts, which are then displayed on film for a radiologist to read. The entire procedure takes about twenty minutes. It is important to have your mammograms done at the same imaging center each year if possible, so that previous films can be compared.

If an abnormality is detected, it does not necessarily mean that you have cancer. About 10 percent of women who undergo screening mammography will have to undergo additional tests because of an abnormality.[4] These tests include a follow-up mammogram, often with magnification views; a breast ultrasound; or a magnetic resonance imaging (MRI). Of the women who undergo additional screening, only two to four out of a thousand will be diagnosed with breast cancer.[5]

Some special situations require other tests as well. If you or your doctor notices a lump or mass, you will need a diagnostic mammogram as opposed to a screening mammogram. This test takes more pictures as well as magnification views to evaluate the suspicious area. An ultrasound may also be performed to provide more information about the abnormal area. If you have breast implants, additional images are taken as the implant is pushed back into the chest while the breast tissue is pulled forward. If you are at high risk for developing breast cancer, your doctor may order an MRI in addition to a screening mammogram.

Mammography is a good way to detect breast cancer in an early stage; however, it will not detect all breast cancers. Other tests are being studied and improvements are being made to help improve detection. Digital mammography captures the images electronically, giving the radiologist the advantage of changing the contrast or magnifying the image on a computer to better evaluate certain areas. This has been shown to more accurately identify cancer in women under the age of fifty and in those with dense breasts. Computer-aided detection can be used in addition to regular mammography to help improve detection. This consists of having a computer read the films and serves as a second opinion to double-check the radiologist. This can pick up some cancers that the doctor might have missed, but it can also lead to unnecessary biopsies. There are other devices being tested, such as nuclear medicine scans, thermal scans, laser scans, and electrical scans.

(i) Most health insurances, including Medicare and Medicaid, cover the cost of mammograms. Low-cost mammograms are available in some communities. You can contact the American Cancer Society at (800) ACS-2345 for information about facilities in your area.

In addition, the National Breast and Cervical Cancer Early Detection Program (NBCCEDP) provides breast and cervical cancer early detection testing to women without health insurance for free or at very little cost. To learn more about this program, please contact the Centers for Disease Control and Prevention (CDC) at (888) 842-6355 or on the Internet at www.cdc.gov/cancer/nbccedp.

## Colonoscopy

A colonoscopy is the best screening tool available for detecting colon cancer, which we will discuss in detail in the next chapter. This device allows visualization of the entire colon. If an abnormal growth or polyp is found during the exam, it can be removed or a biopsy can be performed. If cancer is found and caught early, the five-year survival is greater than 90 percent.[6]

To undergo colonoscopy, you will be given a preparation to drink to help clean out your bowels the day before. A colonoscopy is usually performed by a gastroenterologist or surgeon in their office or in the hospital. You will be given a medication to help you relax, which will often put you to sleep during the procedure. A slender, flexible tube is then inserted into the rectum and colon, and a small amount of air is inserted to allow for visualization. A camera attached to the tube displays the image on a screen. The procedure typically takes about fifteen to thirty minutes. Afterward, you may feel drowsy or "funny" from the medication, and you will need someone to drive you home. You may also feel uncomfortable from the gas inside you, but you should not be in pain during or following the procedure.

If your exam is normal, it should be repeated in ten years; however, if you are at high risk for developing colon cancer, your doctor may recommend performing the test at more frequent intervals. Because colon cancer is very treatable when caught early and often has no symptoms, it is important to undergo recommended screening with colonoscopy. There are other options for screening, including rectal examination, testing the stool for blood, and sigmoidoscopy; however, the best detection rates occur using colonoscopy as a screening tool. Colonoscopy is superior to sigmoidoscopy in women, as a recent study found 65 percent of precancerous lesions were missed in average risk women undergoing screening with sigmoidoscopy.[7]

## Osteoporosis Screening

Osteoporosis is a condition where there is an increased rate of bone turnover, with bone resorption exceeding new bone formation. The bone mineral density is decreased, by definition, 2.5 standard deviations below that of the peak bone mass of a normal healthy twenty-year-old. It is a condition that affects four to six million women.[8]

Each year in the United States, there are approximately 1.5 million fractures per year due to osteoporosis.[9] Risk factors for developing osteoporosis include the following: age over sixty-five, Caucasian race, low weight or low body mass index, history of fracture, family history of osteoporosis, cigarette smoking, lack of estrogen replacement or early menopause, lack of exercise, poor nutrition, and diet low in calcium. There are certain medical conditions and medications that also increase the risk of osteoporosis.

Screening should be performed in all women aged sixty-five and older, and in postmenopausal women under age sixty-five if they have a risk factor. It should not be repeated more frequently than every two years, unless new risk factors develop or treatment is initiated. The standard test for measuring bone mineral density is a dual-energy X-ray absorptiometry (DEXA) scan. It measures the bone density at the sites most commonly affected in osteoporosis—the spine and the hip. It uses little radiation and is highly accurate.

Bone density is measured by comparing the results to that of a young healthy woman at her peak bone mass. The difference is measured in standard deviations and is translated into a T-score. A T-score between -1.0 and -2.5 is designated as low bone mass, or osteopenia. If left untreated, it could progress to osteoporosis. Osteoporosis is defined as a T-score below -2.5. Sustaining a fracture due to a fall from standing height or less also makes the diagnosis of osteoporosis.

There are a variety of medications available for prevention and treatment of osteoporosis. The National Institute of Health recommends daily calcium supplementation with 1000 mg for premenopausal women ages twenty-five to fifty and postmenopausal women who are younger than sixty-five and are on estrogen replacement therapy. Women over sixty-five, or postmenopausal women not on estrogen, are recommended to take 1,500 mg daily. Vitamin D is also important to aid in calcium absorption; 400–800 international units (IU) is the recommended daily dose. Hormone replacement therapy has been shown to decrease the risk of osteoporotic fracture. In addition to estrogen, a class of medications known as selective estrogen receptor modulators (SERMs) work to reduce fractures without increasing the risk of breast cancer. Bisphosphonates are medications that work to reduce bone resorption and bone loss. Parathyroid hormone and calcitonin both act to increase bone formation and are options for treatment.

## Cholesterol and Heart Disease

If you were to ask women what they are most likely to die from, many would say breast cancer is their biggest fear. Some worry about ovarian cancer or colon cancer. The truth is, in women over the age of sixty-five, the number one killer is heart disease. In fact, in that age group, heart disease claims more lives than all cancers combined. An American woman over sixty-five is four to six times more likely to die of heart disease than from breast cancer.[10]

Women are more likely to die of a heart attack than men. They are less likely to make it to the hospital for treatment, and even when they do make it, they are less likely to be diagnosed properly. Health-care providers and women themselves often minimize their symptoms. It is important to be evaluated immediately if you experience any of the following symptoms: pain or discomfort in the center of the chest, neck, jaw, or left arm; shortness of breath; breaking out in a sweat; feeling faint or woozy; or indigestion.

Heart disease is a preventable disease with modifiable risk factors. Smoking; having high blood pressure, diabetes, or high cholesterol; and being sedentary and overweight all increase your risk of developing heart disease. In women under fifty, more than half of all heart attacks occur in women who smoke. If you stop smoking, you cut your risk by one-third in two years.[11] You should know what your blood pressure is. High blood pressure is usually asymptomatic, and if left untreated, it raises your risk of having a heart attack and stroke.

## YOUR BLOOD PRESSURE

Blood pressure is made up of two measurements or numbers. The first number is the systolic blood pressure. This is the peak blood pressure when your heart is pumping out the blood. The second number is the diastolic blood pressure. It's the pressure your blood vessels feel when they are at rest between beats. A normal blood pressure is 120/80 or lower. High blood pressure is 140/90 or higher. If your blood pressure is between 120/80 and 140/90, you have something called "prehypertension."[12]

Diabetes can affect your blood vessels if not under optimal control, so it is important to keep your blood sugar in the desired range if you have diabetes.

Eating a low-fat diet and getting regular exercise—four to six times a week for thirty minutes—will help prevent heart disease, lower your blood pressure, and help control diabetes. Avoiding salt and eating healthily will help lower your blood pressure. Another benefit to following a low-fat diet and getting regular exercise is that it helps lower your cholesterol.

Having some cholesterol in your body is natural and healthy. It serves important functions such as making cell membranes and some hormones. When it is found in high levels, however, it can lead to heart attacks or strokes. There are two types of cholesterol—LDL ("bad" cholesterol) and HDL ("good" cholesterol). LDL, or low-density lipoprotein, is responsible for delivering cholesterol to the body; high levels of LDL can clog arteries, thus increasing your risk of having a heart attack or stroke. HDL, or high-density lipoprotein, carries cholesterol away from the bloodstream; having high levels of HDL actually reduces your risk for heart disease.

Women who are forty-five or older should have their cholesterol checked. To be accurate, your blood should be drawn after you have fasted. If you have a family history of high cholesterol or other risk factors for heart disease, you may need your cholesterol checked earlier. Total cholesterol less than 200 is ideal. Between 200 and 239 is borderline high, and 240 or more is high. As discussed above, it is important to know the breakdown between good and bad cholesterol. Your LDL should be under 130. If it is between 130 and 159, it is borderline high, and if it is 160 or more, it is too high. HDL greater than 60 helps to lower your risk of heart disease, whereas if it is less than 40, your risk increases. Having high triglycerides (a form of fat made in the body) usually accompanies high cholesterol. Elevated triglycerides are usually due to obesity, lack of physical activity, smoking, and a diet rich in carbohydrates.

The first step to lowering your cholesterol is changing your lifestyle. This is very difficult for people to do, but it can make a dramatic impact on your health. If you smoke, stopping will help lower your risk for heart disease. Following a low-fat diet, limiting your alcohol intake, and getting regular exercise can help lower your cholesterol. If you attempt these changes for six months to one year without good results, or if your cholesterol is too high to be changed through these efforts alone, your doctor may place you on a cholesterol-lowering medication. This is not to replace your efforts, because continuing to follow a healthy lifestyle is important.

## Diabetes

Diabetes is a condition where the body does not produce or is unable to utilize insulin properly. Insulin is a hormone that helps your body metabolize sugar and starch (glucose) so that it can be used for energy. Over 20 million people in the United States suffer from diabetes; however, approximately one-third are undiagnosed and unaware that they have the disease.[13]

Diabetes can be diagnosed easily with a simple blood test. Your doctor may order either fasting plasma glucose or an oral glucose tolerance test (GTT). Fasting blood glucose between 100 and 125 is diagnostic of prediabetes, while a level of 126 or higher is indicative of diabetes. In the GTT, you will be given a sugar solution to drink, and your blood glucose level is measured before and afterward. If the blood glucose level is between 140 and 199 two hours after the drink was administered, you have prediabetes. Diabetes is diagnosed if the level is 200 or higher.

If left untreated or if poorly controlled, diabetes can lead to a number of health problems such as heart disease, stroke, blindness, high blood pressure, kidney failure, damage to the nervous system, amputation, dental disease, or sexual dysfunction. Sixty-five percent of diabetics will die from either a heart attack or stroke.[14] Among women with diabetes, there has been a 23 percent increase in deaths due to heart disease over the last thirty years compared with a 27 percent decrease in women without diabetes. Seventy-three percent of people with diabetes have high blood pressure.[15] Diabetic retinopathy is the leading cause for new cases of blindness among people aged twenty to seventy-four, and diabetes is the number one cause of kidney failure. About 60 to 70 percent of people with diabetes have damage to their nervous system, which can lead to amputation.[16]

If you are diagnosed with prediabetes, you can prevent the development of diabetes by making changes in your diet and increasing your level of physical activity. The Diabetes Prevention Program study showed that diet and exercise worked better than medication at preventing or delaying the development of diabetes. A mere 5 to 10 percent reduction in weight, along with thirty minutes a day of moderate physical activity, resulted in a 58 percent reduction in diabetes.[17] If diet and exercise are not enough to control the development of diabetes, your doctor may prescribe medications or insulin injections to keep your blood sugar controlled.

# Chapter 27

# WOMEN AND CANCER

*Ruby, an overweight, sixty-plus-year-old patient, came to the office because she was experiencing vaginal bleeding and knew that bleeding this late in life was abnormal. She weighed about 250 pounds, which made a physical examination of her uterus difficult, so we elected to do a vaginal ultrasound to better visualize the source of her bleeding. Her sonogram revealed a mildly enlarged uterus and a thickened endometrial lining. In women well past menopause, a thickened lining could be the result of a polyp or a sign of uterine cancer.*

*We discussed this with Ruby and offered a simple endometrial biopsy in the office. The procedure consisted of inserting a strawlike catheter through the cervix and into the uterus to remove samples of lining for pathology. Ruby consented, and within five minutes, we had a sample sent to the lab.*

*About one week later, we informed Ruby that the pathology report revealed that she had the early stages of uterine cancer, but that the chances of curing her were very favorable. We consulted a gynecologic oncologist to help us with her hysterectomy. He sampled her pelvic lymph nodes and discovered that all of the cancer was contained within her uterus and was superficial. The hysterectomy removed all of the cancer, and she wouldn't have to undergo chemotherapy or radiation.*

*We shared the good news with Ruby and commended her for acting quickly. By seeking medical attention for the vaginal bleeding immediately, we were able to find the cancer at an early stage and cure her.*

## Breast Cancer

Developing breast cancer is perhaps a woman's greatest fear. And it is a valid concern, as one in eight women will contract breast cancer in their lifetime, regardless of family history. It is the most common cancer in women, and about 182,460 women will develop breast cancer in 2008. The lives of 40,480 women will be claimed by breast cancer this year, making it the second most common cause of death from cancer in women, behind lung cancer. Approximately 2.5 million women currently in the United States have been treated for breast cancer.[1]

Breast cancer occurs when a tumor (abnormal growth of cells) begins in the breast and grows without control. It usually begins in the milk ducts that line the breast, but it can also start in the lobules, or glands that make breast milk. Lymph vessels drain the breast into lymph nodes under the arm, under the neck, and in the chest wall. If the cancer in the breast reaches these lymph nodes and continues to grow, swelling will occur. The cancer can then spread beyond the breast into other tissues of the body.

While the cause of breast cancer is unknown, there are certain risk factors that predispose a person to develop breast cancer. Just because you have a risk factor does not mean that you will develop the disease, and many women without any risk factors will develop breast cancer. The following factors have been associated with an increased risk of developing breast cancer:

- Gender: Being a woman is the single biggest risk factor for developing breast cancer. However, contrary to popular belief, men can develop breast cancer.

- Age: The risk of developing breast cancer increases with age, with 80 percent of cases occurring in women over fifty.[2]

- Family history: If you have a close relative with breast cancer, defined as a parent, sibling, or offspring, your risk doubles.

- Genetic mutations: Carrying a gene that predisposes you to breast cancer makes it likely that you will develop the disease.

- Personal history of breast cancer: If you have already developed breast cancer in one breast, you are more likely to get it again in the other breast.

- Race: Caucasian women are more likely to develop breast cancer.

- Previous breast biopsy: An abnormal breast biopsy in the past puts you at a higher risk of breast cancer.

- Previous radiation exposure: Undergoing treatment to the chest with radiation raises your risk of breast cancer.

- Prolonged menstrual cycles: Having periods beginning before age twelve or lasting past age fifty-five increases your risk.

- DES (diethylstilbestrol) exposure: If your mother took diethyl-stilbestrol when she was pregnant with you, then you are at an increased risk.

- Not having children: If you do not have children or you have your first child after age thirty, your risk is increased.

- Hormone replacement therapy (HRT): Recent studies suggest that taking HRT can increase your risk of developing breast cancer if taken for several years. It does not appear that estrogen replacement alone increases this risk. However, if you have had breast cancer, you should not take estrogen, as it may increase your chance of recurrence.

- Alcohol: Drinking even one drink daily increases your risk.

- Obesity: Being overweight increases your risk of developing breast cancer.

The following factors have been associated with a decreased risk of breast cancer:[3]

- Weight loss: Losing eleven pounds or more can decrease risk, especially among postmenopausal women.

- Physical activity: Studies show that exercising (at least thirty minutes on five or more days of the week) may reduce your risk by 30 to 40 percent.

- Limited alcohol consumption: The more alcohol you drink, the greater your risk. Limit yourself to not more than one drink per day—12 ounces of beer, 5 ounces of wine, or 1.5 ounces of liquor.

- Breast-feeding: Breast-feeding for at least four months offers women some protection against breast cancer.

- Avoiding cigarette smoke: Smoking is responsible for 30 percent of all cancer deaths.

- Bypassing HRT: HRT increases the risk of breast cancer and heart disease. Talk to your doctor about the risks and benefits.

(i) The Web site www.cancer.gov/bcrisktool/ contains the Breast Cancer Risk Assessment Tool, which can be used to help you identify your own personal risk of developing breast cancer.

Breast cancer can be detected through screening techniques, such as mammography, clinical breast exams, and self breast exams. Some signs to look for are: swelling in a part of the breast, skin irritation or dimpling, nipple pain or inversion, redness or scaliness of the breast skin, discharge other than a milky substance, or a lump under the arm. If something suspicious is found through screening, diagnostic tests will be performed through an ultrasound and MRI. Suspicious areas or lumps may need a biopsy to obtain a sample of the tissue to see if it is cancerous or not.

If cancer is detected, there are various options for treatment. You may be a candidate for a *lumpectomy*, or removal of the tumor mass itself. When the entire breast needs to be removed, it is called a *mastectomy*. There are different types of mastectomy, including the following: simple mastectomy, partial mastectomy, modified radical mastectomy, and radical mastectomy. In addition to surgery, chemotherapy and/or radiation may be recommended by your doctor.

After undergoing treatment for cancer, it is important to take care of yourself and to undergo recommended follow-up tests and exams. Breast cancer can recur, but many more women are diagnosed with breast cancer than actually die as a result of it. This indicates that breast cancer is curable, especially if caught early.

## Colon Cancer

Colon cancer, or colorectal cancer, is the third most common cause for cancer deaths among women in the United States. This year, approximately 150,000 Americans will be diagnosed with colon cancer, and 50,000 will die as a result of it.[4] Colon cancer is a preventable disease. It starts out as a growth in the colon called a polyp, and if caught early, it can be removed before it becomes cancerous. More than 90 percent of all cases of colon cancer are detected in people age fifty or older.[5] Therefore, the American Cancer Society recommends that all men and women over the age of fifty undergo screening. If you have a family history of colon cancer, your doctor may recommend that you get tested at a younger age. Colon cancer begins in the large intestine (colon) or rectum (end of colon).

Risk factors for developing colon cancer include:[6]

- Age: people over the age of fifty
- Having had colorectal cancer before, even if it was completely removed
- Having colorectal polyps
- Family history of colon cancer
- Ulcerative colitis or Crohn's disease

- Having a genetic syndrome that predisposes you to developing colon cancer
- Ethnic background: Jews of Eastern European descent are more likely to develop colorectal cancer.
- Race: colon cancer is more prevalent among African Americans.
- Diet: a diet high in fat and red meat predisposes you to developing colon cancer.
- Lack of exercise
- Overweight
- Diabetes
- Smoking
- Alcohol

Colon cancer can develop without any symptoms, though the following symptoms are associated with it:

- Diarrhea, constipation, or change in bowel habits
- Blood in the stool
- Anemia not explained by another cause
- Abdominal pain
- Intestinal obstruction
- Weight loss
- Narrowing stools

Tests can be done to detect colon cancer if any of the above symptoms are present, or detection may be done as screening tests. Your doctor may perform a rectal exam and test your stool for blood (FOBT—fecal occult blood test). If this test is positive, it does not mean you have colon cancer, nor does it mean that you do not if it is negative. Other tests include barium enema (an X-ray after contrast is inserted into the rectum), flexible sigmoidoscopy, and colonoscopy. The American Cancer Society recommends the following options for screening:

- FOBT yearly plus flexible sigmoidoscopy every five years OR
- Barium enema every five years OR
- Colonoscopy every ten years

Women should consider being screened with colonoscopy rather than sigmoidoscopy, as cancers in the right side of the colon are more common in women and can be missed by a sigmoidoscopy.[7]

If you are diagnosed with colon cancer, you will likely undergo additional evaluation to see if the cancer has spread. This can be done with CT scan, X-ray, or MRI. You will be tested to see if you have developed anemia. Treatment of colon cancer consists of surgery to remove the cancer and chemotherapy and radiation to kill cancerous cells. If caught early, colon cancer is highly treatable, with a five-year survival rate of over 90 percent. Unfortunately, only 39 percent of cases are caught at an early stage.[8] It is important to undergo the recommended screening procedures, because colon cancer can almost always be caught early.

# Cervical Cancer

Cancer of the cervix develops when normal cells in the lining of the cervix, where the innermost cells of the cervical canal connect with the cells on the surface of the cervix, become abnormal and develop changes that eventually turn into cancer. Cervical cancer does not develop overnight. With proper screening, it can usually be caught and treated at an early or precancerous stage. Despite this, an estimated 11,070 cases of invasive cervical cancer will be detected in the United States this year, and approximately 3,870 women will die as a result of the disease.[9]

Because of widespread use of the Pap smear test, the number of deaths from cervical cancer has dropped significantly since 1955.[10] The majority of cases of cervical cancer diagnosed today are in women who have never had or not recently had a Pap smear. If an abnormality is found, it can almost always be treated before progressing to cancer. Therefore, it is important to undergo routine testing as recommended by your doctor and to have follow-up testing if an abnormality is found. If cancer is found early, it can be cured over 90 percent of the time.

The majority of cases of cervical cancer are preventable. There are definitive risk factors that predispose you to develop cervical cancer. Infection with certain strains of HPV can lead to the development of cancer. If you have had an STD in the past, your risk is greater, and if you were exposed to DES (diethylstilbestrol) before birth, you are also at greater risk.

Precancerous lesions and early-stage cancers do not have any symptoms. They are detected through routine screening. Symptoms of invasive cervical cancer include abnormal bleeding or discharge and pain or bleeding during intercourse. If you are found to have a precancerous lesion or invasive cancer, your doctor will recommend further workup and treatment.

If an abnormality is detected with a Pap smear, your doctor will usually perform a colposcopy. This is a procedure where your doctor visualizes the abnormal area on your cervix with binoculars and takes a biopsy for further testing to see if dysplasia (a precancerous condition) is present. The tissue is then graded as mild dysplasia, moderate dysplasia, or severe dysplasia. Most cases of mild dysplasia will not progress to cancer, while moderate or severe cases have a higher risk of becoming cancerous. Your doctor may recommend a procedure to remove these abnormal cells so that they do not progress to cancer.

If invasive cancer is found, the treatment is hysterectomy (removal of the uterus and cervix) if caught early. More advanced cases are treated with radical hysterectomy (removal of the uterus, cervix, and surrounding tissue) or chemotherapy and radiation.

Cervical cancer is one of the easiest cancers to detect at an early stage. With regular Pap smears, it is extremely unlikely you will develop cervical cancer.

## Uterine Cancer

The most common type of uterine cancer is endometrial cancer, which starts in the lining of the uterus, or endometrium. It is the fourth most common cancer in women, behind lung, breast, and colon cancers.[11] If caught early and confined to the uterus, it is effectively treated with a hysterectomy.

Endometrial cancer is most common in women who are postmenopausal, though it can be found in younger women on occasion. It is usually caught early because most women develop symptoms of vaginal bleeding either between periods or after menopause.

Endometrial cancer develops over a period of time. First, the cells that make up the lining of the uterus grow and proliferate in response to estrogen. They become abnormal and, if not treated, can grow out of control, becoming cancerous. Conditions that increase your exposure to estrogen increase your risk of developing endometrial cancer. Some of these conditions include the following:[12]

- Starting your period at a young age or going through menopause late

- Never being pregnant

- Ovulating irregularly or having irregular menstrual cycles, such as in women with PCOS

- Obesity, due to enzymes in fat tissue converting hormones into estrogen

- Having type 2 diabetes, as this is frequently associated with being overweight

- Taking estrogen replacement therapy without a progestin, as unopposed estrogen causes the lining of the uterus to grow, while progestins cause the lining to shed

- Rare ovarian tumors that can secrete estrogen

Other risk factors for developing endometrial cancer include the following:[13]

- Age

- History of breast or ovarian cancer

- Tamoxifen use, as it can stimulate the lining of the uterus to grow and cause cancer in one out of every five hundred women who take it

- Race—white women are more likely to develop endometrial cancer

- Genetic syndromes that increase your risk for endometrial cancer as well as colon cancer

If you develop irregular vaginal bleeding, bleeding at times other than when you have your period, or bleeding after you go through menopause, you should contact your doctor. He or she may want to perform an exam and special tests such as a Pap smear, biopsy, or ultrasound. If cancer is suspected or further testing is needed, you may need to undergo a D&C.

If cancer is found, it can be treated with a hysterectomy if caught early. Other treatments used if it is more advanced include progesterone therapy, chemotherapy, and radiation. After treatment, you will need to be followed closely for return of the cancer. Your doctor may perform exams, a Pap smear, and chest X-rays to detect a recurrence.

Your risk for developing endometrial cancer is lowered if you maintain a healthy weight, take birth control pills for ten years or more, or take a combination HRT (with both estrogen and progestin).

## Ovarian Cancer

Ovarian cancer is epithelial cancer, which means it starts on the surface of the ovary and spreads throughout the pelvis and abdomen. It usually progresses to an advanced stage before it is diagnosed. In 2008, an estimated 21,650 women will be diagnosed with ovarian cancer, and 15,520 will die from it.[14]

Symptoms of ovarian cancer can be vague, making it difficult to diagnose at an early stage. Some of the symptoms include the following:[15]

- Bloating
- Abdominal pain
- Difficulty eating or feeling full quickly
- Urinary symptoms (urgency or frequency)
- Fatigue
- Indigestion
- Back pain
- Pain with intercourse
- Constipation
- Irregular menstrual cycles

If you have these symptoms, especially the first four, for three weeks or more, you should contact your doctor. A pelvic exam and ultrasound can be used to detect ovarian cancer. A blood test called a CA-125 can also be ordered if cancer is suspected.

If any of these tests show suspicion for cancer, your doctor may refer you to a women's cancer specialist (gynecologic oncologist) for staging and treatment. Staging is performed surgically and consists of removing the affected ovary or ovaries and any additional tissue or organs that it has spread to. If the cancer has spread beyond the ovaries, treatment also consists of chemotherapy and, rarely, radiation.

After diagnosis and treatment of ovarian cancer, your doctor will monitor you closely for recurrence of the disease. The likelihood of recurrence depends on the stage of diagnosis, with early stage cancers having a survival rate of 93 percent for five years or more, with most being cured.[16] However, most ovarian cancers are diagnosed at an advanced stage.

# Skin Cancer

The most common form of cancer in the United States is skin cancer. There are several different types of skin cancer. Basal cell carcinoma and squamous cell carcinoma are the two most common forms, while melanoma is less common but more dangerous.[17]

The following factors put you at an increased risk of developing skin cancer:

- History of sunburns or spending a lot of time in the sun
- Being fair-skinned
- Family history of skin cancer
- Age over fifty years

If you have any suspicious areas on your skin, you should have your doctor look closely at them. If caught early, most skin cancers can be treated by excision before they spread to other parts of the body.

The best way to avoid having skin cancer is to take steps to prevent it. Wear clothing and hats that cover sun-exposed areas when possible. Be sure to use sunscreen every time you are outside. Use something that has a high protectant against both UVA and UVB rays. Have your doctor examine your skin each year as part of your general exam.

### UVA, UVB, AND SUNSCREENS

UVB rays are those that are most responsible for sunburn and cancer. UVA rays penetrate deeper and cause more of the aging effects like wrinkles, age spots, and leathering. SPF—or sun protection factor—is a measure of a sunscreen's ability to prevent UVB rays from damaging the skin.

SPF 15 blocks approximately 93 percent of all incoming UVB rays. SPF 30 blocks 97 percent, and SPF 50 blocks 99 percent. While these are small differences in percentage, the improvement in cancer protection is much greater. But no amount of SPF can block all UVB rays. Use at least an SPF 15 to prevent skin cancer.

Sunscreen, regardless of strength, will not stay effective longer than two hours without reapplication. Remember, preventing sunburn is only dealing with the UVB rays; UVA damage may still be happening.[18]

# Chapter 28

# AGING AND INTIMACY

As a couple reaches their forties and fifties, they will notice certain changes happening to their bodies that will cause them to reevaluate their sex life. Many couples will wrongly conclude that they have reached an age when sexual activity is no longer possible or no longer desirable. With the average life expectancy now reaching deep into the eighties and nineties, to abandon sexual activity as one ages is to forfeit some of the best years of marital intimacy. As the average age to marriage has increased to age twenty-seven, there would appear to be only two good decades of marital sex available to us if we embrace the myths about sex and aging.

Most of the baby-boomer generation has grown up with the idea that anything is possible if you work hard at it. It is a generation ever seeking youth and beauty, aware of the benefits of health and exercise as no previous generation on Earth. But the realm of sexual activity and aging is at a crossroads. Most of those couples have parents who grew up in the 1940s and 1950s when sexual activity was rarely talked about or demonstrated at home. Women did not work as hard as they do today to stay attractive and fit. The mother of the baby boomer may have let herself age prematurely by today's standards. The husband may have paid little attention to her as she got older, and the two may have lived very separate lives. As a consequence, the romantic involvement of their parents may have diminished considerably over time. Even if their parents stayed sexually active, it was never discussed and affection was often not shown. Thus, the current generation of middle-aged couples has little in the way of a role model to pattern their sexual lives together.

## Myths About Sex and Aging

Certain myths about sex continue to this day and influence the lives of otherwise committed Christians.[1] We see this in our offices each week.

One myth is that sex isn't important as people get older. Other things in life like companionship or recreational activity can keep the marriage together. Even grandchildren can be a source of common interest for an older couple. Sex is really something one does when he or she is younger or wanting a family. After a while, it isn't that big of a deal anymore.

The second myth is that sexual activity is supposed to fade away due to the process of aging. The body naturally tends to stop being able to be sexually active, and the desire for sex is supposed to follow the ability to have it. Since God created our bodies, when our bodies no longer can do the things it used to do, that must be a signal that it is time to stop being sexually active. Otherwise, God would have made us capable of staying at the same level sexually.

The third myth is that sex after a certain age is dangerous. Many men are afraid they will have a heart attack while having sex and will be found by paramedics in an embarrassing position that all the neighbors will hear about.

The fourth myth is more prevalent for women. Since they are getting older and may not be as attractive physically as they once were, they must not be sexually attractive to their husbands. If he still wants sex, it is just to satisfy his own needs and not because he still finds her attractive.

The final myth is that with menopause and erectile dysfunction, it is just too much of a bother to stay sexually active. It is easier for everyone involved if the issue never comes up and they move on in the marriage without it. The amount of work involved is not worth the rewards.

All of these myths are just that—flat-out lies. With the tenacity of the current baby boomers as role models, our children should grow up in a loving home where the husband and wife continue to model romance and passion, letting the next generation know that sex does not end at an arbitrary age.

One has only to look at the Bible to see that God did not intend for us to stop being sexually active as we age. Examples from the Old Testament show couples who were still sexual as they aged.

In the Book of Ruth, a young widow returns to Israel and seeks the kindness of a distant relative named Boaz, who would become the great-grandfather of King David; ultimately, Christ would come to Earth through this union. Boaz was flattered that Ruth chose him when she could have chosen a younger man (Ruth 3:10). He takes her as his bride, and she gives birth to a son. There was never a question of whether Boaz could still perform sexually or not, or that he was even sexually attractive to a younger woman. It was a very natural thing for Ruth and Boaz to come together as a sexual couple.

## IT'S IN THE WORD

The story of Abraham and Sarah is a prime example of enjoying sex in the "golden years." Even at the age of sixty-five, Sarah was so beautiful that when she and Abraham went down to Egypt, her appearance so struck Pharaoh that he took her into his palace. One of the most powerful men in the world at that time, a man who could have had any woman he desired, chose a sixty-five-year-old Hebrew woman to be in his palace (Gen. 12:11–15). Even when Sarah was well into her eighties, Abraham made her lie about being his wife so he would not get killed because of her beauty. (See Genesis 20.) By the time the Lord enabled Sarah to conceive their son, Isaac, Sarah was well into her nineties and Abraham was a century old (Gen. 21:5). There is no record in the Bible that the Lord had to convince Abraham to have sexual relations with Sarah, just that He would cause her to conceive. The fact that they could still have sex was a given.

# Benefits of Aging

Hopefully we have at least opened the door to the idea that God wants you to enjoy sexual activity in marriage as you age. Now we'd like to look at some practical considerations. As we reach middle age (for purposes of discussion we'll agree on the late forties and early fifties), we may find that our lives offer us far more freedom than when we were younger. The children have either left the home or are teens who do not need (or want) our constant attention. There is more time alone to be sexual as a couple than when our children were small. The fear has long passed of being "caught" having sex by some preschooler who wanders into the bedroom at night. With age has also come a diminished need for birth control. Menopause signals the end of fertility and a freedom to enjoy sexual intercourse without the fears of unplanned pregnancy or the hassles of condoms and diaphragms.

Usually at this stage in our lives, we have achieved career stability and financial success. We are no longer climbing our way to the top of the corporate ladder or swimming in a mountain of debt. Wherever we are financially at this stage, we have made peace with it and can relax and enjoy life more than when we were younger and just starting out. We have more time to cultivate activities we both share and once again enjoy each other's company without the focus always being on work or children. It is a time to reconnect with our spouses on every level.

By the time we have been married fifteen or twenty years, we should have built a level of trust between one another that allows us to share almost anything. We will have gone through at least one marital, financial, or career crisis by this point and weathered the storm together, forging a strong bond of loyalty.

With such solid foundations in every other aspect of our relationship together, it is a shame that most couples abandon satisfying sexual activity just when it could become the best it has ever been. While the challenges of staying sexually active as one ages require work, the rewards are well worth the effort.

## Challenges of Aging

It is easy for couples to grow apart. When you are focusing on the kids or the business, there is a common goal. But many couples do not keep their relationship healthy in the process. Various outside interests, hobbies, and clubs can pull you in two different directions. Once the children are grown, you discover that you have little in common anymore. The level of intimacy has diminished, and sex becomes either an obligation or a nuisance as it no longer serves to unite you into "one flesh."

Intimacy is key to keeping the sexual fires burning as you age. Little things done during the day can remind your spouse that you are thinking about him and desiring him. Notes left in a briefcase or a call at work can remind him that he has value to you. And the same is true for you. Unexpected flowers or a surprise dinner at a romantic restaurant can be the start of a passionate evening. Even a bath together can be a prelude to greater things.

Diana Hagee, wife of popular evangelist and pastor John Hagee, writes of this in her book *The King's Daughter*. She recalls her own struggle to keep intimacy alive in her marriage amidst a very hectic schedule. The solution is a program she calls OWE: "One Way Every day."[2] This phrase reminds her and her husband to do one thing that is loving, kind, and romantic each day. They are forever courting, forever on the path of romance.

The simple things really make the most impact. When your spouse sees that you love him and think about him, he will naturally be drawn to you and feel safe with you. The level of intimacy will grow to the point where you are each free to share what is really going on as you age.

There will be physical changes that will occur as you age that are inevitable. Learn to accept them and accept yourself. Do not compare yourself or your spouse to what you used to be. You can never go back there. Don't compare yourself to what Hollywood says you should look like. Most of what you see is fake.

Jamie Lee Curtis, at age forty-three, had the courage to do a photo shoot for *More Magazine* that showed before and after pictures. She wanted women to see what she looked like before she put on the girdle and before the makeup team and hairdressers arrived, before the photos were retouched in the studio. It was important to her to remove the mask and let women know that what they see on television or in magazines is not the mark they should be shooting for. It doesn't really exist.[3]

At nearly fifty, she posed for *AARP the Magazine* topless. "I want to be older," she tells the magazine. "I actually think there's an incredible amount of self-knowledge that comes with getting older. I feel way better now than I did when I was 20. I'm stronger, I'm smarter in every way."[4]

We need to try to be the best we can be at the age that we are and accept the difference. We must also accept who we are becoming based on the limits we are willing to bear. There are some who can afford plastic surgery and some who cannot. There are some who will dedicate themselves to a feverish exercise schedule and those who will not or cannot. There are those who are willing to be strict in their diet and never eat certain foods, and there are those who don't want to live under those tight restrictions. We will get different results based on what we are willing to invest in the process.

There needs to be a healthy and honest conversation where we can determine as husband and wife what we are and are not willing to do to remain as healthy and vibrant as possible. Once we are in agreement, neither side can push the other to do things that are objectionable. Each couple must make an honest assessment of where they are headed and what they can do to stay healthy and vibrant sexually within their own comfort zone.

As we have discussed in the chapter on menopause, local vaginal estrogens are extremely helpful in ensuring that intercourse is not uncomfortable for the woman. Some of the vaginal surgeries we detailed earlier are also useful in maintaining a properly functioning vagina.

Staying in good health is obviously a worthwhile goal even if you never have sex, but the reverse is equally true: if you want to stay sexually active, you have to stay in good health. Almost every disease will have an impact on our sex lives. Heart disease causes lack of energy and diminished stamina. Diabetes leads to hardening of the arteries and loss of nerve function, major contributors to the high impotence rates among diabetic men. If most couples would lose fifty pounds and eat correctly, not only would their diseases improve, but also they might never have developed in the first place.

Hypertension also impedes blood flow to the penis, and the medications that are often necessary to treat it have their own side effects on sexual arousal for both men and women. Weight loss, dietary changes, and exercise could eliminate this disease for a large percentage of people. I am reminded of the words of the apostle Paul when he wrote, "The wife's body does not belong to her alone but also to her husband. In the same way, the husband's body does not belong to him alone but also to his wife" (1 Cor. 7:4). There are medical aspects of aging that we do have some control over, and our spouse has every right to expect us to do whatever we can to stay as healthy as possible.

# The Male Retreat

It is important for a woman to understand the difficulties her man faces as he ages if she is to continue to enjoy sexual intimacy. The first thing that a man notices with aging is the changes in erectile function. The penis will take longer to achieve an erection, and it will likely not be as strong as it used to be. The sight of his naked wife will no longer be enough to ensure an erection, and the erection may fade in mid-coitus.

For men, the ability to have and maintain a strong erection has been tied to their self-image as a sexual being. It seemed that in their teens and twenties, erections happened even when they were not desired. Visual stimulation was often all that was needed to become aroused, and a simple kiss could bring the penis to life. Now those things no longer are enough, and it can be a frightening experience for most men. This "crisis" of masculinity is really no crisis at all. It will happen to every man just as surely as menopause will come to every woman.

Men falsely believe that once they begin to struggle with erections, it is the end of their sex lives. Instead of reaching out for support and help, they retreat, often abandoning their wives emotionally as well. If there is no physical touch from kissing, hugging, cuddling, then there is no danger that things will progress to the place where she will want to make love and he will have to face his fear of failure and his weakening self-image as a man. This period of vulnerability can be a crossroads for any marriage.

When men learn that sex is not just about the penis and penetration, a whole new area of sexual exploration unfolds. Women have instinctively known that they are having sex when they are held in a warm embrace, or caressed in a soothing bath, or kissed passionately for hours. They do not restrict the idea of sex to vaginal penetration and ejaculation. Maybe because orgasm is not the only factor in successful sexual relationships for women, the transitions of aging are not as abrupt as they are for men. But the wise woman will learn to take advantage of the changes in her husband to explore a new realm of experience.

It is a biological fact that men reach orgasm much faster than women. While men can ejaculate in as little as ninety seconds, women often need forty-five minutes to reach orgasm.[5] This wide disparity has often left women without their fair share of orgasmic experiences. Most men are neither patient or knowledgeable enough to do what is necessary to see that their partner is sexually satisfied. And because most women do not expect to achieve orgasm each time, it is often left unspoken.

But now with age comes the great equalizer. It is as if God has remembered the woman and given to her the gift of time. Because it will now take the man longer to achieve and maintain an erection, the process cannot be rushed, as it once might have been when her husband was younger or when she was tired from the kids and just wanted to "get it over with." Now sexual intercourse is an experience that must be lingered over by the very changes that nature brings to the man. It is all about the journey and not just the destination. This is when sex becomes intimate and not simply a race to the finish. And because the house is not filled with little children or demands of work, there is the time available to really explore one another and discover what brings each one pleasure.

The man must now learn to be creative and give his wife pleasure regardless of the ability he still possesses to have vaginal intercourse. Foreplay is now the most important thing, and this gives the wife the much-needed time she needs to be fully aroused and orgasmic. As the husband concentrates his efforts on caressing her body and stimulating her clitoris by either tongue or hand, she is free to enjoy and receive instead of always giving. She can delight in a truly satisfying sexual experience where her needs have been made primary and her only duty is to receive. It is such a rare gift that the man who is wise enough to give it will be repaid handsomely.

With the concentration placed on pleasing the woman first, the pressure to have an erection spontaneously is greatly diminished. Since the focus is no longer on the penis, any pressure or anxiety that the man was carrying can also be discarded. Just removing the mental stress can do wonders for the ability to have an erection.

This time of erectile difficulty is also the perfect time for the woman to reach out to the vulnerable man and be the helpmate God created her to be. Because the man is no longer able to achieve erection based solely on sight, she must be careful not to interpret these changes as signs that he is not interested in her anymore or that he is having an affair. The wife must realize that her husband has no control over his erections and cannot "will" them into existence. In fact, pressure to perform to his previous standard can be an erection killer. She must also not make fun of him or tease him in any way. No other area of life is as vulnerable and exposed for men as this one. Only the most gentle and soothing words of encouragement will allow him to let his wife meet his need.

The successful wife will open the door to communication in a way that does not place blame or accuse, but honestly offers help. She will show him other ways to please her sexually that do not involve penetration. And she will encourage him to seek medical help and offer to go with him to see a urologist.

## Medical Help for the Man You Love

There are many things that can be done to help erectile difficulties.[6] A trained urologist can suggest an assortment of products, depending on the man's unique medical condition. There is almost no one who cannot be helped to have an erection. The main barrier is pride.

Most of the products overcome the weakness of blood flow to the penis that comes with aging. Hardening of the arteries slows the flow of blood to the penis, making time to full erection longer and lessening the firmness of the erection. Devices like the vacuum pump are placed over the penis to pull blood into it. Once an erection is achieved, a rubber ring is placed around the base of the penis to prevent the flow of blood back out of the penis until intercourse is complete. This device may intimidate both the man and his wife, but it can be successfully woven into foreplay. Men who are on any type of blood thinners cannot use it.

Penile self-injection is a technique where a small needle is used to inject a medication directly into the penis to achieve erection. It takes effect within ten minutes and lasts for four hours. The hindrances to this method are the reluctance to inject one's penis and the fact that the erection will not go away for four hours. On the positive side, millions of people self-inject insulin every day and have grown accustomed to it. The fact that the erection lasts so long and is so reliable is also a plus for the wife, who is assured of all the time she needs to achieve her own orgasm. The man can be confident that his erection cannot fade prematurely, and this frees him to linger in lovemaking as well.

The creation of the drug Viagra has been revolutionary in the field of medicine. Except for a very few specific medical conditions, almost every man can use Viagra. Most will achieve measurable improvement in the strength of their erection as well as longevity in the erection. Viagra can decrease blood pressure and must be used under medical supervision for those men who are taking blood pressure medication or who have heart disease.[7]

Other medications in this class of drugs include Levitra and Cialis, the latter giving couples the option of having intercourse anytime from thirty minutes to thirty-six hours after taking the drug.

For those few who are unable to use or achieve results with the previous methods, there is the penile implant. This is a device that is surgically implanted into the shaft of the penis, and a pump is placed inside the scrotum. When an erection is desired, the pump is squeezed to release a liquid that fills the device in the shaft of the penis for as long as needed. The liquid is then drained back into the pump when erection is no longer needed. This is a more complicated task but one that many who suffer from prostate cancer have found will bring them back to sexual function again.

Besides these medical tools, the wife can aid her husband in achieving an erection. The older penis needs more tactile stimulation to become erect. This means that the sense of touch now becomes more dominant than the sense of sight. Again, God balances it so that just as women begin to feel less physically beautiful, the realm of visual images loses it power and is replaced by touch. Both manual stimulation, following the techniques of masturbation, and oral sex are important tools for achieving erection.

## Nonsexual Intimacy

We are certainly aware that there will come a time when the physical aspect of aging or disease will takes its toll and vaginal-penile intercourse is no longer possible. It is then that the old saying "Sex is in the mind" is fully realized. One can be having a sexual encounter when kissing, caressing, or sharing a bath or massage. These activities can be very fulfilling and continue intimacy in the marriage.

I (SAF) am reminded of the De Beers diamond commercial where a couple in their late twenties is walking in the park and they come upon a couple in their eighties walking hand in hand on the path in front of them. The younger couple separates as they walk around the older couple on each side. They then reunite and give a glance back to the elderly couple. These senior citizens look at them with a twinkle in their eyes. At the end of the commercial, the young woman is looking at her husband as if to say, "That is what I want for us as we grow old together."

We firmly believe God is for us and that He cares about our relationships in every detail. He can help us bring joy, pleasure, and love, in all its forms, to that person He has united us with. Only God can make two separate human beings into one flesh. Through extending and receiving forgiveness, we can be vulnerable enough to share our secrets. Through honest communication, we can make our needs known and our desires understood. Through failure we can discover those empty places in our soul that the other can fill.

As we grow older, we are on a journey together, unashamed of the changes we encounter along the way. We are willing to adapt but unwilling to give up. Despite what the generations before us have decided, the thought of not being sexually intimate after a certain age is foreign to us. As baby boomers, our generation is refusing to concede anything as we age.

Our prayer is that this generation of Christian baby boomers will continue to present to the church marriages filled with life and passion as we age. May our children and grandchildren see us as role models, living vibrant lives even into retirement. The decades of marriage should mold two into one so tightly that younger generations will wish for the day they can achieve that level of intimacy and love. The youthful, physical stamina of their early sexual relations will pale in comparison to the deep, unfaltering breadth of love they can achieve in their senior years.

May the fire in our eyes tell them that passion still burns after thirty, forty, fifty, and sixty years of marriage. May we be able to say at the end of the journey that we achieved what Adam and Eve knew in the garden—we were naked (heart, soul, mind, and body) and unashamed.

# Notes

## Chapter 1: Woman as Designed by God

1. M. Yusoff Dawood, "Primary Dysmenorrhea: Advances in Pathogenesis and Management," *Obstetrics and Gynecology* 108 (August 2006): 428–441.

2. M. Steiner, "Premenstrual Syndromes," *Annual Review of Medicine* 48 (1997): 447–445.

3. R. L. Reid and S. S. C. Yen, "Premenstrual Syndrome," *American Journal of Obstetrics and Gynecology* 139 (1981): 85–104.

## Chapter 2: Body Image

1. APA Task Force on the Sexualization of Girls, "Report of the APA Task Force on the Sexualization of Girls Executive Summary," 2007, http://www.apa.org/pi/wpo/sexualizationsum.html (accessed April 3, 2008).

2. E. E. Abramson and P. Valene, "Media Use, Dietary Restraint, Bulimia and Attitudes Toward Obesity: A Preliminary Study," *British Review of Bulimia and Anorexia Nervosa* 5, no. 2 (1991): 73–76.

3. APA Task Force on the Sexualization of Girls, "Report of the APA Task Force on the Sexualization of Girls Executive Summary."

4. Nanci Hellmich, "Do Thin Models Warp Girls' Body Image?" USAToday.com, September 26, 2006, http://www.usatoday.com/news/health/2006-09-25-thin-models_x.htm (accessed April 3, 2008).

5. Ibid.

6. Ibid.

7. M. Levine, L. Smolak, and H. Hayden, "The Relation of Sociocultural Factors to Eating Attitudes and Behaviors Among Middle School Girls," *Journal of Early Adolescence* 14, no. 4 (1994): 471–490.

8. Hellmich, "Do Thin Models Warp Girls' Body Image?"

9. National Alliance on Mental Illness, "Anorexia Nervosa," http://www.nami.org/Template.cfm?Section=By_Illness&template=/ContentManagement/ContentDisplay.cfm&ContentID=7409 (accessed April 3, 2008).

10. National Institutes of Health, "Anorexia Nervosa," MedlinePlus, http://www.nlm.nih.gov/medlineplus/ency/article/000362.htm (accessed April 3, 2008).

11. Ibid.

12. eMedicineHealth.com, "Bulimia," http://www.emedicinehealth.com/bulimia/article_em.htm (accessed April 3, 2008).

13. American Association of Clinical Endocrinologists, "Position Statement on Metabolic and Cardiovascular Consequences of Polycystic Ovary Syndrome," *Endocrine Practice* 11, no. 2 (2005): 126–134.

## Chapter 3: Sex and Teens

1. T. Sorensen and B. Snow, "How Children Tell: The Process of Disclosure in Child Sexual Abuse," *Child Welfare Journal* 70, no. 1 (1991): 3–15.

2. A. Negrusz and R. E. Gaensslen, "Analytical Developments in Toxicological Investigation of Drug-Facilitated Sexual Assault," *Analytical and Bioanalytical Chemistry* 376, no. 8 (August 2003): 1192–1197.

## Chapter 4: Your Gynecologist and You

1. ClevelandClinic.org, "Thyroid Disease," http://www.clevelandclinic.org/health/health-info/docs/2000/2011.asp?index=8541 (accessed April 3, 2008).

2. eHealthMD.com, "What Is the Pap Smear?" http://www.ehealthmd.com/library/papsmear/PAP_whatis.html (accessed April 3, 2008).

## Chapter 5: Emotional Health

1. Steiner, "Premenstrual Syndromes," 447–445.

2. FactsforHealth.org, "What Is Premenstrual Dysphoric Disorder?" http://pmdd.factsforhealth.org (accessed April 3, 2008).

3. FactsforHealth.org, "Nutritional Approaches," http://pmdd.factsforhealth.org/treatment/nutritional.asp (accessed April 3, 2008).

4. James LaValle, RPh, "Guide to Herb, Vitamin, and Mineral Use," *OB/GYN Special Edition*, Spring 1999.

5. World Health Organization, "Depression," http://www.who.int/mental_health/management/depression/definition/en/ (accessed April 3, 2008).

6. Depression.com, "Depression-Related Mood Disorders," http://www.depression.com/types_of_depression.html (accessed April 3, 2008).

7. L. J. Williams et al., "Depression and Pain: An Overview," *Acta Neuropsychiatrica* 18, no. 2 (April 2006): 79–87.

8. MayoClinic.com, "Selective Serotonin Reuptake Inhibitors (SSRIs)," http://www.mayoclinic.com/health/ssris/MH00066 (accessed April 4, 2008).

9. MayoClinic.com, "Generalized Anxiety Disorder," http://www.mayoclinic.com/health/generalized-anxiety-disorder/DS00502 (accessed April 4, 2008).

## Chapter 6: Diet and Exercise

1. Obesity Education Initiative, "Rationale," Guidelines on Overweight and Obesity: Electronic Textbook, National Institutes of Health, http://www.nhlbi.nih.gov/guidelines/obesity/e_txtbk/ratnl/20.htm (accessed April 4, 2008).

2. BMI chart and text courtesy of John Pilcher, MD, New Dimensions Weight Loss Surgery, www.NewDimensionsWLS.com.

## Chapter 7: Dating and Sex

1. P. J. Sulak et al., "Impact of an Adolescent Sex Education Program That Was Implemented by an Academic Medical Center," *American Journal of Obstetrics and Gynecology* 195, no. 1 (July 2006): 78–84. Visit www.worththewait.org. Also, Joe McIlhaney, MD, *Sexual Health Today* (Austin, TX: The Medical Institute for Sexual Health, 1999).

2. Leon Speroff, MD, et al., *Clinical Gynecological Endocrinology and Infertility*, sixth ed. (Baltimore: Lippincott Williams & Wilkins, 1999), 390.

3. American Decency Organization, "Abercrombie & Fitch," http://www.americandecency.org/main.php?f=campaigns/abercrombie/index (accessed April 4, 2008).

4. Joshua Harris, *I Kissed Dating Goodbye* (Sisters: Multnomah, 1997), 93.

5. Lewis B. Smedes, *Sex for Christians* (Grand Rapids, MI: William B Eerdmans, 1976), 128.

## Chapter 8: Sexually Transmitted Diseases

1. H. Hunter Handsfield, MD, *A Practical Guide to Sexually Transmitted Diseases* (Minneapolis, MN: McGraw-Hill, 1996), 5.

2. National Institutes of Health, "Scientific Evidence on Condom Effectiveness for STD Prevention," July 20, 2001.

3. Centers for Disease Control and Prevention, "Trends in Reportable Sexually Transmitted Diseases in the United States, 2006," November 2007, http://www.cdc.gov/std/stats/trends2006.htm (accessed April 4, 2008).

4. National Institute of Allergy and Infectious Diseases, "An Introduction to Sexually Transmitted Diseases," Fact Sheet, July 1999.

5. Centers for Disease Control and Prevention, "Trends in Reportable Sexually Transmitted Diseases in the United States, 2006."

6. National Institute of Allergy and Infectious Diseases, "Chlamydia: Complications," http://www3.niaid.nih.gov/healthscience/healthtopics/chlamydia/complications.htm (accessed April 4, 2008).

7. National Institute of Allergy and Infectious Diseases, "Pelvic Inflammatory Disease," Fact Sheet, July 1998.

8. Centers for Disease Control and Prevention, "Trends in Reportable Sexually Transmitted Diseases in the United States, 2006."

9. Charlotte Gaydos, MD, et al., "Chlamydia Trachomatis Infections in Female Military Recruits," *New England Journal of Medicine* 339, no. 11 (1998): 739–744.

10. *OB/GYN News*, "CDC Issues New Guidelines on Treatment of STDs: Rescreen Women 3–4 Months After They Have Completed Treatment for Chlamydia (First Update Since 1998)," June 15, 2002, http://www.accessmylibrary.com/coms2/summary_0286-2087953_ITM (accessed April 4, 2008).

11. Centers for Disease Control and Prevention, "Trends in Reportable Sexually Transmitted Diseases in the United States, 2006."

12. National Institute of Allergy and Infectious Diseases, "Workshop Summary: Scientific Evidence on Condom Effectiveness for Sexually Transmitted Disease (STD) Prevention," July 20, 2001, http://www3.niaid.nih.gov/research/topics/STI/pdf/condomreport.pdf (accessed April 4, 2008).

13. MedicineNet.com, "Definition of Syphilis," http://www.medterms.com/script/main/art.asp?articlekey=5689 (accessed April 29, 2008).

14. Centers for Disease Prevention and Control, "Trichomoniasis—CDC Fact Sheet," December 2007, http://www.cdc.gov/std/trichomonas/STDfact-Trichomoniasis.htm (accessed April 4, 2008).

15. Association of Professors of Gynecology and Obstetrics, "Sexually Transmitted Infections: The Ob-Gyn's Role," three-part teaching module in the APGO Educational Series on Women's Health Issues, 2003.

16. Handsfield, *A Practical Guide to Sexually Transmitted Diseases*, 29.

17. Dexter Frederick, MD, et al., "Fatal Disseminated Herpes Simplex Virus Infection in a Previously Healthy Pregnant Woman," *Journal of Reproductive Medicine* 47, no. 7 (2002): 591–596.

18. Richard Sweet and Ronald Gibbs, *Infections of the Female Genital Tract* (Baltimore: Williams & Wilkins, 1985), 183–184.

19. Centers for Disease Control and Prevention, "Genital HPV Infection—CDC Fact Sheet," March 2008, http://www.cdc.gov/std/HPV/STDFact-HPV.htm (accessed April 4, 2008).

20. Ibid.

21. Association of Professors of Gynecology and Obstetrics, "Sexually Transmitted Infections: The Ob-Gyn's Role."

22. Centers for Disease Control and Prevention, "Genital HPV Infection—CDC Fact Sheet."

23. Ibid.

24. KaiserNetwork.org, "Congress Approves HPV Education and Prevention Provision," *Kaiser Daily Women's Health Policy*, December 19, 2000, http://www .kaisernetwork.org/daily_reports/rep_index.cfm?hint=2&DR_ID=1771 (accessed April 4, 2008).

25. Centers for Disease Control and Prevention, "Viral Hepatitis B: Fact Sheet," July 2007, http://www.cdc.gov/ncidod/diseases/hepatitis/b/fact.htm (accessed April 7, 2008).

26. Ibid.

27. Association of Professors of Gynecology and Obstetrics, "Sexually Transmitted Infections: The Ob-Gyn's Role."

28. Katherine Chen, MD, "Hepatitis C: The Silent Epidemic," *OBG Management* 14, no. 2 (2002): 27–45.

29. Centers for Disease Control and Prevention, "A Glance at the HIV/AIDS Epidemic," June 2007, http://www.cdc.gov/hiv/resources/factsheets/At-A-Glance.htm (accessed April 7, 2008).

30. Anthony S. Fauci, MD, Margaret Johnston, PhD, and Gary J. Nabel, MD, PhD, "HIV Vaccine Awareness Day: Monday, May 15, 2006," National Institute of Allergy and Infectious Diseases, http://www3.niaid.nih.gov/about/directors/news/HVAD2006.htm (accessed April 7, 2008).

31. Joint United Nations Programme on HIV/AIDS, "Report on the Global AIDS Epidemic: Executive Summary," May 2006, http://data.unaids.org/pub/ GlobalReport/2006/2006_GR-ExecutiveSummary_en.pdf (accessed April 7, 2008).

32. Centers for Disease Control and Prevention, "Trends in HIV/AIDS Diagnoses—33 States, 2001–2004," *Morbidity and Mortality Weekly Reports* 54, no. 45 (November 18, 2005): 1149–1153, http://www.cdc.gov/mmwr/preview/mmwrhtml/mm5445a1.htm (accessed April 7, 2008).

33. Centers for Disease Control and Prevention, "Revised Recommendations for HIV Testing of Adults, Adolescents, and Pregnant Women in Health-Care Settings," *Morbidity and Mortality Weekly Reports* 55, Recommendations and Reports 14 (September 22, 2006): 1–17, http://www.cdc.gov/mmwr/preview/mmwrhtml/rr5514a1.htm?s_cid=rr5514a1_e (accessed April 7, 2008).

34. J. P. Montgomery et al., "The Extent of Bisexual Behaviour in HIV-Infected Men and Implications for Transmission to Their Female Partners," *AIDS Care* 15 (2003): 829–837.

35. L. A. Valleroy et al., "Young Men's Survey: The Bridge for HIV Transmission to Women From 23- to 29-Year-Old Men Who Have Sex With Men in 6 U.S. Cities," National HIV Prevention Conference, July 2003, Atlanta, Georgia. Abstract M2-B0902.

36. R. N. Anderson and B. L. Smith, "Deaths: Leading Causes for 2002," *National Vital Statistics Reports* 53, no. 17 (2005).

37. American College of Obstetricians and Gynecologists (ACOG), "Human Immunodeficiency Virus Infections in Pregnancy," *ACOG Educational Bulletin* 232 (1997).

38. Centers for Disease Control and Prevention, "Mother-to-Child (Perinatal) HIV Transmission and Prevention," October 2007, http://www.cdc.gov/hiv/topics/perinatal/ resources/factsheets/perinatal.htm (accessed April 7, 2008).

39. Joint United Nations Programme on HIV/AIDS, "Report on the Global AIDS Epidemic: Executive Summary." See also: National Institute of Allergy and Infectious Diseases, "Statement From the National Institutes of Health on World AIDS Day," December 1, 2006, http://www3.niaid.nih.gov/news/newsreleases/2006/wad06.htm (accessed April 7, 2008).

40. Bruce Wetterau, *The New York Public Library Book of Chronologies* (New York: Prentice Hall Press, 1990), 528.

## Chapter 9: STD Prevention

1. David M. Fergusson, PhD, et al., "Circumcision Status and Risk of Sexually Transmitted Infection in Young Adult Males: An Analysis of a Longitudinal Birth Cohort," *Pediatrics* 118, no. 5 (November 2006): 1971–1977.

2. Xavier Castellsagué, MD, et al., "Male Circumcision, Penile Human Papillomavirus Infection, and Cervical Cancer in Female Partners," *New England Journal of Medicine* 346, no. 15 (April 11, 2002): 1105–1112.

3. Hans-Olov Adami, MD, PhD, "Cervical Cancer and the Elusive Male Factor," *New England Journal of Medicine* 346, no. 15 (April 11, 2002): 1160–1161.

4. R. Bailey et al., "Male Circumcision for HIV Prevention in Young Men in Kisumu, Kenya: A Randomised Controlled Trial," *Lancet* 369 (2007): 643–656.

5. Robert Bazell, "Health Officials Back Circumcision in AIDS Fight," NBC News, December 29, 2006, http://www.msnbc.msn.com/id/16184582 (accessed April 7, 2008).

6. Centers for Disease Control and Prevention, "Trends in Sexual Risk Behaviors Among High School Students," *Morbidity and Mortality Weekly Reports* 51, no. 38 (September 27, 2002): 856–859.

7. M. M. Dooley, "History of the Condom," *Journal of the Royal Society of Medicine* 87, no. 1 (January 1994): 58; N. Himes, *Medical History of Contraception* (New York: Gamut Press, Inc., 1963); and H. Youssef, "The History of the Condom," *Journal of the Royal Society of Medicine* 86, no. 4 (April 1993): 266–228.

8. Robert Hatcher et al., *Contraceptive Technology*, 17th ed. (New York: Ardent Media, 1998), 216.

9. Tamar Nordenberg, "Condoms: Barriers to Bad News," *FDA Consumer*, U.S. Food and Drug Administration, March–April 1998.

10. Karen Davis and Susan Weller, "The Effectiveness of Condoms in Reducing Heterosexual Transmission of HIV," *Family Planning Perspectives*, Nov/Dec 1999, 272–279.

11. Ibid.

12. C. M. Roland and M. J. Schroeder, "Intrinsic Defect Effects on NR Permeability," *Rubber & Plastics News*, January 12, 1998, 15.

13. National Institutes of Health, "Scientific Evidence on Condom Effectiveness for STD Prevention," July 20, 2001.

14. Nordenberg, "Condoms: Barriers to Bad News."

15. L. Warner, et al., "Assessing Condom Use Practices: Implications for Evaluating Method and User Effectiveness," *Sexually Transmitted Diseases* 25, no. 6 (July 1998): 273–277.

16. Prolife.com, "Condom Warnings—Beware!" Pro-Life America, http://www.prolife.com/condoms.html (accessed April 7, 2008).

17. Patrick Dixon, "Condoms Are Unsafe for HIV Prevention?" *The Truth About AIDS*, http://www.globalchange.com/ttaa/ttaa%206.htm (accessed April 7, 2008).

18. Lawrence Stanberry, MD, et al., "Glycoprotein-D-Adjuvant Vaccine to Prevent Genital Herpes," *New England Journal of Medicine* 347, no. 21 (2002): 1652–1661.

19. *Sydney Morning Herald*, "Researchers Hope for Chlamydia Vaccine," February 3, 2006, http://www.smh.com.au/news/World/Researchers-hope-for-chlamydia-vaccine/2006/02/03/1138836416259.html (accessed April 7, 2008).

20. Centers for Disease Control and Prevention, "HPV Vaccine Questions and Answers," August 2006, http://www.cdc.gov/std/HPV/STDFact-HPV-vaccine.htm (accessed April 7, 2008).

21. Ibid.

22. Heather Feldman, "Scientists Fighting STD With Research, Education," *The Mission*, vol. 27, no. 2, Spring 2000, http://www.uthscsa.edu/mission/spring00/std.htm (accessed April 7, 2008).

23. Fauci, Johnston, and Nabel, "HIV Vaccine Awareness Day: Monday, May 15, 2006."

24. Ronald Kotulak, "AIDS Virus Fights Attempts to Create Vaccine," *Chicago Tribune*, May 10, 1987.

25. Centers for Disease Control and Prevention, "Human Immunodeficiency Virus Type 2," October 1998, http://www.cdc.gov/hiv/resources/factsheets/PDF/hiv2.pdf (accessed April 7, 2008).

## Chapter 10: Abortion

1. L. B. Finer et al., "Disparities in Unintended Pregnancy in the United States, 1994 and 2001," *Perspectives on Sexual and Reproductive Health* 38, no. 2 (2006): 90–96.

2. Department of Obstetrics and Gynecology/Reproductive Endocrinology and Infertility, "Recurrent Pregnancy Loss (Recurrent Miscarriage)," Washington University School of Medicine in St. Louis, http://wuphysicians.wustl.edu/dept.asp?pageID=8&ID=35 (accessed April 7, 2008).

3. Lawrence B. Finer et al., "Reasons U.S. Women Have Abortions: Quantative and Qualitative Perspectives," *Perspectives on Sexual and Reproductive Health* 37, no. 3 (2005): 110–118.

4. Lilo T. Strauss et al., "Abortion Surveillance—United States, 2002," *Morbidity and Mortality Weekly Report* 54, SS07 (November 25, 2005): 1–31.

5. Rachel K. Jones, Jacqueline E. Darroch, and Stanley K. Henshaw, "Contraceptive Use Among U.S. Women Having Abortions in 2000-2001," *Perspectives on Sexual and Reproductive Health* 34, no. 6 (2002).

6. Finer et al., "Reasons U.S. Women Have Abortions: Quantative and Qualitative Perspectives."

7. I. M. Spitz et al., "Early Pregnancy Termination With Mifepristone and Misoprostol in the United States," *New England Journal of Medicine* 338, no. 18 (1998).

8. FDA.gov, "Mifeprex (mifepristone) Tablets, 200 mg," http://www.fda.gov/cder/foi/label/2005/020687s013lbl.pdf (accessed April 7, 2008).

9. FDA.gov, "Mifeprex (mifepristone) Information," http://www.fda.gov/cder/drug/infopage/mifepristone/ (accessed April 7, 2008).

10. U.S. House of Representatives Government Reform Committee, "The FDA and RU-486: Lowering the Standard for Women's Health," staff report prepared for the Hon. Mark Souder, Chairman, Subcommittee on Criminal Justice, Drug Policy, and Human Resources, October 2006, http://souder.house.gov/index.cfm?Fuseaction=Files.View&FileStore_id=f01ec1e7-0fdd-4f50-bc59-d2734e084032 (accessed April 7, 2008).

11. WebMD.com, "Manual and Vacuum Aspiration for Abortion," October 6, 2006, http://women.webmd.com/manual-and-vacuum-aspiration-for-abortion (accessed April 7, 2008).

12. AbortionFacts.com, "Gianna Jessen: Testimony of Abortion Survivor Gianna Jessen Before the Constitution Subcommittee of the House Judiciary Committee on April 22, 1996," http://www.abortionfacts.com/survivors/giannajessen.asp (accessed April 7, 2008). Also, Lois Rogers, "Fifty Babies a Year Are Alive After Abortion," *Sunday Times*, November 27, 2005.

13. S. Ballas, J. B. Lessing, and M. Michowitz, "Amniotic Fluid Embolism and Disseminated Intravascular Coagulation Complicating Hypertonic Saline-Induced Abortion," *Postgraduate Medical Journal* 59 (1983): 127–129, abstract available at http://pmj.bmj.com/cgi/content/abstract/59/688/127 (accessed April 7, 2008).

14. ChildrenbyChoice.org, "Second Trimester Abortion," http://www.childrenbychoice.org.au/nwww/abortion2.htm (accessed April 7, 2008).

15. Guttmacher Institute, "Facts on Induced Abortion in the United States," January 2008, http://www.guttmacher.org/pubs/fb_induced_abortion.html (accessed April 7, 2008).

16. Cornell University Law School, "Supreme Court Collection: *Gonzales v. Carhart* (Nos. 05-380 and 05-1382)," http://www.law.cornell.edu/supct/html/05-380.ZO.html (accessed April 7, 2008).

17. Francis X. Clines, "Reagan Appeal on Abortion Is Made to Fundamentalists," *New York Times*, January 31, 1984, A16, as referenced in "President Reagan's Quote on Abortion and Fetal Pain and Various Doctors' Confirmations," http://www.mpomerle.com/NoAbort/Reagan_Fetal_Pain.shtml (accessed April 7, 2008).

18. BBC News, "Foetuses 'No Pain Up to 29 Weeks,'" August 24, 2005, http://news.bbc.co.uk/2/hi/health/4180592.stm (accessed April 7, 2008).

## Chapter 11: Post-Abortion Recovery

1. Ronald Burkman, MD, and Anne Moore, "Unintended Pregnancy," *Clinical Courier*, vol. 20, no. 20, October 2002.

2. Laurie Elam-Evans, PhD, et al., "Abortion Surveillance—United States, 1999," *Morbidity and Mortality Weekly Report* 51, SS09, November 29, 2002, http://www.cdc.gov/mmwr/preview/mmwrhtml/ss5109a1.htm (accessed April 7, 2008).

3. Guttmacher Institute, "Facts on Induced Abortion in the United States."

4. A. Tzonou et al., "Induced Abortions, Miscarriages, and Tobacco Smoking as Risk Factors for Secondary Infertility," *Journal of Epidemiology and Community Health* 47, no. 1 (1993): 36–39.

5. E. Pauli, U. Haller, and R. Zimmermann, "Morbidity of Dilatation and Evacuation in the Second Trimester: An Analysis," *Gynakol Geburtshilfliche Rundsch* 45, no. 2 (2005): 107–115.

6. S. Mittal and S. L. Misra, "Uterine Perforation Following Medical Termination of Pregnancy by Vacuum Aspiration," *International Journal of Gynaecology and Obstetrics* 23, no. 1 (1985): 45–50.

7. World Health Organization, "Medical Methods for Termination of Pregnancy," WHO Technical Report Series 871, 1997.

8. M. J. Lanska, D. Lanska, and A. A. Rimm, "Mortality From Abortion and Childbirth," *Journal of the American Medical Association* 250, no. 3 (1983): 361–362.

9. J. Bartley et al., "Parity Is a Major Determinant of Success Rate in Medical Abortion: A Retrospective Analysis of 3161 Consecutive Cases," *Contraception* 62, no. 6 (2000): 297–303.

10. Ibid.

11. Guttmacher Institute, "Facts on Induced Abortion in the United States."

12. Jeani Chang, MPH, et al., "Pregnancy-Related Mortality Surveillance—United States, 1991–1999," *Morbidity and Mortality Weekly Report* 53, SS02, February 21, 2003, http://www.cdc.gov/mmwr/preview/mmwrhtml/ss5202a1.htm (accessed April 7, 2008).

13. Rogers, "Fifty Babies a Year Are Alive After Abortion."

14. V. Beral et al., "Breast Cancer and Abortion: Collaborative Reanalysis of Data From 53 Epidemiological Studies, Including 83,000 Women With Breast Cancer From 16 Countries (abstract)," *Lancet* 363 (2004): 1007–1016.

15. Breast Cancer Prevention Institute, "Early Reproductive Events and Breast Cancer: A Minority Report," March 10, 2003, http://www.bcpinstitute.org/nci_minority_rpt.htm (accessed April 7, 2008).

16. Abortion and Breast Cancer, "American Abortion-Breast Cancer Studies," http://www.etters.net/cancerTP.htm#3 (accessed April 7, 2008).

17. Lavin C. Gomez and Garcia R. Zapata, "Diagnostic Categorization of Post-Abortion Syndrome," *Actas Esp Psiquiatr* 33, no. 4 (2005): 267–272.

18. D. C. Reardon and J. R. Cougle, "Depression and Unintended Pregnancy in the National Longitudinal Survey of Youth: A Cohort Study," *British Medical Journal* 19, no. 324 (January 19, 2002): 151–152.

19. D. M. Fergusson, L. J. Horwood, and E. M. Ridder, "Abortion in Young Women and Subsequent Mental Health," *Journal of Child Psychology & Psychiatry* 47, no. 1 (2006): 16–24.

20. Sarah-Kate Templeton, health editor, "Royal College Warns Abortions Can Lead to Mental Illness," *Sunday Times*, March 16, 2008, http://www.timesonline.co.uk/tol/life_and_style/health/article3559486.ece (accessed April 9, 2008).

21. ReligiousTolerance.org, "Post-Abortion Syndrome: Summary, Symptoms, Frequency," http://www.religioustolerance.org/abo_post.htm (accessed April 9, 2008).

22. Information is taken from AfterAbortion.com, http://afterabortion.com/pass_details.html (accessed April 9, 2008). Used with permission.

## Chapter 12: The Wedding Night

1. Barbara Levy, MD, "Breaking the Silence: Discussing Sexual Dysfunction," *OBG Management* 14, no. 3 (March 2002).

2. Culley Carson, MD, and Diana Wiley, *The Couples' Guide to Great Sex Over 40* (New York: Masquerade Books, 1997), 50.

## Chapter 13: Methods of Birth Control

1. Hatcher et al., *Contraceptive Technology*, 215–218.

2. Ibid.

3. American College of Obstetricians and Gynecologists, "Family Planning by Periodic Abstinence," *ACOG Patient Education*, March 1997, http://www.medem.com/search/article_display.cfm?path=n:&mstr=/ZZZH6QKJ27C.html&soc=ACOG&srch_typ=NAV_SERCH (accessed April 10, 2008).

4. Hatcher et al., *Contraceptive Technology*, 215–218.

5. Ibid.

6. David Grimes, MD, et al., *Modern Contraception* (Totowa: Emron, 1997), 158.

7. Hatcher et al., *Contraceptive Technology*, 215–218.

8. Leon Speroff, MD, et al., *Clinical Gynecological Endocrinology and Infertility*, sixth ed. (Baltimore: Lippincott Williams & Wilkins, 1999), 1044.

9. American College of Obstetricians and Gynecologists, "Birth Control Pills," *ACOG Patient Education*, 1999.

10. Hatcher et al., *Contraceptive Technology*, 215–218.

11. Ibid., 516.

12. Ibid., 215–218.

13. Essure.com, "Clinical Testing," http://www.essure.com/Home/Understanding/ClinicalTesting/tabid/58/Default.aspx (accessed April 10, 2008).

## Chapter 15: Female Sexual Drive

1. E. Pluhar, "Low Sexual Desire," *The Female Patient* S38 (2003): 13–15.

2. Andrew Comiskey, *Pursuing Sexual Wholeness* (Lake Mary: Siloam, 1989), 109–125.

3. L. Zussman et al., "Sexual Response After Hysterectomy-Oophorectomy: Recent Studies and Reconsideration of Psychogenesis," *American Journal of Obstetrics and Gynecology* 140 (1981): 725–729. Also, J. Nathorst-Boos et al., "Elective Ovarian Removal and Estrogen Replacement Therapy," *J Psychosom Obstet Gynaecol* 14 (1993): 283–290.

4. M. Zoler, "Hypertension Tied to Female Sexual Dysfunction," *Ob.Gyn. News*, 1 October 2006, 14.

5. A. J. Cohen and B. Bartlik, "Ginkgo Biloba for Antidepressant-Induced Sexual Dysfunction," *J Sex Marital Ther* 24, no. 2 (April–June 1998): 139–143.

6. Elaine Magee, MPH, RD, "Give Your Libido a Lift," MedicineNet.com, February 12, 2005, http://www.medicinenet.com/script/main/art.asp?articlekey=55981 (accessed April 10, 2008).

7. M. Tremblay, J. Copeland, and W. Van Helder, "Effect of Training Status and Exercise Mode on Endogenous Steroid Hormones in Men," *J Appl Physiol* 96 (2004): 531–539.

8. Levy, "Breaking the Silence: Discussing Sexual Dysfunction."

9. Ibid.

10. Ibid.

11. T. Ito, A. Trant, and M. Polan, "A Double-Blind Placebo-Controlled Study of ArginMax, a Nutritional Supplement for Enhancement of Female Sexual Function," *J Sex Marital Ther* 27, no. 5 (October 2001): 541–549.

## Chapter 16: When You're Ready for a Baby

1. J. A. Martin et al., "Births: Final Data for 2002," *National Vital Statistics Reports*, volume 52, number 10, December 17, 2003.

2. March of Dimes, "Smoking During Pregnancy," http://www.marchofdimes.com/professionals/14332_1171.asp (accessed April 10, 2008).

3. U.S. Department of Health and Human Services, "The Health Consequences of Smoking: A Report of the Surgeon General—2004," Centers for Disease Control and Prevention, Office on Smoking and Health, May 2004.

4. Ibid.

5. T. Jensen et al., "Does Moderate Alcohol Consumption Affect Fertility? Follow Up Study Among Couples Planning First Pregnancy," *British Medical Journal* 317 (1998): 505–510.

6. J. Gill, "The Effects of Moderate Alcohol Consumption on Female Hormone Levels and Reproductive Function," *Alcohol and Alcoholism* 35, no. 5 (2000): 417–423.

7. U.S. Department of Health and Human Services, "U.S. Surgeon General Releases Advisory on Alcohol Use in Pregnancy," February 21, 2005, http://www.surgeongeneral.gov/pressreleases/sg02222005.html (accessed April 10, 2008).

8. L. Burkman et al., "Marijuana (MJ) Impacts Sperm Function Both in Vivo and in Vitro: Semen Analyses From Men Smoking Marijuana," *Fertility and Sterility* 80, suppl 3 (September 2003): 231.

9. E. Pergament, A. Schechman, and L. Jordan, "Angiotensin-Converting Enzyme (ACE) Inhibitors and Pregnancy," *ITIS* 4, no. 5 (March 1996).

10. H. Sorensen et al., "Do Hypertension and Diuretic Treatment in Pregnancy Increase the Risk of Schizophrenia in Offspring?" *Am J Psychiatry* 160, no. 3 (2003): 464–468.

11. Beacon Pharmaceuticals information page, http://www.beaconpharma.co.uk (accessed April 10, 2008).

12. K. Fuhrmann et al., "Prevention of Congenital Malformations in Infants of Insulin-Dependent Diabetic Mothers," *Diabetes Care* 6, no. 3 (May–June 1983): 219–223.

13. MarchofDimes.com, "Thyroid Conditions and Pregnancy," http://www .marchofdimes.com/pnhec/188_8923.asp (accessed April 18, 2008).

14. X. Weng, R. Odouli, and D-K Li, "Maternal Caffeine Consumption During Pregnancy and the Risk of Miscarriage: A Prospective Cohort Study," *American Journal of Obstetrics and Gynecology* 198 (March 2008): 279.e1–8.

15. EPA.gov, "What You Need to Know About Mercury in Fish and Shellfish," http:// www.epa.gov/waterscience/fish/advice/ (accessed April 18, 2008).

16. Georgia Department of Human Resources, "Position Paper: Preconception Nutrition," http://health.state.ga.us/pdfs/epi/PreconceptionNutritionpositionpaper2006 .pdf (accessed April 18, 2008).

## Chapter 17: Infertility: Causes and Treatments

1. WomensHealth.gov, "Infertility," http://www.womenshealth.gov/faq/infertility.htm (accessed April 18, 2008).

2. Ibid.

3. Centers for Disease Control and Prevention, "2003 Assisted Reproductive Technology (ART) Report," http://www.cdc.gov/ART/ART2003/index.htm (accessed April 18, 2008).

4. Barbara Collura, "The Costs of Infertility Treatment," Resolve.org, http://www .resolve.org/site/PageServer?pagename=lrn_mta_cost (accessed April 18, 2008).

5. National Institute of Child Health and Human Development, "Understanding Klinefelter Syndrome," http://www.nichd.nih.gov/publications/pubs/klinefelter.cfm (accessed April 18, 2008).

6. Maria G. Essig, MS, ELS, "Semen Analysis: Test Overview," February 20, 2007, http://health.yahoo.com/reproductive-diagnosis/semen-analysis/healthwise--hw5612.html (accessed April 18, 2008).

7. E. Carlsen et al., "Evidence for Decreasing Quality of Semen During Past 50 Years," *British Medical Journal* 305 (1992): 609–613.

8. S. H. Swan et al., "Geographic Differences in Semen Quality of Fertile US Males," *Environmental Health Perspectives* 111 (2003): 414–420.

9. W. G. Sanger and P. C. Friman, "Fit of Underwear and Male Spermatogenesis: A Pilot Investigation," *Reproductive Toxicology* 4 (1990): 229–232.

10. Yefim Sheynkin et al., "Increase in Scrotal Temperature in Laptop Computer Users," *Human Reproduction* 20, no. 2 (2005): 452–455.

## Chapter 18: The First Trimester

1. American College of Obstetricians and Gynecologists, *Your Pregnancy and Birth* (Washington DC: American College of Obstetricians and Gynecologists, 2005), 84–85.

2. A. J. Wilcox et al., "Incidence of Early Loss of Pregnancy," *New England Journal of Medicine* 319 (1988): 189–194.

3. Centers for Disease Control and Prevention, "Current Trends Ectopic Pregnancy—United States, 1990–1992," *Morbidity and Mortality Weekly Report* 44, no. 3 (January 27, 1995): 46–48, http://www.cdc.gov/mmwr/preview/mmwrhtml/00035709.htm (accessed April 18, 2008).

5. J. C. Smulian et al., "Birth Defects Surveillance," *N J Med* 99, no. 12 (2002): 25–31.

6. Aaron B. Caughey, Linda M. Hopkins, and Mary E. Norton, "Chorionic Villus Sampling Compared With Amniocentesis and the Difference in the Rate of Pregnancy Loss," *Obstet. Gynecol.* 108 (September 2006): 612–616.

## Chapter 19: The Second Trimester
1. American College of Obstetricians and Gynecologists, *Your Pregnancy and Birth*.
2. Ibid.

## Chapter 20: The Third Trimester
1. J. A. Martin et al., "Births: Final Data for 2000,"*National Vital Statistics Report* 50 (2002): 1–02.
2. D. E. Hickock, "The Frequency of Breech Presentation by Gestational Age at Birth: A Large Population-Based Study," *American Journal of Obstetrics and Gynecology* 166 (1992): 851–856.
3. American College of Obstetricians and Gynecologists, "Multiple Gestation: Complicated Twin, Triplet, and High-Order Multifetal Pregnancy," *Obstetrics and Gynecology* 104 (2004): 869–883.

## Chapter 21: Childbirth
1. BabyCenter.com, "Lamaze Childbirth Method," September 2005, http://www .babycenter.com/0_lamaze-childbirth-method_640.bc (accessed April 21, 2008).
2. BabyCenter.com, "Bradley Childbirth Method," September 2005, http://www .babycenter.com/0_bradley-childbirth-method_631.bc (accessed April 21, 2008).
3. American College of Obstetricians and Gynecologists, "Episiotomy," *Obstetrics and Gynecology* 107 (2006): 957–962.

## Chapter 22: The Postpartum Mother
1. Agustin Conde-Agudelo, Anyeli Rosas-Bermúdez, and Ana Cecilia Kafury-Goeta, "Birth Spacing and Risk of Adverse Perinatal Outcomes: A Meta-Analysis," *Journal of the American Medical Association* 295 (April 19, 2006): 1809–1823.
2. Family Health International, "Consensus Statement: Lactational Amenorrhea Method for Family Planning," http://search.fhi.org/cgi-bin/MsmGo.exe?grab _id=87841746&extra_arg=&page_id=293&host_id=1&query=Bellagio+consensus&hiword =BELLAGIO+CONSENSUS+CONSENSUAL+ (accessed April 21, 2008).
3. Anna M. Georgiopoulos et al., "Population-Based Screening for Postpartum Depression," *Obstetrics and Gynecology* 93 (May 1999): 653–657.

## Chapter 23: The Life of a Perimenopausal Soccer Mom
1. American Society of Plastic Surgeons, "Plastic Surgery Procedures Maintain Steady Growth in 2007," March 25, 2008, http://www.plasticsurgery.org/media/press_releases/ Plastic-Surgery-Growth-in-2007.cfm (accessed April 21, 2008).
2. Victoria Corderi, "Plastic Surgery Tourism?" *Dateline NBC*, March 18, 2005, http:// www.msnbc.msn.com/id/7222253/ (accessed April 21, 2008).
3. For example, IrishHealth.com, "Plastic Surgery Complications Killed Woman," May 26, 2005, http://www.irishhealth.com/index.html?level=4&id=7603 (accessed April 21, 2008). Also, NigerianVillageSquare.com, "First Lady Died of Plastic Surgery Complications," October 24, 2005, http://www.nigeriavillagesquare.com/articles/omoyele -sowore/first-lady-died-of-plastic-surgery-complica-2.html (accessed April 21, 2008).

## Chapter 24: Everything Menopause

1. M. R. Soules et al., "Executive Summary: Stages of Reproductive Aging Workshop (STRAW), Park City, Utah, July 2001," *Menopause* 8 (2001): 402–407.

2. Menopause.org, "The Changing Body," http://www.menopause.org/MG2.pdf (accessed April 21, 2008).

3. Yale-New Haven Hospital, "Women's Health Initiative Study on HRT Stopped," September 24, 2002, http://www.ynhh.org/healthlink/womens/womens_9_02.html (accessed April 21, 2008).

4. Stephen Hulley, MD, et al., "Randomized Trial of Estrogen and Progestin for Secondary Prevention of Coronary Heart Disease in Postmenopausal Women," *Journal of the American Medical Association* 280, no. 7 (August 19, 1998).

5. Jacques Rossouw, MD, et al., "Risks and Benefits of Estrogen and Progestin in Healthy Menopausal Women," *Journal of the American Medical Association* 288, no. 3 (July 17, 2002).

6. A. Z. LaCroix, MD, and W. Burke, MD, "Breast Cancer and Hormone Replacement Therapy," *Lancet* 350, no. 9084 (October 11, 1997): 1047–1059. Also, James Lacey Jr., PhD, et al., "Menopausal Hormone Replacement Therapy and Risk of Ovarian Cancer," *Journal of the American Medical Association* 288, no.3 (July 17, 2002).

7. J. Hsia et al., "Conjugated Equine Estrogens and Coronary Heart Disease: The Women's Health Initiative," *Archives of Internal Medicine* 166 (2006): 357–365.

8. F. Grodstein et al., "Hormone Therapy and Coronary Heart Disease: The Role of Time Since Menopause and Age at Hormone Initiation," *Journal of Women's Health* 15 (2006): 35–44.

9. R. T. Chlebowski et al., "Influence of Estrogen Plus Progesterone on Breast Cancer and Mammography in Healthy Postmenopausal Women: The Women's Health Initiative Randomized Trial," *Journal of the American Medical Association* 289 (2003): 3243–3253. Also, M. L. Stefanik et al., "Effects of Conjugated Equine Estrogens on Breast Cancer and Mammography Screening in Postmenopausal Women With Hysterectomy," *Journal of the American Medical Association* 295 (2006): 1647–1657.

10. L. Boothby et al., "Bio-identical Hormone Therapy: A Review," *Menopause* 11, no. 3 (2004): 356–365.

11. National Institutes of Health, "Questions and Answers About Estrogen-Plus-Progestin Hormone Therapy," http://www.nhlbi.nih.gov/health/women/q_a.htm#q12 (accessed April 21, 2008).

12. G. Burke et al., "Soy Protein and Isoflavone Effects on Vasomotor Symptoms in Peri- and Postmenopausal Women: The Soy Estrogen Alternative Study," *Menopause* 10, no. 2 (2003): 147–153.

13. E. Liske, "Therapeutic Efficacy and Safety of *Cimicifuga Racemosa* for Gynecologic Disorders," *Advances in Ther* 15 (1998): 45–53.

14. V. Stearns et al., "A Pilot Trial Assessing the Efficacy of Paroxetine Hydrochloride (Paxil) in Controlling Hot Flashes in Breast Cancer Survivors," *Annals of Oncology* 11 (2000): 17–22.


## Chapter 25: Surgery 101

1. *OB GYN News*, "No Retreatment in 75% After Global Ablation (Thermachoice)," vol. 38, issue 12, June 15, 2003.

2. A. Chechia et al., "Management of Dermoid Ovarian Cysts. Report of 58 Cases," *Tunis Med* 80 (2002): 131–135.

3. Menopause.org, "The Changing Body."

4. Nilsson et al., "7 Year Follow-up on the Tension-free Vaginal Tape (TVT) Procedure," *International Urology*, Abstract 116, no. 89 (October 2003).

5. American College of Obstetricians and Gynecologists, "Surgery for Urinary Incontinence," ACOG Education Pamphlet AP166, July 2006, http://www.acog.org/publications/patient_education/bp166.cfm (accessed April 22, 2008).

6. American College of Obstetrics and Gynecology, "ACOG Committee Opinion No. 378: Vaginal 'Rejuvenation' and Cosmetic Vaginal Procedures," *Obstetrics and Gynecology* 110, no. 3 (September 2007): 737–738.

## Chapter 26: Life Beyond Forty: Maintaining Your Health

1. L. Ries et al., *SEER Cancer Statistics Review, 1975–2003* (Bethesda, MD: National Cancer Institute, 2006).

2. National Cancer Institute, U.S. National Institutes of Heath, "Breast Cancer," http://www.cancer.gov/cancertopics/types/breast (accessed April 22, 2008).

3. Texas Department of Criminal Justice, "Wellness Initiative Now," October 2006, http://www.tdcj.state.tx.us/win/newsletters/news1006.pdf (accessed April 22, 2008).

4. American Cancer Society, "Overview: Breast Cancer: How Is Breast Cancer Found?" September 26, 2007, http://www.cancer.org/docroot/CRI/content/CRI_2_2_3X_How_is_breast_cancer_found_5.asp?sitearea= (accessed April 22, 2008).

5. Ibid.

6. Haley Jorgensen, "Colonoscopy Best Defense Against Colorectal Cancer," Sauk Prairie Memorial Hospitals and Clinics, March 2, 2006, http://www.spmh.org/News/Colonoscopy.html (accessed April 22, 2008).

7. Philip Schoenfeld, MD, et al., "Colonoscopic Screening of Average-Risk Women for Colorectal Neoplasia," *New England Journal of Medicine* 352, no 20 (May 19, 2005): 2061–2068.

8. Ernesto Canalis, MD, Andrea Giustina, MD, and John P. Bilezikian, MD, "Mechanisms of Anabolic Therapies for Osteoporosis," *New England Journal of Medicine* 357, no. 9 (August 30, 2007): 905–916.

9. *Obstetrics and Gynecology* 104, "Hormone Therapy: Osteoporosis" (2004): S66–S76.

10. FamilyDoctor.org, "Heart Disease and Heart Attacks: What Women Need to Know," November 2006, http://familydoctor.org/online/famdocen/home/common/heartdisease/risk/287.html (accessed April 22, 2008).

11. Ibid.

12. FamilyDoctor.org, "High Blood Pressure: Things You Can Do to Lower Yours," November 2006, http://familydoctor.org/online/famdocen/home/common/heartdisease/risk/092.html (accessed April 22, 2008).

13. American Diabetes Association, "All About Diabetes," http://www.diabetes.org/about-diabetes.jsp (accessed April 22, 2008).

14. National Institutes of Health, "National Diabetes Education Program," http://ndep.nih.gov/campaigns/BeSmart/BeSmart_index.htm (accessed April 22, 2008).

15. American Diabetes Association, "Complications of Diabetes in the United States," http://www.diabetes.org/diabetes-statistics/complications.jsp (accessed April 22, 2008).

16. Ibid.

17. American Diabetes Association, "Standards of Medical Care in Diabetes—2008," *Diabetes Care* 31 (2008): S12–S54.

## Chapter 27: Women and Cancer

1. American Cancer Society, "Overview: Breast Cancer: How Many Women Get Breast Cancer?" September 26, 2007, http://www.cancer.org/docroot/CRI/content/CRI_2_2_1X_ How_many_people_get_breast_cancer_5.asp?sitearea= (accessed April 22, 2008).

2. Illinois Department of Health, "Breast Cancer," http://www.idph.state.il.us/cancer/ factsheets/breastc.htm (accessed April 22, 2008).

3. Health Canada, "It's Your Health: Breast Cancer," http://www.hc-sc.gc.ca/iyh-vsv/ diseases-maladies/breast-sein_e.html#min (accessed April 22, 2008).

4. American Cancer Society, "Overview: Colon and Rectum Cancer: How Many People Get Colorectal Cancer?" March 5, 2008, http://www.cancer.org/docroot/CRI/content/ CRI_2_2_1X_How_Many_People_Get_Colorectal_Cancer.asp?sitearea= (accessed April 22, 2008).

5. American Cancer Society, "Overview: Colon and Rectum Cancer: What Causes Colorectal Cancer?" March 5, 2008, http://www.cancer.org/docroot/CRI/content/CRI_2_ 2_2X_What_causes_colorectal_cancer.asp?sitearea= (accessed April 22, 2008).

6. Ibid.

7. Schoenfield et al., "Colonoscopic Screening of Average-Risk Women for Colorectal Neoplasia."

8. Medline Plus, "Colon Cancer," http://www.nlm.nih.gov/medlineplus/ency/ article/000262.htm (accessed April 22, 2008).

9. American Cancer Society, "Overview: Cervical Cancer: How Many Women Get Cancer of the Cervix?" November 30, 2006, http://www.cancer.org/docroot/CRI/content/ CRI_2_2_1X_How_many_women_get_cancer_of_the_cervix_8.asp?sitearea= (accessed April 22, 2008).

10. Ibid.

11. MayoClinic.com, "Endometrial Cancer," December 7, 2006, http://www.mayoclinic .com/health/endometrial-cancer/DS00306 (accessed April 22, 2008).

12. MayoClinic.com, "Endometrial Cancer: Risk Factors," December 7, 2006, http:// www.mayoclinic.com/health/endometrial-cancer/DS00306/DSECTION=4 (accessed April 22, 2008).

13. Ibid.

14. National Cancer Institute, "Ovarian Cancer," http://www.cancer.gov/cancertopics/ types/ovarian (accessed April 22, 2008).

15. Women's Cancer Network, "Ovarian Cancer Symptoms Consensus Statement," June 13, 2007, http://www.wcn.org/ov_cancer_cons.html (accessed April 22, 2008).

16. American Cancer Society, "Detailed Guide: Ovarian Cancer: How Is Ovarian Cancer Staged?" January 19, 2008, http://www.cancer.org/docroot/CRI/content/CRI_2_4_ 3X_How_is_ovarian_cancer_staged_33.asp?sitearea= (accessed April 22, 2008).

17. Medline Plus, "Skin Cancer," http://www.nlm.nih.gov/medlineplus/skincancer.html (accessed April 22, 2008).

18. Skin Cancer Foundation, "Sunscreens Explained," http://www.skincancer.org/ sunscreen/sunscreens-explained.html (accessed April 22, 2008).

## Chapter 28: Aging and Intimacy

1. Carson and Wiley, *The Couples' Guide to Great Sex Over 40*, 13.

2. Diana Hagee, *The King's Daughter* (Nashville: Thomas Nelson, 2001), 108.

3. Jamie Lee Curtis interview, *More Magazine*, September 2002.

4. Nancy Griffin, "Jamie Lee Curtis Turns 50," *AARP the Magazine,* May/June 2008, http://www.aarpmagazine.org/entertainment/essential_jamie_lee_curtis.html (accessed April 22, 2008).

5. Carson and Wiley, *The Couples' Guide to Great Sex Over 40*, 50.

6. Ibid., 54–55.

7. Viagra.com, "About Viagra," http://www.viagra.com/content/about-viagra -ed-treatment.jsp?setShowOn=../content/about-viagra-ed-treatment.jsp&setShowHighlight On=../content/about-viagra-ed-treatment.jsp (accessed April 22, 2008).

# Glossary

**abdominoplasty:** the removal of excess abdominal skin and tightening of the abdominal wall muscles, which in lay terms is a "tummy tuck"

**amniocentesis:** placing a needle into the amniotic sac of a fetus to remove fluid and grow cells to check for chromosomal abnormalities such as Down syndrome

**anorexia nervosa:** defined as a refusal to maintain body weight within 15 percent of an individual's minimum normal weight

**anovulation:** the absence of ovulation or the lack of egg release from the ovary

**areola:** the pigmented skin around the nipple

**bacterial vaginosis (BV):** the overgrowth of certain bacteria in the vagina that causes a "fishy" odor and vaginal irritation

**biophysical profile:** a combination of a nonstress test and ultrasound to assess fetal well-being. It has five components: the nonstress test, ultrasound evaluations of fetal body movements, fetal breathing, fetal muscle tone, and amount of amniotic fluid. These are scored on a 10-point scale, with a maximum of 2 points per section. A reassuring test is a score of 8 to 10. It is used for the same conditions as the nonstress test.

**bladder:** the organ that holds urine until it is ready to be eliminated from the body

**body mass index (BMI):** a table of weight and height measurements designed to accurately define normal weight and various levels of obesity; the higher the BMI, the more health risks are involved.

**Braxton-Hicks contractions:** uterine tightening that does not cause cervical dilation, often called "false labor"

**bulimia:** a cycle of overeating (bingeing) followed soon after by vomiting or laxative use (purging) as a way to maintain weight; this is an eating disorder

**calcium:** a mineral found in various sources, such as dairy, that is essential to bone health and proper muscle function, including the heart muscle

**chlamydia:** the most common bacterial STD; is a leading cause of infertility and tubal pregnancy as well as neonatal blindness in developing countries

**chromosome:** a strand that contains DNA, the building block of every cell in our body; there are forty-six chromosomes in humans

**clitoris:** the female counterpart to the head of the penis, located at the top of the vaginal opening above the urethra and an important sensory organ for the achievement of female orgasm

**colostrum:** a thin, yellow substance secreted from the breasts during lactation that contains antibodies to help fight off disease and supplies all the nutrients a baby needs to grow during its first few days of life

**colposcopy:** a procedure that involves placing a topical vinegar solution onto the cervix and examining it through a colposcope, the medical equivalent of "binoculars," to assess for precancerous and cancerous changes to the cervix; this is done in response to an abnormal Pap smear

**contractions:** rhythmic tightening of the pregnant uterus; these may or may not result in labor, depending on whether there are changes to the thickness or dilation of the cervix

**cryotherapy:** freezing of the surface of the cervix as a treatment for the abnormal Pap smear

**cystic fibrosis:** an inherited disease of the mucus and sweat glands affecting mostly the lungs, pancreas, liver, intestines, sinuses, and sex organs. An abnormal gene causes the normally watery mucus of the body to become thick and sticky, building up in the lungs and blocking the airways. Death is usually from respiratory failure in the late twenties or early thirties.

**D&C (dilation and curettage):** this procedure is often used to remove a miscarriage but is also a technique for abortion. *Dilation* stands for stretching or opening the cervix. *Curettage* is a French word to describe removal of the fetal tissue.

**delivery:** the removal of a baby from the womb, either through vaginal pushing or by cesarean section

**DES (diethylstilbestrol):** a man-made form of estrogen that was given to about five million pregnant women between 1938–1971 in the hopes of preventing miscarriage or premature delivery. Exposure to the drug by female fetuses has led to increased risk of rare female cancers, abnormal development of their reproductive organs, and difficulty with their own fertility. Women born between 1938 and 1971 need to know if their mothers took this drug while pregnant with them.

**Down syndrome (trisomy 21):** a chromosomal condition often seen in the pregnancies of older women that results in too many copies of chromosome #21. This results in a child with mental retardation, distinguishing facial features, and often cardiac or other organ abnormalities.

**dysfunctional uterine bleeding (DUB):** defined as excessively heavy, prolonged, or frequent bleeding that is not caused by a uterine abnormality

**dysmenorrhea:** another word for painful periods. This is a more severe form of the typical menstrual cramps most women experience.

**ectopic pregnancy (also known as tubal):** a pregnancy that has implanted in the tube. This is a potentially dangerous condition that can be life-threatening.

**egg:** produced in the ovary, this carries the mother's genetic material and is responsible for one-half of the developing embryo when joined by a sperm

**embryo:** a collection of cells formed by the union of egg and sperm after conception. After eight weeks of pregnancy, this ball of cells has grown to become a fetus.

**endometrium:** the lining of the uterus containing glands that will nourish the pregnancy until the placenta is fully formed. If no pregnancy occurs, this lining is shed each month as a "period."

**erection:** the aroused state of the penis that allows for intercourse

**estrogen:** the dominant female hormone made by the ovary that interacts with nearly every organ in the body

**fallopian tube:** the organ that connects the ovary to the uterus and is the site of fertilization of the egg by the sperm

**fertilization:** the union of the egg and sperm to create an embryo

**fetus:** the name of an unborn baby from eight weeks of pregnancy until delivery

**fibroid:** a noncancerous muscle tumor of the uterus common in older women and certain ethnic groups

**generalized anxiety disorder (GAD):** an excessive or unrealistic anxiety and worry about life circumstances, often without an identifiable cause. Other forms of the disease include phobias, panic attacks, and obsessive-compulsive disorder.

**gestational diabetes:** a form of diabetes brought on by pregnancy hormones that disappears after delivery. High blood sugars can cause excessive weight gain in the fetus.

**herpes (HSV):** there are two types of herpes—type 1, which has traditionally been called "oral herpes" and is associated with lesions around the mouth called "cold sores," and type 2, which is the genital variety that has historically been called an STD. However, these distinctions are beginning to blur due to oral sex and the transmission of type 1 from mouth to genitals and type 2 from genitals to mouth.

**human chorionic gonadotropin (hCG):** the hormone made by the placenta that signals the body a woman is pregnant. This is the chemical that makes a pregnancy test turn "positive."

**human papillomavirus (HPV):** the most common STD, it is a virus that can cause genital warts and cancer of the cervix

**hyperemesis gravidarum:** a condition that begins with morning sickness and progresses into severe nausea and vomiting, leading to dehydration and weight loss

**hyperthyroidism:** an overproduction of thyroid hormone that causes palpitations and weight loss

**hypothalamus gland:** an organ in the brain that secretes chemicals that interact with other glands, such as the pituitary, to achieve ovulation

**hypothyroidism:** an underproduction of thyroid hormone that causes problems with ovulation and weight gain

**hysterosalpingography:** an X-ray examination of the uterus and fallopian tubes to detect blocked tubes as part of an infertility evaluation

**in vitro fertilization (IVF):** the joining of an egg and sperm in the laboratory to create embryos that are implanted into the uterus to achieve pregnancy in infertile couples

**incest:** sexual abuse that occurs between family members

**intercourse:** the insertion of the penis into another organ such as the vagina or anus

**intracytoplasmic sperm injection (ICSI):** a technique used for those with very low sperm counts, poor motility, or high numbers of abnormal shapes in which a single sperm is extracted from the testis and inserted into an egg to achieve fertilization

**intrauterine device (IUD):** a form of contraception that is inserted into the uterus, lasting for five to ten years

**Klinefelter's syndrome:** a chromosomal disorder in which males are born with an extra X chromosome, which sometimes results in infertility in adulthood

**labia:** the "lips" of the female genital tract that pull on the hood of the clitoris during intercourse to produce pleasurable sensations

**lactational amenorrhea:** a method of birth control that relies on the low levels of estrogen during breast-feeding to inhibit ovulation

**luteinizing hormone (LH):** a hormone made by the pituitary gland that prepares the ovary for ovulation

**macrosomia:** large fetus or baby who weighs more than the ninetieth percentile for his age. This condition is often seen in uncontrolled diabetes and can lead to difficulties with delivery.

**major depressive disorder:** also known as "clinical depression"; a set of symptoms that accompany sadness, persisting as a chronic state of mind

**mastitis:** an infection developed during breast-feeding that produces redness in the breast area and results in high fevers (greater than 101 degrees Fahrenheit)

**masturbation:** self-stimulation to achieve sexual release

**menopause:** the cessation of menstruation due to the loss of eggs in the ovary and the decline of estrogen production

**menorrhagia:** heavy or excessive menstrual bleeding

**menstrual cramps:** see *dysmenorrhea*

**menstrual cycle:** the fertile cycle involving ovulation and menstruation, generally occurring every twenty-eight days

**menstruation:** the shedding of the endometrial lining each month that occurs if pregnancy does not occur

**molestation:** forcing undesired sexual acts by one person onto another

**nonstress test:** often done to assess fetal well-being, such as when a patient complains of decreased fetal movement, has a high-risk pregnancy, or is overdue. It consists of monitoring the fetal heartbeat for increases of at least fifteen beats when the fetus moves. A test is "reactive" or reassuring to the physician when there are at two or more such increases in a twenty-minute time period.

**osteoporosis:** loss of bone density that increases the risk of spine or hip fractures, a leading cause of disability and death in older women

**ovaries:** the organ that holds the eggs and produces the hormones estrogen and progesterone

**ovulation:** the release of the egg by the ovary each month

**pelvic cavity:** the space surrounded by the pelvic (hip) bones that contains the bladder, uterus, fallopian tubes, ovaries, and rectum

**pelvic inflammatory disease (PID):** a serious infection of the reproductive organs, where the infection spreads from the cervix into the uterus, through the fallopian tubes, and into the pelvic cavity where it circulates throughout the abdomen. PID can cause scarring of the fallopian tubes, which can block the tubes and prevent fertilization from taking place.

**penis:** the male sex organ necessary for intercourse and the transmission of semen for conception

**perimenopause:** the transition from regular menses to menopause, marked by irregular menstrual cycles and hot flashes

**pituitary gland:** an organ in the brain that secretes chemicals into the bloodstream that produce ovulation

**placenta previa:** a condition where the placenta covers all or part of the cervix, blocking the baby from coming through the birth canal

**polycystic ovarian syndrome (PCOS):** a condition of the ovaries resulting in hormone imbalance with weight gain and irregular cycles

**polymenorrhea:** the occurrence of menstrual blood loss more than once a month

**post-abortion syndrome (PAS), also known as post-abortion stress syndrome (PASS):** a term used to describe a set of mental health characteristics that have been observed in women following an abortion

**postpartum depression:** a moderate to severe form of depressed mood that occurs after delivery. This often continues for many months, in contrast to "baby blues," which is a common feeling of sadness in the first six weeks postpartum due the loss of hormones from the placenta.

**post-traumatic stress disorder (PTSD):** an anxiety disorder caused by severe psychological trauma; examples of severe trauma are physical or sexual abuse, assault, and effects of war

**preeclampsia (also known as toxemia):** occurs during pregnancy when high blood pressure leads to stress on the kidneys, causing protein to leak into the urine. It can affect all organs of the body and, in its most severe form, lead to seizures (eclampsia).

**premenstrual dysphoric disorder (PMDD):** a more severe form of PMS that includes depression, anxiety, anger, and certain physical changes as well. This is a debilitating condition that occurs right before the menstrual period.

**premenstrual syndrome (PMS):** a milder condition with emotional and physical changes such as depressed mood, anger, bloating, and breast tenderness

**progesterone:** a hormone produced by the ovary after ovulation to prepare the uterus to receive the embryo

**puberty:** the process of body development leading from childhood to adulthood, brought on by increases in sex hormones and growth hormone

**rectum:** the organ that holds stool and reabsorbs water from the GI tract

**reproduction:** the process of creating new life by the joining of egg and sperm to produce a baby

**scrotum:** the sac that holds the testicles

**selective serotonin reuptake inhibitor (SSRI):** a class of medications used to raise serotonin levels in the brain, useful in the treatment of depression, anxiety, PMDD, and addictions such as smoking

**serotonin:** a brain chemical whose imbalance is thought to play a role in depression, anxiety, PMDD, and other mental health conditions

**sexually transmitted disease (STD):** contagious infections caused by sexual contact

**sigmoidoscopy:** a procedure that screens for colon cancer, polyps, inflammatory bowel disease, and other ailments of the lower GI tract using a scope introduced through the rectum

**sonohysterogram:** a technique of instilling saline into the uterine cavity through a catheter inserted in the cervix. The saline helps to outline any irregularities of the uterine cavity such as polyps or fibroids.

**speculum:** an instrument inserted into the vagina to visualize the vaginal walls and cervix. It is often thought of in association with the Pap smear.

**sperm:** carries the genetic material of the male contributing to conception

**spina bifida:** the failure of the spinal column to fully close during fetal development, which leads to damage of the spinal cord

**squamous cell carcinoma:** a type of cancer deriving from skin cells, often seen as a form of skin cancer or a type of cervical cancer

**syphilis:** a bacterial form of STD that infects through skin-to-skin contact. It initially leaves an ulcer on the skin and then moves inside the body; left untreated, it eventually damages the internal organs.

**Tamoxifen:** an anti-estrogen hormone that is used in the treatment of breast cancers that are "fed" by estrogen

**testosterone:** the dominant male hormone that in women is responsible for vocal deepening, facial and body hair coarsening, and acne. Normal amounts are thought to be important in female sexual drive.

**toxemia:** see *preeclampsia*

**trichomonas:** a parasite that is easily contracted through sexual activity and causes vaginal infections marked by itching

**uterine lining:** see *endometrium*

# INDEX

## A

abdominal pain    63–64, 69, 182, 251, 255
abdominal wall defect 170, 173
abdominoplasty    208–210, 282. *See also* tummy tuck
abnormal bacteria    33
abnormal bleeding patterns    31
abortion(s)    4, 55, 84–95, 105, 111–112, 137–138, 283, 286
    abortion–breast cancer (ABC) theory    93
    abortion clinic    84, 86
    elective abortion(s)    85, 87
    failed abortion(s)    92
    induced abortion(s) 85, 92–93
    medical abortion(s)    86–87
    partial-birth abortion    88. *See also* intact dilation and extraction
    post-abortion recovery 90
    post-abortion stress syndrome (PASS)    93–95, 286
    post-abortion syndrome (PAS)    93, 286
    spontaneous abortion    85. *See also* miscarriage
    therapeutic abortion(s) 85
    vacuum abortion(s)    87
abstinence    53–54, 56, 60, 76, 103, 107–108
ACE inhibitors    146
acne    12, 14, 18–19, 112, 134, 287
acquired immunodeficiency syndrome (AIDS)    60, 70–73, 75–76, 78, 80, 82

AIDS epidemic    73, 77
Activella    226
acyclovir    66
adolescent(s)    6, 10–11, 16–17, 42–43, 69
adrenal glands    5
aerobic exercise    12, 208
afterbirth    193. *See also* placenta
alcohol    12, 23, 28, 37, 43, 58, 94, 144–146, 149, 161, 165, 245, 249, 251
Aldara    68
Aldomet    147
Alli    46
alpha-fetoprotein (AFP) 173
Alzheimer's disease    222
Ambien    220
amenorrhea    219
American Academy of Husband-Coached Childbirth    190
American Cancer Society 240–241, 250–251
American College of Obstetricians and Gynecologists (ACOG)    162, 237
American Psychiatric Association    15
American Psychological Association    15
American Society for Reproductive Medicine    162
amnionitis    194
amniotic fluid    88, 146, 173, 181, 183–184, 194, 282
amputation    245
anal sex    67
anemia    112, 185, 251–252
anencephaly    150
anesthesia    32, 87, 116–117, 192, 196, 205, 209
Angeliq    226
anogenital sex    71

anorexia nervosa, anorexia 15–18, 94, 153, 282
antibiotic(s)    32–34, 60–63, 82, 84, 91, 103, 115, 184
antihistamine(s)    220
antileptics    147
anxiety    12, 22, 35, 39–40, 49, 58, 94, 149, 206, 263, 284, 286
areola    7, 164–165, 201, 282
ArginMax    138
arthritis    46, 63
artificial insemination 55, 161
assisted reproductive technology (ART)    157–158
asthma    175
Atkins    43
attention-deficit hyperactivity disorder (ADHD)    145
auscultation    191
autoinoculation    65

## B

baby blues    206, 286. *See also* postpartum depression
backache    11, 166
bacterial infection(s)    60, 155, 220
bacterial vaginosis (BV)    33, 282
bariatric surgery(ies)    47
barium enema    251
barrier method(s)    100, 106, 108–110, 205
basal body temperature (BBT)    107–108, 153–155, 204
basal cell carcinoma    255
behavioral therapy    17
bestiality    127
beta blockers    135, 147

bimanual examination 30

bingeing 17, 282

bioidentical hormone therapy 224

biological clock 55

biophysical profile 181, 282

biopsy(-ies) 27, 31, 68, 160, 232, 239, 241, 248, 250, 253–254

birth canal 30, 66, 182, 184–185, 192, 195, 230, 285

birth control pill(s) 1, 10, 14, 18, 38, 103, 105, 110, 112–114, 119, 134, 167, 204, 226, 229, 254. *See also* contraceptive(s): oral contraceptive(s)

birth defect(s) 145–148, 169, 173, 175–176, 184

birth plan 188, 190

birth weight 16, 64, 144–146, 199, 202

bisexual 71–72

bisphosphonates 243

black cohosh 217, 225

black death 73

bladder 2, 4, 33, 103, 165, 192, 221, 229–230, 233–237, 282, 285

bladder control 221

bladder infection(s) 103, 109

bladder leakage 233

bladder lift 228, 234

overactive bladder 221, 233

perforated bladder 92

blindness 61, 63, 81, 245, 282

bloating 12–13, 18, 36–38, 255, 286

blood 7, 10–11, 14, 30–31, 60, 62, 69–70, 72, 74, 76, 87–89, 92, 99, 110–112, 135–136, 150, 153, 155, 158–160, 164–165, 167–

168, 170, 173–176, 179, 185, 217–220, 225, 230–233, 236, 242, 244–245, 251, 255, 261, 264, 286

blood clot(s) 47, 112–113, 176, 225–226

blood patch 192

blood thinner(s) 176, 264

blood pressure 28, 35, 44, 46–47, 112, 134, 146–147, 174, 179–185, 192, 194, 243–245, 264, 286

blood sugar(s), blood glucose 148, 156, 175, 181–182, 244–246, 284

body aches 12, 65

body fat 6, 16, 152

body image 14–16, 18, 138

body mass index (BMI) 9, 28, 44–47, 150, 242, 282

body piercing 69

bone density 205, 242–243, 285

bone loss 16, 43, 205, 224, 229, 243

Bontril 47

Botox 14, 211

Botox injection(s) 211

Bradley method 188–189

brain chemical(s) 35, 38–39, 46, 286

brain damage 16

Braxton-Hicks contractions 179–180, 188, 282. *See also* false labor

breast-feeding 66, 73, 112–113, 115, 137, 164, 189–190, 198–205, 207, 210, 249, 284–285

breast augmentation 14, 210

breast implants 210, 241

breast development 2, 6–7

breast disease 29

breast exam(s) 28–29, 240, 249

breast reduction 211

breast self-examination(s) 29, 211

breast tenderness 12, 36, 163–164, 286

breast tissue 7, 29, 164, 240–241

breech presentation 184, 195

brow lift(s) 210

bulimia 15, 17–18, 94, 282

**C**

CA-125 232, 255

caffeine 12, 35, 37, 149

calcitonin 243

calcium 3, 12, 37, 43, 150, 203, 205, 224, 242–243, 282

calories 17, 42–44, 47–49, 185, 203

cancer(s) 29–30, 32, 67, 70–72, 75, 82, 93, 213, 221–222, 229, 231–232, 239–241, 243, 247–256, 283–284, 287

bone cancer 239

breast cancer 29, 46, 93, 112, 211, 222–225, 239–241, 243, 247–250, 253–254, 287

cervical cancer 30–31, 60, 64, 67, 75, 82, 219, 241, 252, 253, 287

colon cancer 46, 241–243, 250–254, 286

colorectal cancer 30, 222, 250–251

endometrial cancer 46, 253–254

epithelial cancer 254

genital cancers 68

liver cancer 70

lung cancer 247, 253

ovarian cancer 112, 222, 232, 243, 254–255

skin cancer 29, 255–256, 287

uterine cancer  112, 219, 223, 225–226, 247, 253
vaginal cancer  67
vulvar cancer  67
cancer therapy  158
cannula  87–88
carbohydrates  33, 37, 43–44, 245
cardiologist  176
cardiovascular abnormalities  147
carrier testing  170
Celexa  39
celibacy  126
Centers for Disease Control and Prevention, the (CDC)  60, 62, 67, 70–71, 78, 80–81, 83, 152, 157–158, 241
cerebral palsy  144
cervical cap  108–109, 121
cervical mucus  62, 107, 111, 153, 156, 204
cervix  3–4, 27–32, 59, 61–62, 66–67, 74–75, 81, 84, 87–88, 91, 102, 107–109, 111, 115, 117, 153, 155, 160–161, 166–167, 170, 173, 178, 180, 183, 188, 194–196, 229–230, 235, 247, 252–253, 282–286
cesarean section, cesarean delivery  66, 68, 73, 150, 182, 185–186, 190, 194–197, 199, 206, 233, 283
chemotherapy  218, 239, 247, 250, 252–255
childbirth  4, 54, 92, 137, 165, 187, 189–190, 193, 209–210, 212, 229, 233–235, 237
chills  61, 65
chlamydia  61–62, 71, 74, 78, 81, 115, 233, 282
chlamydial infection(s)  61–62
cholesterol  18, 222, 240, 243–245
bad (LDL)  3, 221, 244

good (HDL)  3, 221, 244
chorionic villus sampling  170
chromosome(s)  2, 143, 158, 166–167, 169–170, 282–284
chronic hepatitis  69
chronic liver disease  69
chronic pain  39
Cialis  264
cigarette smoke, smoking  28, 38–39, 48, 58, 67, 144–145, 149, 161, 165, 242–245, 249, 251, 286
cilia  143, 153
circumcision  74–75
cirrhosis  70
cleft lip  147, 176
Climara  226
Climara Pro  226
clinical breast exams  249
clinical depression  38, 94, 285
clitoris  2, 4–5, 102, 127, 134, 237, 263, 282, 284
Clomid  152, 156
clomiphene citrate  156
coitus interruptus  57, 108. See also withdrawal method
cold sores  64–66, 284
colonoscopy  240–242, 251
colorectal polyps  250
colostrum  165, 200, 282
colposcopy  27, 31, 60, 252, 282
Combipatch  226
conception  106, 110–112, 117, 143–144, 148, 150, 152, 283, 285–286
condom(s)  33, 63, 68–70, 74–80, 86, 100, 106, 108–111, 120, 259
condyloma  68, 82. See also genital warts
Condylox  68

congenital heart disease  176
conization  153
conjunctivitis (pinkeye)  61
constipation  47, 165, 234–235, 251, 255
contraceptive(s)  55, 77, 106, 110, 113–114, 119–121
oral contraceptive(s)  10–11, 14, 38. See also birth control pills
contractions  4, 86, 179–181, 183, 188, 191–192, 194, 196, 199, 283
cosmetic surgery  209–211
craving(s)  12–13, 42
cretinism  176
Crohn's disease  250
cryotherapy  27, 32, 153, 283
CT scan(s)  232, 252
Cymbalta  39
cystadenomas  232
cystic fibrosis  170, 283
cystic teratoma  232. See also dermoid
cystocele  234

## D

date rape  23
date rape drug(s)  23
dehydration  164, 203, 284
dental disease  245
Department of Health and Human Services (HHS)  42
Depo-Provera  114–115, 204
depression  6, 12, 15, 17–18, 22–23, 35–36, 38–39, 46, 49, 94, 134, 205–206, 220, 225, 286
dermatologist(s)  19
dermoid  232. See also cystic teratoma
Desoxyn  47
Desyrel  39

Detrol 234

dexfenfluramine 47

DHEA 138, 224

diabetes 18, 33, 35, 44, 46–47, 49, 72, 147–148, 150–151, 156, 166, 169, 174–175, 181–182, 194, 225, 240, 243–246, 251, 261, 284–285

type 1 diabetes 148

type 2 diabetes 148, 253

Diabetes Prevention Program 246

diabetic retinopathy 245

diaphragm (contraceptive device) 100, 108–109, 120–121, 259

diarrhea 11–12, 251

diet 14, 33, 37, 42–44, 46–47, 128, 149, 175, 181, 203, 209, 225, 242, 244–246, 251, 261

Dietary Guidelines for Americans 42

diethylstilbestrol (DES) 248, 252, 283

difficulty concentrating 12, 39

difficulty sleeping 12–13, 206, 220. *See also* insomnia

dilated 84, 178, 183, 192, 194, 230

dilation and curettage (D&C) 87, 90, 163, 167, 229, 254, 283

dilation and evacuation (D&E) 88

dildo(s) 67

Ditropan 234

diuretic(s) (water pill) 18, 38, 135, 146–147

DNA 81, 282

douching 62

doula 190

Down syndrome 169–170, 173, 282–283. *See also* trisomy 21

drug abuse 28, 69, 71–72, 94, 144, 146, 165

drug screens 23

dry mouth 47, 234

dual-energy X-ray absorptiometry (DEXA) scan 242

dysfunctional uterine bleeding (DUB) 10–11, 283

dysmenorrhea 7, 10–11, 283, 285. *See also* painful periods

dysplasia 27, 32, 67, 82, 253

**E**

eating disorder(s) 15–18, 22, 282

ectopic pregnancy(ies) 60–61, 92, 153, 157, 167–169, 283. *See also* tubal pregnancy(ies)

effaced, effacement 183, 194

Effexor 39

egg(s) 2–4, 7–8, 11, 77, 85, 107–108, 110–111, 116, 119, 143, 146, 151, 153, 155, 157–158, 160–161, 169, 185, 218–219, 231–233, 282–286. *See also* ovum

ejaculation 58, 80, 102, 107–108, 110, 116, 151, 153, 158, 160, 262

electronic fetal monitor 191

embryo(s) 2–4, 8, 61, 85, 87, 107, 111–112, 115, 143–144, 146, 151, 153, 155, 157, 161, 167, 283–284, 286

embryonic defects 155

emergency contraception 111

Enablex 234

endometrial ablation 230

endometrial biopsy 219, 247

endometriomas 231–232

endometriosis 30, 137, 153, 156–157, 168, 231, 233

endometrium 7–8, 11, 253, 283, 287

enema(s) 193

Enjuvia 226

epidural, epidural anesthesia 116, 189, 191–192, 196

epilepsy 147, 176

episiotomy 137, 192–193, 237

erectile dysfunction 137, 228, 258

Essure system 117

estradiol 226

Estrasorb 226

Estring 227

estriol 173, 226

EstroGel 226

estrogen 2–3, 7–8, 11, 93, 110, 112–113, 134, 137, 145, 152–153, 156, 173, 199, 203–204, 217–227, 242–243, 249, 253–254, 261, 283–285, 287

estrogen cream(s) 226–227

estrogen deficiency 138

estrogen therapy 134, 243, 254

exercise 6, 14, 16–17, 42, 44, 46–49, 135–136, 144, 150, 153, 161, 167, 175, 181, 190, 203, 207–210, 233, 235, 242, 244–246, 251, 257, 261

eye lift(s) 210

eyes 20, 61, 127, 130, 198, 210–211, 265–266

**F**

face-lift(s) 14, 210

facial hair 14, 18–19, 112

fallopian tube(s)   2, 4, 60–61, 115–117, 143, 152–153, 157, 161, 167, 230, 233, 283–285

false labor   180, 282. See also Braxton-Hicks contractions

false positive(s)   27, 31

Famvir   66

fat cells   18

fatigue   11–12, 69, 136, 217, 220, 255

fecal occult blood test (FOBT)   251

fellatio   127. See also oral sex

female genital disorders   30

Femhrt   226

Femring   226

Femtrace   226

fenfluramine   47

fertility specialists   156, 161

fertilization   2, 61, 107–108, 111–112, 143, 153, 157–158, 160–161, 283–285

fetal abnormalities   147

fetal alcohol syndrome (FAS)   145

fetal fibronectin   183

fetal heart rate   181, 184, 191

fetal position   1, 11, 173

fetus(es)   1, 4–5, 16, 58, 66, 84–88, 90, 92, 112, 115, 144–145, 147, 149–150, 153, 156, 163, 167, 173–174, 180–181, 183, 185, 190, 282–285

fever   32–33, 61, 65, 199–200, 285

fibroid tumor(s), fibroids   31, 137, 153, 155–156, 219, 230–231, 284, 286

fibromyalgia   39

fibrous cysts   29

Fitz-Hugh-Curtis syndrome   62

folate, folic acid   12, 43, 147, 150, 163, 176

follicle (egg sac)   7–8, 19

follicle-stimulating hormone (FSH)   6–7, 155–156

Follistim   156

Food and Drug Administration (FDA)   38, 46, 68, 77–78, 81, 86–87, 106, 111, 223, 225

forceps   88, 176, 195

foreplay   57, 74, 100–101, 128, 136, 263–264

foreskin   74–75

Furadantin   104

G

gallbladder disease   46, 112

Gardasil   81–82

gastric banding   47

gastric bypass surgery(ies)   47–48

gender   38, 74, 129, 248

generalized anxiety disorder (GAD)   36, 40, 284

genetic disorder(s)   166, 169–170

genital tract   62, 284

genital warts   29, 67–68, 82, 284. See also condyloma

gestational diabetes   174–175, 181–182, 284

gestational hypertension   182

ginkgo biloba   135

ginseng   225

Glucophage (metformin)   156

glucose   148, 175, 245

glucose tolerance test (GTT)   175, 245

glycohemoglobin   148

Gonal-f   156

gonorrhea   62–63, 71, 74, 78, 115, 233

growth spurt(s)   6, 10

Gynecare TVT-OT   234

gynecologic oncologist   247, 255

gynecologist   27–28, 30, 32, 62, 103, 123, 226–227, 234, 237

Gynediol   226

H

Harvard School of Public Health   75

headache(s)   11, 13, 36, 39, 47, 182, 192

healthy fats   42–43

Heart and Estrogen/Progesterone Replacement Study (HERS)   222

heart attack(s)   3, 40, 112, 176, 221–222, 243–245, 258

heart disease   18, 44, 46–47, 49, 71, 176, 221–225, 240, 243–245, 249, 261, 264

heavy menstrual periods   10. See also menorrhagia

hemoglobin A1C   148

hemorrhage   61, 91, 167

hemorrhoids   65

hepatitis B   69–70

hepatitis C   70

heredity   38

hernia(s)   29, 47, 233–236

hernia repair   158

herpes (HSV)   29, 64–66, 78–79, 81, 195, 284

  herpes support groups   66

  herpes vaccine   81

  oral herpes   64, 284

  type 1 herpes   64–65, 284

  type 2 herpes   64–66, 284

Herpevac Trial for Women   81

heterosexual   22, 69, 71–73, 75–77

Hollywood 14, 55, 137, 209, 260
homosexual, homosexuality 21, 56, 69, 72–73, 75–76, 127
honeymoon cystitis 103
hormonal birth control 100, 119–120, 134
hormonal imbalance 18, 36, 132
hormone replacement therapy (HRT) 217–218, 221–225, 249, 254
hormone supplement(s) 166, 221
hot flashes 156, 217, 219–221, 223–225, 231, 285
human immunodeficiency virus (HIV) 60, 64, 70–75, 77–78, 80, 82–83, 195
human menopausal gonadotropin (hMG) 156
human papillomavirus (HPV) 27–28, 30–31, 59, 67–68, 74–75, 78–79, 81–82, 252, 284
    genital HPV 67
    HPV vaccines 68, 81–82
hymen 10, 99–102
*hyperemesis gravidarum* 164, 284
hyperthyroidism 47, 148, 176, 284
hypothalamic-pituitary-gonadal axis 5
hypothalamus 5, 220, 284
hypothyroidism 148, 176–177, 284
hysterectomy 32, 115, 134, 223–224, 228, 231, 234–235, 247, 253–254
    abdominal hysterectomy 231, 233
    laparoscopic hysterectomy 231
    vaginal hysterectomy 231, 235

hysterosalpingogram (HSG) 117, 155
hysteroscopic ligation 117
hysteroscopy 155, 167, 219, 230

**I**

ibuprofen 11, 32
Implanon 113–114
implantation 111–112, 115, 144, 153, 157
impotence 261
incest 22, 86, 127, 284
incompetent cervix 91
induced labor 194
infection(s) 4, 29, 33–34, 47, 60–68, 70–72, 74–75, 78, 81–82, 84, 87, 91–92, 115, 155, 158, 160, 166, 183–184, 194–195, 200, 220, 238, 252, 285–287
infertility 4, 18–19, 62, 78, 85, 91, 115, 151–153, 156–158, 161–162, 168, 282, 284
Inhibin A 173
insomnia 39, 47, 206. *See also* difficulty sleeping
insulin 14, 18, 152, 156, 175, 181, 245–246, 264
intact dilation and extraction (intact D&X) 88. *See also* partial-birth abortion
intercourse 4–5, 21, 54–56, 58–59, 61–62, 67, 69, 71, 73–80, 99–100, 102–103, 105–111, 124–127, 129, 133–134, 136–139, 154, 159–160, 180, 193, 199, 203–205, 217–221, 223, 227–228, 237–238, 252, 255, 259, 261, 263–265, 283–285
International Council on Infertility Information Dissemination, Inc. 162
intracytoplasmic sperm injection (ICSI) 161, 284

intrauterine device (IUD) 115, 119–120, 153, 205, 284
intrauterine insemination (IUI) 156–157, 161
in vitro fertilization (IVF) 85, 157–159, 284
iron 43
irritability 12, 36–38, 217, 220

**J**

jaundice 69, 182
Jenny Craig 43
joint pain 69
Joint United Nations Programme on HIV/AIDS 73
Juvéderm 211

**K**

K-Y Jelly 80, 100–101
Kegel exercises 235, 237
kidney disease 146
kidney failure 245
Klinefelter's syndrome 158, 284

**L**

labetalol 147
lactation 93, 166, 200, 282
lactational amenorrhea method 204
Lamaze method 189
laparoscopy 152, 155, 167, 232–233
laser hair removal 19
latch, latch(ed) on 198, 200–202
latex 33, 76–80, 110
learning disabilities 144
LEEP (loop electrocautery excision procedure) 32
lesion 27, 32, 64–68, 82, 153, 242, 252, 284
Levitra 264

Lexapro   39, 135
libido   39, 134–136, 219
linea nigra   179
lip enhancement   14
liposuction   210
liquid nitrogen   32
liver   63, 69–70, 73, 112,
   225–226, 283
   liver failure   69
   liver transplants   69–70
local vaginal estrogens
   261
loss of appetite   69, 206
low-dose birth control pill
   1, 226
lumpectomy   250
Lunesta   220
lungs   61, 68, 113, 146,
   175, 182–184, 209, 283
luteinizing hormone
   (LH)   6, 8, 285
Lybrel   114
lymph nodes   65, 239,
   247–248

**M**

Macrobid   104
Macrodantin   104
macrosomia   175, 182, 285
major depressive disorder
   38, 285
male-pattern baldness   18
malnutrition   16–17
mammogram(s), mam-
   mography   29, 42, 211,
   239–241, 249
marriage covenant   56
mastectomy   250
   modified radical mastec-
      tomy   250
   partial mastectomy   250
   radical mastectomy   250
   simple mastectomy   250
mastitis   200, 285
masturbation   57–58, 160,
   265, 285
maternal-fetal medicine specialist   174

Medicaid   241
Medical Institute for Sexual
   Health   54
Medicare   241
menarche (first period)   7–
   8, 11
menopause   3, 36, 38,
   134, 137, 212, 217–221,
   223–224, 226, 242, 247,
   253–254, 258–259, 261–
   262, 285
menorrhagia   7, 10, 285.
   See also heavy menstrual
   periods
menstrual cramping   1, 114
menstrual cycle   1, 3, 7–8,
   10–11, 18, 28, 30–31, 35,
   38, 46, 86, 105, 107–108,
   112, 114, 152–154, 156,
   218, 229–231, 248, 253,
   255, 285
menstruation   3, 6–7, 36,
   54, 62, 107–108, 113, 115,
   153–154, 218–219, 285
mental retardation   144,
   176, 283
Meridia   46
metabolism   49, 229
methotrexate   168
metronidazole   82
Mifeprex (mifepristone)
   86, 87. See also RU-486
migraine   38–39
milk letdown   199
Mirena   115
miscarriage   61, 85, 87,
   90–91, 115, 144, 148–149,
   151, 163, 166–167,
   170, 175, 283. See
   also abortion(s): spontaneous abortion(s)
misoprostol   86–87
missionary position   126
mitral valve prolapse   176
models   14–15, 17, 82, 126,
   258, 266
molestation   22, 285
monogamy   76

mood changes/swings   6,
   10–12, 35–36, 156, 219,
   221, 224
morning after pill, the
   150, 111–112. See also
   Plan B
morning sickness   163–164,
   172, 284
MPA progesterone   224
MRI(s) (magnetic resonance
   imaging)   232, 240–241,
   250, 252
multiple pregnancy(ies)
   157, 185, 196

**N**

naproxen   32
National Alliance on Mental
   Illness   16
National Breast and Cervi-
   cal Cancer Early Detection
   Program (NBCCEDP)
   241
National Cancer Institute
   93
National Center for Health
   Statistics of the Centers for
   Disease Control and Pre-
   vention   152
National Institute of Allergy
   and Infectious Diseases
   (NIAID)   75, 81, 83
National Institutes of
   Health (NIH)   16, 75,
   78, 83, 243
National Women's Health
   Information Center
   (NWHIC)   162
natural family planning
   (NFP)   105–108, 154,
   204
nausea, nauseated   11–12,
   61, 69, 163–164, 171, 185,
   284
neonatal death   64, 144,
   146
nervous system   37, 63, 89,
   149, 245

neural tube defect(s)   147, 170, 173, 176

*New England Journal of Medicine*   62

night sweats   217, 220–221, 223, 225

nitrofurantoin   103–104

nodules   30

nonoxynol 9   108

nonsteroidal anti-inflammatory drug (NSAID)   11

nonstress test   181, 282, 285

norepinephrine   38–39

Norplant   113

nose jobs   210. *See also* rhinoplasty

nurse-midwife   190

nursing bras   164, 187, 203

nursing pads   203

NuvaRing   113–114

**O**

obese, obesity   28, 44, 46–47, 49, 161, 182, 232, 245, 249, 253, 282

obsessive-compulsive disorder   40, 284

obstetrician/gynecologist (OB/GYN)   31, 36, 198, 229, 238, 240

oral contraceptive(s)   10–11, 14, 38. *See also* birth control pill(s)

oral sex   61, 64, 122–123, 127–128, 265, 284. *See also* fellatio

orgasm   5, 58, 102, 127–128, 135, 137–139, 237, 262, 264, 282

orlistat   46

Ortho Evra   113–114

osteoporosis   3, 16, 49, 221, 223–224, 240, 242–243, 285

outercourse   56

ovarian cyst(s)   112–113, 155–156, 231–232

ovarian torsion   231

ovary(ies)   2–3, 5–7, 14, 18, 30–31, 102, 107, 110, 119, 134, 143, 152–153, 155–157, 168, 218–220, 231–233, 254–255, 282–283, 285–286

over-the-counter (OTC) medications   1, 11, 32–33, 39, 46, 65, 82, 164

overweight   22, 44, 46–47, 114, 175, 182, 243, 247, 249, 251, 253

ovulation   2, 8, 10–11, 16, 18, 36, 62, 107–108, 110–111, 143, 148, 152–157, 159, 203–204, 218, 229, 231, 233, 282, 284–286

ovum   7. *See also* egg

oxytocin   194, 199

Oxytrol   234

**P**

painful periods   1, 7, 10–11, 283. *See also* dysmenorrhea

painful urination   61–63

panic attack(s)   40, 284

Papanicolaou, George Dr.   30

Pap smear(s)   27, 28, 30–31, 42, 59–60, 67–68, 82, 239, 252–254, 286

abnormal Pap smear(s)   4, 27, 31, 67, 153, 282–283

ParaGard   115

parathyroid hormone   243

Paxil   39, 135, 225

Paxil CR   38

pediatrician   28, 200, 212

pelvic cavity   2, 61, 153, 167, 285

pelvic exam   27–28, 30–31, 167, 255

pelvic inflammatory disease (PID)   60–63, 168, 285

pelvic prolapse   229, 233

pelvic stretches   135

penile implant   264

penile self-injection   264

penis   2, 4–5, 61, 65, 67, 71, 74, 79–81, 100–103, 108, 127–128, 133, 237, 261–265, 282–285

perforated bowel   92

Pergonal   156

perimenopause   218, 285

perinatologist   147

permanent sterilization   116, 233

pharyngitis (throat infections)   61

pharynx   68

phentermine   47

phobia(s)   40, 284

phytoestrogens   224

pitocin   194

pituitary gland   5, 7, 156, 285

placebo   110, 112, 114, 138, 221–222

placenta   4, 61, 87, 88, 111, 147, 170, 173–174, 181, 184, 193, 195, 197, 283–286

placental abruption   144, 176, 184

placenta previa   144, 184, 195, 285

Plan B   111. *See also* morning after pill

pneumonia   61

polycystic ovarian syndrome (PCOS)   14, 18–19, 152, 156, 253, 286

polymenorrhea   10, 286

polyp(s)   31, 155, 219, 229–230, 241, 247, 250, 286

pornography   58, 123

post-traumatic stress disorder (PTSD)   23, 93, 286

postmenopausal   43, 218–220, 242–243, 249, 253

postpartum   116–117, 190, 198, 204–205, 286

postpartum depression 206, 286. *See also* baby blues

preeclampsia 150, 176, 182, 286–287. *See also* toxemia

pregnancy complications 16, 91

pregnancy test 31, 144, 163, 284

prehypertension 244

Premarin 222, 224, 226–227

premarital sex 54–56, 127

premature birth/delivery 64, 85, 88, 91, 144, 150, 156, 184, 283

premature labor 37, 178, 183

premenstrual dysphoric disorder (PMDD) 10–13, 35–38, 286

premenstrual syndrome (PMS) 10–12, 35–38, 105, 112, 114, 286

Prempro 222, 226

prenatal visit 61, 163

prenatal vitamins 150

prescription drugs 37, 39–40, 46–47, 68, 103, 105, 108–109, 111, 135, 146, 220, 224, 228

pro-choice 94

pro-life 87, 93–94, 105

progesterone 2–3, 7–8, 11, 19, 36, 86, 107, 110–115, 152–155, 184, 217–218, 222–224, 226, 229, 254, 285–286

prostaglandins 11, 87–88

prostate, prostate gland 46, 61, 116, 158

Prozac 38–39, 135

psychotherapy 17

puberty 2, 5–6, 8, 10, 16, 18, 21, 38, 54, 57, 286

purging 17, 282

**R**

radiation 85, 158, 161, 218, 239–240, 242, 247–248, 250, 252–255

rape 20, 22–23, 86

rectocele 235

rectum 4, 30, 33, 62, 221, 229–230, 235, 237, 242, 250–251, 285–286

red clover 225

relaxation techniques 12, 190, 192

Remifemin 225

reproduction 2–3, 21, 125, 286

reproductive endocrinologist(s) 157

Repronex 156

Resolve: The National Infertility Association 162

respiratory distress syndrome 175, 183

respiratory problems 46

Restylane 211

rheumatic heart disease 176

rhinoplasty 14, 210. *See also* nose jobs

rhythm method 106, 204

rooting reflex 200

Roux-en-Y gastric bypass 48

Rozerem 220

RU-486 86. *See also* Mifeprex

**S**

safe sex 61, 76, 78, 80

saline abortion 88

Sanctura 234

sanitary pad 8, 10

Sarafem 38

saturated fats 43

scar tissue 62–63, 137, 152–153, 168, 230, 232–233, 237

schizophrenia 147

scrotum 2, 67, 79, 116, 158, 161, 264, 286

Seasonique 114

secondhand smoke 145

sedation 32, 87

seizure disorders 146–147, 176

selective embryo reduction 85

selective estrogen receptor modulators (SERMs) 224, 243

selective serotonin-norepinephrine reuptake inhibitors (SNRIs) 39

selective serotonin reuptake inhibitors (SSRIs) 13, 36, 39–40, 135, 286

semen 57–58, 60, 65, 72, 74, 78–80, 109, 116, 152–153, 158, 160, 285

seminal fluid 146

seminal vesicles 116

septic shock 92

serotonin 13, 36, 38–39, 135, 225, 286

sex hormone(s) 2, 5, 54, 132, 134, 286

sexual(ly) abuse(d) 21–23, 137–138, 284, 286

sexual addiction 55

sexual arousal 102, 134, 136, 261

sexual assault 22–23

sexual confusion 22

sexual dysfunction 134–135, 245

sexual exploration 21, 126, 128, 262

sexual intercourse 21, 54–56, 73, 76, 124, 129, 139, 180, 259, 263

sexually transmitted disease(s) (STD[s]) 28–29, 32, 53, 55–56, 59–70, 74–76, 78–79, 81, 91, 115, 121, 137–138, 158, 168, 233, 252, 282, 284, 286–287 sexual positions 122

sexual predators 23

sexual trauma 21–22

shoulder dystocia 182

sigmoidoscopy 242, 251, 286

signs of anorexia 16

Simply Sleep 220

sleep apnea 46–47

sleep cycle(s) 6

Slim Fast 44

sonography 29

sonohysterography 219

South Beach 43

soy 217, 225

speculum 29–30, 286

sperm 2, 4, 62, 77–79, 85, 107–109, 111, 115–117, 119–120, 143, 146, 151, 153, 156–158, 160–161, 169, 185, 232, 283–284, 286

sperm count 145–146, 152, 160–161, 284

sperm mobility, motility 160, 284

spermicide(s) 108–109, 115, 120

spina bifida 147, 150, 287

squamous cell carcinoma 255, 287

stillbirth 64, 144, 146, 148, 175

strep throat 65

stretch marks 14, 179, 208–209

stroke(s) 3, 46–47, 112, 174, 176, 213, 221–222, 225, 244–245

suction-aspiration 87

sudden infant death syndrome (SIDS) 144–145

sun protection factor (SPF) 256

surgical enhancement(s) 14, 211

surgical procedure(s) 4, 91, 155, 158, 211

surgical weight loss 47

Susan G. Komen for the Cure 29

swollen breasts 13

syphilis 63–64, 74, 78–79, 287

**T**

T-score 243

Tamoxifen 254, 287

tampon(s) 8, 10, 100, 199

teenage pregnancy 28, 54, 76

Tenuate 47

teratogens 146

testes 116, 158, 160

testicles 61, 102, 136, 151, 158, 286

testosterone 1, 18–19, 132, 134, 136, 138, 145, 160, 219, 224, 287

thalamus 88

thyroid disease 28, 147–148, 151–152, 217, 219

thyroid disorder(s) 148, 176–177

thyroid gland 28–29, 31

thyroid storm 176

tinidazole 82

toxemia 37, 182, 286–287. *See also* preeclampsia

toxic shock syndrome 8

trans fats 43

transformation zone (T-Zone) 30

transfusion(s) 70, 76, 92

transvaginal ultrasonography 155

transverse 195

trazodone 39

trichomonas 64, 82, 287

tricyclic antidepressants 39

triglycerides 244

trisomy 18 170, 173

trisomy 21 170, 173, 283. *See also* Down syndrome

tubal ligation 116–117, 168, 205, 209, 212, 219, 233

tubal pregnancy(ies) 117, 152, 282. *See also* ectopic pregnancy(ies)

tummy tuck 208–210, 282. *See also* abdominoplasty

tumor(s) 29, 31, 72, 112, 153, 155, 230–232, 239, 248, 250, 254, 284

Tylenol PM 220

**U**

ulcer 63, 287

ulcerative colitis 250

ultrasound 31, 91, 152, 157, 163, 165, 167, 170, 173–174, 181, 183, 185–186, 191, 232, 240, 247, 250, 254–255, 282

umbilical cord 174, 185

Unisom 220

unplanned pregnancy(ies) 90, 106, 259

unwed mother(s) 54

urethra 5, 33, 61, 63, 103, 109, 116, 233–235, 282

urinary tract infection(s) (UTI) 31, 33, 65, 103, 221

urodynamics 234

uterine abnormality 10, 283

uterine cramping 32, 155

uterine lining 3, 7, 107, 111, 115, 153, 230, 287

uterus 2–4, 7–8, 11, 30–31, 61, 84–88, 91–92, 102, 107, 110–111, 115, 117, 119, 143–144, 152–153, 155, 157, 161, 165–168, 180, 184–185, 194–195, 197, 199, 219, 221, 223, 226, 229–231, 233, 235, 247, 253–254, 283–286

perforated uterus 92, 115

UVA   256
UVB   256

## V

Vagifem   227
vagina   1–2, 4–5, 7, 29–30,
  32–33, 61–62, 65–66, 68,
  71, 74, 80–81, 84, 99–
  103, 107–110, 113, 134,
  136, 146, 160–161, 170,
  193–195, 199, 220–221,
  228, 233–237, 261, 282,
  284, 286
vaginal antibiotic   33
vaginal area   64
vaginal bacteria   103
vaginal bleeding   166, 168,
  183, 188, 247, 253–254
vaginal delivery(ies)   184–
  186, 196, 199, 206, 209,
  283
vaginal discharge   29, 62,
  178
vaginal disease(s)   71
vaginal dryness   139, 199,
  203, 220, 223, 227
vaginal estrogens   261
vaginal examinations   192,
  194
vaginal fluids   146
vaginal infection(s)   31–33,
  64, 287
vaginal intercourse   61, 74,
  78, 127, 137–138, 263,
  265
vaginal irritation   33, 109,
  282
vaginal lining   220
vaginal muscles   237
vaginal muscle tone   235
vaginal opening   65, 67,
  101, 237, 282
vaginal pain   137
vaginal penetration   56–57,
  79, 262
vaginal pH   220
vaginal prolapse   234

vaginal rejuvenation   237–
  238
vaginal repair(s)   228
vaginal ring(s)   120,
  226–227
vaginal secretion(s)   60, 68,
  72, 74
vaginal skin tearing   101,
  137, 217
vaginal space   233
vaginal surgery(ies)   109,
  261
vaginal swab   32
vaginal tissue(s)   64, 137,
  228, 235
vaginal ultrasound   247
vaginal vault pro-
  lapse   235–237
vaginal walls   4, 29, 236–
  237, 286
vaginal weakness   236
valerian root   220
Valium   40
Valtrex   66
varicocele   158
varicose veins   158
vas deferens   116
vasectomy   116, 161, 205,
  208, 212
vasomotor symptoms   225
VESIcare   234
Viagra   264
vibrator(s)   67, 122,
  127–128
viral infections   60
viral load   72
virginity, virgins   8, 20, 28,
  53–54, 59, 83, 99–100,
  103
vitamin D   43, 243
Vivelle   226
vomiting   11, 17–18, 61,
  69, 164, 185, 282, 284
vulva   29, 74, 81

## W

water retention   18, 38

weight gain   12–14, 16–18,
  39, 114–115, 138, 205,
  207, 209, 229, 284, 286
weight loss   38–39, 43,
  46–49, 150, 164, 207, 210,
  249, 251, 261, 284
Weight Watchers   44
Wellbutrin (bupropion)
  135
white blood cell(s)   33, 72,
  158
withdrawal method   108.
  See also coitus interruptus
womb(s)   4, 90, 111–112,
  115, 133, 144, 151, 153,
  162, 174, 219, 283
Women's Health Initiative
  (WHI)   221–226
World AIDS Day   80
World Health Organiza-
  tion   80
Worth the Wait   54

## X

X-ray   117, 152, 155, 167,
  232, 239–240, 242, 251–
  252, 254, 284
Xanax   40
Xenical   46

## Y

Yasmin   18
yeast infection(s)   29, 32–
  33, 65, 82, 103, 220
  yeast remedies   33, 65, 82
yoga   12, 135

## Z

Zoloft   38–39, 135
Zone, The   44
Zovirax   66
zygote intrafallopian transfer
  (ZIFT)   157

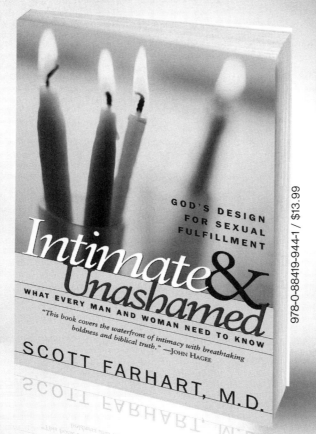

# FREE NEWSLETTERS
## TO HELP EMPOWER YOUR LIFE

## Why subscribe today?

☐ **DELIVERED DIRECTLY TO YOU.** All you have to do is open your inbox and read.

☐ **EXCLUSIVE CONTENT.** We cover the news overlooked by the mainstream press.

☐ **STAY CURRENT.** Find the latest court rulings, revivals, and cultural trends.

☐ **UPDATE OTHERS.** Easy to forward to friends and family with the click of your mouse.

## CHOOSE THE E-NEWSLETTER THAT INTERESTS YOU MOST:

- Christian news
- Daily devotionals
- Spiritual empowerment
- And much, much more

SIGN UP AT: **http://freenewsletters.charismamag.com**

8178